Denenberg, Barry.
   The story of Muhammad Ali.

# THE ART OF
# POLITICS

## ELECTORAL STRATEGIES
## and
## CAMPAIGN MANAGEMENT

## JAMES BROWN & PHILIP M. SEIB
*Southern Methodist University*

**Alfred**
PUBLISHERS

ALFRED PUBLISHING CO., INC.

**Library of Congress Cataloging in Publication Data**

Brown, James, 1934 (May 1)–
    The art of politics.

    Bibliography: p.
    1. Campaign management–United States.
    2. Electioneering–United States.  I. Seib,
Philip M., 1949    joint author.  II. Title.
    JK2281.B76    329'.01    76-1872
    ISBN 0-88284-036-3

*TO*

*BONNIE JO, SHANNON,*
*and*
*NANCY*

## ACKNOWLEDGMENTS

The authors are indebted to a number of people whose advice, assistance, and encouragement made it possible and enjoyable for us to write this book. We would like to thank the members of the Department of Political Science and Dean Emmie V. Baine of the Human Resources Center of Southern Methodist University who instituted and funded a course in "Practical Electoral Politics." The content of this course served as a starting point for the development of this book.

We are particularly grateful to Cynthia Ward for her cheerful and invaluable assistance in preparing the manuscript and for many of the tables and charts included.


J.B.
P.M.S.

Southern Methodist University
Dallas, Texas, 1975

# CONTENTS

# PREFACE

Students of American politics have long marveled at the seemingly illogical manner in which political campaigning is conducted. However well trained one might be in the academic discipline of political science or some related field, it often is difficult to discern any true substance in the art of campaigning that might lend itself to productive study. As a result, students learn the theories that are the foundation of our political system and they are able to understand the end results of political activity as reflected in election returns or policy development, but they are unaware of that aspect of politics that serves as the link between these two areas—the practice of electoral politics.

It was the recognition of the existence of this gap in the learning process that led to the writing of this book. We have endeavored to present the type of material found in campaign manuals utilized by candidates and party organizations, but to do so within a format that is suited to classroom use. Hopefully, this material will prove useful to the beginning student of political science as well as to the more advanced student who may be concentrating on parties, electoral behavior, or campaign history. Furthermore, we hope that the student who reads this textbook will have the opportunity to participate in some political activity. The practice of politics can be taught only partially in a classroom; the true learning experience occurs in the utilization of campaign skills. More and more universities are incorporating work-study programs in their curricula, and it is this kind of subject matter that lends itself well to the pursuit of experiential learning.

We hope that both students and nonstudents will develop certain insights and skills in the course of reading this book. Basic to these is a fundamental amount of expertise in the field of political participation. This is not to say that study of these pages will produce a professional campaign manager, but it might produce in the reader a realistic appreciation of what constitutes a campaign, how the elements of a campaign are integrated into a coherent whole, and why a given campaign succeeds or fails. Too often the well-intentioned novice sets out on his first political venture confident that his shining ideals will guide his cause to victory. More often than not, this aspiring politician will find that ideals alone are no match for an experienced opponent who has learned that idealism is worth little unless it is coupled with the ability to mobilize a constituency and generate votes. The newcomer, after being flattened by a political steamroller, is likely to terminate his short-lived career as a political activist, leaving the field to those who understand the mechanics of politics even if they do not understand that there is a need for a motivation more substantive than that of running for the sake of running. In recent years we have seen far too many elected officials who apparently view politics as an end in itself rather than as merely a means to achieve a desired goal. This outlook will continue to predominate unless an influx of new political participants can be found, participants who bring to politics not only their ideals and ideas, but also a level of competence that will enable them to last long enough in the political wars to exert some influence on the course of events. The dynamism of the American political system requires participation by as many citizens as possible. Such participation is made far more feasible and palatable when the individual understands what is going on and how he fits into the given political activity.

This book also is designed to be of use to the concerned observer who, for whatever reasons, may choose not to become an active participant in a campaign. As a campaign unfolds, there seems to be a frenetic rush of activity: appearances by the candidate, proselytizing by supporters, reports of public opinion polls, insistent voices of advertising media. All these factors contribute to a campaign's degree of efficiency and all should be interrelated to some extent. Anyone interested in evaluating the ongoing effectiveness of a campaign requires some basic standards upon which he can base his judgment. This book makes no claims of presenting a foolproof formula for how a campaign should be run, but it does set forth an outline of basic elements of campaigning that almost every candidate must utilize. There are surprisingly many campaigns that are poorly run, neglecting tactics and tasks simply because they are not thought of. For someone interested in judging whether a given campaign is a "good" one, a comprehensive knowledge of the political essentials is invaluable. We have tried to include these essential matters in our presentation.

The format of this book is designed to provide the reader with a step-by-step guide to the practice of electoral politics. Chapter 1, by Professor Brown, presents a broad overview of the political system, concentrating on voting behavior and the role of the political parties. Chapters 2 through 13, by Professor Seib, outline possible ways for the individual to become involved in politics, and explain the process by which a political campaign is created and conducted. In Chapters 14 through 16, Professor Brown provides in-depth explanations of some of the more complex aspects of campaigning: the uses of aggregate data, the techniques of public opinion polling, and the post-Watergate methods of campaign finance.

Expertise in politics, just as in any other field, is a relative matter. It can be acquired, to a limited degree, from an academic approach to the subject matter, but it also requires a certain amount of practical experience. We urge students and all others interested in politics to pursue this combined approach. We hope that in this book you will find the tools that will make such a venture a success.

J.B.<br>P.M.S.

August 1975

# THE ART OF
# POLITICS

## ELECTORAL STRATEGIES
## and
## CAMPAIGN MANAGEMENT

# 1

# An Overview
# The Voter, Parties,
# and the Polity

### Suffrage—The Legal Setting

The Constitution of the United States originally left the regulation of elections and the qualifications for voting primarily to the states, but since the Civil War the federal government has played an increasingly larger role in these areas.

Through the years there has been a steady expansion of suffrage. Some of this liberalization has been initiated on the state level. A greater part of it, however, has resulted from amendments to the United States Constitution, Supreme Court decisions, and Congressional action.

At the time of the adoption of the Constitution, suffrage was restricted to adult white males who met certain property-holding and religious qualifications. These qualifications were to be swept aside by the influence of Jacksonian democracy, with its faith in the masses. The Fourteenth, Fifteenth, and Nineteenth amendments limit the states' powers to restrict the vote on the basis of race and sex. Most recently the Twenty-sixth Amendment set the minimum voting age at eighteen for all elections.[1]

The Fifteenth Amendment, relating to discrimination on the basis of race, has been the most difficult to implement. Efforts at implementation have been resisted, especially in the South, by social, economic, and physical pressures directed against voting by blacks, as well as by political means such as regulations and practices sanctioned by state laws (these exclusionary or discriminatory practices have been invalidated). Among the latter have been: (1) the "grandfather clause" which provided that one could not register to vote unless one could read and write or unless one owned property. However, if one's father or grandfather had voted prior to 1867 that individual was exempt from the above qualifications;[2]    (2)  the "White Primary" which excluded blacks in several southern states from voting in the Democratic primary, leaving them no effective choice among candidates because the nominees of the Democratic party were usually unopposed in the general election;[3] (3) the poll tax which tended to discourage poor whites as well as blacks from voting;[4] and  (4)  the literacy test requirements which were primarily aimed at blacks.

The literacy test is still in effect in several states although its use has been severely restricted. In the 1964 Civil Rights Act, Congress required the states to accept a sixth-grade education as meeting the literacy requirements unless illiteracy could otherwise be proven. The 1965 Civil Rights Act went even further in limiting discrimination in the application of literacy tests. It grew out of dissatisfaction with the rate of progress in registering blacks, as dramatized by the events in Selma, Alabama, and the march on the state capitol led by Martin Luther King. As a result the national government could suspend literacy tests and directly register voters in the event the test was found to be discriminatory. In the first two years following the passage of this act, black registration nearly tripled. Continuing congressional concern over voting rights led to passage of the Voting Rights Acts of 1970 and 1975. These acts basically extended the 1965 act for five-year intervals and prohibited literacy tests where states had required that they be taken in English only. The 1970 act also confined residency requirements for voting in presidential elections to thirty days and established uniform standards for absentee registration and balloting in presidential elections. The 1975 Voting Rights Act continues for seven years, through August 1982, the basic protections of the Voting Rights Act of 1965 and requires that states provide for bilingual ballots if they had not done so by

2

1972 and if the ethnic minority exceeds 5 percent of their population. The 1975 act extends this basic protection to certain language minorities defined as persons of Spanish heritage, American Indians, Asian Americans, and Alaskan natives. In essence, the Voting Rights Act of 1965, as amended in subsequent years and bolstered by court decisions, has displaced with federal authority the power of the states over voting requirements and the supervision of elections, especially in those areas with a past history of discrimination against blacks and other minorities. Federal officials are now mandated to enroll and protect the right to vote of all those who are qualified. States still impose the basic qualifications for voting, but Congress has determined that it is necessary and proper for the national government to enforce the Fourteenth and Fifteenth amendments.

State governments now commonly require: (1) U.S. citizenship; (2) a minimum residency in the state, county, or precinct (but no more than thirty days for voting in presidential elections or fifty days in state and local elections); (3) registration; and (4) a minimum age, now uniformly eighteen. State governments may disqualify those who have been declared insane or who are convicted of a felony, those dishonorably discharged from the armed forces, or wards of the state.

Generally speaking, these legal requirements closely approximate the democratic ideal of universal adult suffrage. Yet in every election in the United States a large proportion of the electorate *does not* participate. This may range from 40 percent or so of the eligible voters in presidential elections to as much as 90 percent or more in local contests. In the last two presidential elections about 40 percent of those eligible went to the polls. Over 60 percent of the electorate stayed home in the congressional election of 1974. Many of these individuals do not vote because they think it is not worth the bother.

Another substantial portion of nonvoters would like to vote, but for various reasons they are unable to do so. These involuntary nonvoters fall into two groups. The first consists of blacks and other ethnic minorities (Chicanos, Indian-Americans) who have been illegally but effectively excluded by such devices as intimidation and arbitrary interpretations of the election laws (e.g., literacy tests). The Voting Rights acts mentioned earlier have been effective deterrents in ending most of this kind of discrimination.

The other group of involuntary nonvoters includes those who would like to vote but cannot because they have moved and have not satisfied the residency requirements in their new electoral district *or* who will be absent from their voting district on election day. Registering to vote or obtaining an absentee ballot is bothersome and time-consuming and often compels a potential voter to initiate action long before he or she faces election issues.

However, the prime reasons for not voting are not institutional, rather they are personal. Millions of Americans are just not interested enough to go to the polls to vote for a president and even fewer vote in state and local elections. It seems to be their feeling that (1) politics is not important, (2) there is no real choice among candidates, (3) they do not know enough to vote, or (4) they are "disgusted with politics" altogether. Some may fear losing wages or business if they take time out to go to the polls. Much nonvoting is a result of a combination of low interest and inconvenience: elderly people might vote if the polls were around the corner—but they may be three miles away, it might be raining, and they often lack transportation. Of course, sometimes this inconvenience is simply a way of rationalizing lack of interest.

Should such apathy surprise us? How much interest should a voter evidence to qualify for voting? Enough to take the initiative to register and then wait in line for half a day to perform his duty? Should we encourage or perhaps even require everyone eligible to vote? For example, should we make voting mandatory as in Belgium or Australia? The answers to these questions have been debated throughout our history by many without reaching a concensus on the best way to increase voter turnout. This is the dilemma that faces all democratic governments. Fortunately, there are certain "agents," among them political parties, which act as buffers between the "raw" citizen-voter and governmental actions.

## Political Parties and the Law

It was George Washington's desire to have a partyless government or a government above parties. No provision was made in the Constitution for parties and Congress has done very little to regulate them. At the state level other problems emerge which have resulted in a considerable volume of legislation regulating all facets of party activity: nominating procedures, election practices, organization, and selection of party committees.

Up until the mid-nineteenth century, political parties were considered private organizations, and as such were unregulated by public law. To a certain extent at both the national and state levels today parties are viewed as being quasi-private, quasi-public institutions.[5] The Civil War, followed by the era of boss rule and corruption in the late 1880s and early 1900s, led to regulations and restrictions on party activity. Many of these regulations, as mentioned above, stemmed from acts of Congress and court rulings. Both state and federal laws regulate political parties. The states, for example, impose their own requirements concerning how a political party may qualify candidates on the ballot. New or third parties may be asked to meet rigorous requirements, such as securing the names of thousands of eligible voters from various parts of the state on a petition to qualify as a party. The broad outline of political party organization, both permanent and temporary, is also set by state law (see Figure 1-1). At the bottom of the permanent organization are precinct committee persons, precinct captains, or in some cases county chairpersons who are usually chosen in the primary committees from each county, district, or other unit from which public officials are elected, e.g. ward (city council districts), state legislation or senatorial districts, congressional districts, and state central committees. Generally, each of these permanent committees is selected by a convention or meeting of the committees just under it in the organizational structure.

The temporary organizations of the party usually follow the party committee structure. These are the various conventions whose legally defined duties are not too impressive: they

5

are formed to elect delegates to the next level of convention (precinct, county, or district, to state, to national), to draft the party platform, to choose delegates to the national convention, and to select presidential electors. At the apex of the party organizational structure are the national convention and national committee, which are founded on no basis of law. Both of these are made up of individuals selected at the state level, either in convention or by state executive committees. What appears to be a pyramiding of state party representation into a single, integrating national party authority is in reality nothing of the kind, but rather merely a confederation of party representatives who are brought together for a limited purpose.

These conventions do offer a rationale for organized political effort by providing the party an opportunity to recruit and socialize political activists. They serve as a means of developing leadership and are also used as barometers for conditions within each party insofar as they act as crude indicators of the strength of various factions and personalities.

Two other areas of state law that primarily affect political parties and political activity are nominations and campaign financing. The earliest method of securing a nomination for governor, state legislator, or other elective administrative post was through the endorsement of a political caucus, an informal meeting of a small number of political leaders. The caucus gave way to the convention method in the early nineteenth century, and beginning in the late nineteenth century the convention method was replaced, through the dictate of state laws, by the direct primary through which voters could participate in the nominating process. The most common type of primary, used in forty states, is the closed primary in which only registered voters of the party may participate, but the criteria for membership vary greatly. In some cases, the voter must declare party affiliation at the time of registration and may not vote in the primary of any other party without registering a change of party affiliation in a timely fashion. Those who register as independents have no primary at all in which to vote. A half dozen other states, mostly in the upper Midwest, have open primaries in which the voter may freely choose in the privacy of the voting booth the primary in which he will participate.

At present, two states (Washington and Alaska) utilize the "blanket" or "free-love" primary which, as in regular elections, allows the voter to split his vote for candidates in each party, nominating his favorite for each office regardless of party affiliation.

As the nominating process has moved from caucus to convention to primary, the system has become more democratic. In many areas the only opportunity the voter has to make a choice among candidates is to vote in the primary of the dominant party. Primaries have also helped party reformers to defy party officials by permitting them to appeal directly to the voters.

**Figure 1-1** FORMAL PARTY ORGANIZATION

TEMPORARY                                    PERMANENT

| National Convention | | National Chairperson |
|---|---|---|
| | | National Committee |

| State Convention | ---> | State Chairperson |
|---|---|---|
| | | State Executive Committee |

| District Convention |
|---|

| County Convention | | Executive Committee |
|---|---|---|
| | | County, City, or Town Chairperson |

——— Direct Control
- - - - Tenuous Control

| Precinct or Ward Conventions | ---> | Ward Committee |
|---|---|---|
| | | Precint or Ward Chairperson |

Voters

At the same time primaries have undoubtedly made campaigns more expensive, giving an advantage to those with access to funds, and have lessened party cohesion. Often the primaries precipitate and expose internal party divisions resulting in public disputes which not only embarrass the party but make it

7

more difficult to unite party members behind the nominee. Party officials also must worry about the possibility of "raiding," where the members of one party vote in another party's primary. The fear is that the voters from the other party will attempt to secure the worst possible candidate, one who could easily be defeated in the general election. It may well be, however, that the crossover voter actually is merely voting for the candidate he prefers.

Some evidence suggests that there is a direct correlation between the money spent by a candidate for primary and general elections and eventual success at the polls.[6] There are, of course, two campaigns—one for nomination and one for election—and each may last many months. Campaigns are expensive and growing more so. A presidential aspirant, for example, may campaign for at least a year before election: Goldwater in 1964, Nixon in 1968, McGovern in 1972, and Udall, Jackson, and Wallace in 1976. A candidate for the state legislature from an urban district can expect to spend anywhere from $5,000 to $50,000, while a candidate for governor of a large state needs over a million dollars to win a primary and conduct a general election campaign. Traditionally, unless a candidate was independently wealthy, he has had to rely on contributions, the bulk of which have come from large contributors who may hold various expectations concerning the candidate's political behavior after the election. The perennial problem is not so much the amount of money involved— politics inevitably will be expensive. The problem in a democracy is *inequality*. Do large sums of money donated to a political campaign generate a disproportionate amount of political power for the donor? Although this proposition has not been wholly proved, how does it square with the doctrine of government by the people?

Fear of corruption and abuses in campaign financing have prompted the states and the federal government to adopt acts that will have a limiting effect on such practices. These acts do all or some of the following:

——Impose limits on how money is spent by candidates and/or committees working on the candidates' behalf. Maximum amounts may be set at a specific dollar amount for a political office or an estimate based on the number of votes cast for the office at the last election (e.g., 25c to 50c per voter). Under federal regulation, public financing is now available for major party candidates and for holding of national conventions.

——Impose limits on the sources and size of contributions. Corporations, unions, and those who hold public contracts or licenses from state agencies may be forbidden to contribute. Size of contributions may also be limited, and measures have been adopted to prevent "laundering" of funds by channeling them through campaign committees.

——Impose upon candidates the responsibility for the accuracy of all campaign financial reports. The candidate or his campaign treasurer is required to keep track of funds, to divulge the sources of support and publish expenditures, and to make public reports during the primary and general campaigns and upon their conclusion.[7]

The criticisms raised and explanations sought regarding campaign funding are so complex that they do not lend themselves to easy solutions. There will be a return to this issue of campaign financing and the allied questions of Watergate and election reform in Chapter 16.

## Parties and the Political Arena

A further perspective on parties is the historical one in which parties are viewed as a series of "grand coalitions" of groups and sectional leaders and interests that slowly shift their focuses and allegiances over time. Although a complete history of party organization and doctrine cannot be undertaken in this volume, a short review is in order.

Two-party contests for the presidency did not begin with any regularity until 1832, but there was a basis for party struggle in the early days of the Republic, when Federalists vied against Jeffersonians for the presidency in 1796 and 1816. The Federalists viewed the industrial society as important and favored using the powers of the central government to promote it. Hamilton favored the dominance of the rich and wellborn. On the other hand, the Jeffersonians, and later Jackson's followers, argued for an agrarian society, had faith in the masses, and emphasized states' rights and the philosophy that the government that governs least is best. Embracing small farmers, laborers, frontiersmen, slaveowners, and debtors, and with a base primarily in the central and southern states, this coalition dominated American politics for two generations. The Whigs rose to challenge the Jeffersonian Republicans with their view of a strong legislature, with minority interests which would have an opportunity to block the majority, and with their rejection of a strong executive. But the Democratic party, utilizing its Jeffersonian symbols and holding on to its component groups, was able to overcome Whig opposition in most elections. Neither party, however, seemed able to deal with the explosive issue of slavery. Out of this issue and the Civil War came a new major party—the Republican party. As the party "of the union," the Republicans had support from a multitude of groups: financiers, merchants, industrialists, workers, farmers, and the newly freed Negroes. For about five decades beginning in 1860, this coalition was to win the presidency in all cases except for the Grover Cleveland victories of 1884 and 1892. On the other hand, the Democratic party survived with its durable base in the South.

During the twentieth century, both parties have remained true to the rule that under a two-party system neither party can take an extremist position. Both parties have contained elements that were conservative and liberal, and further, both appealed to interests that included business and labor. It was not until 1930 that the Democratic party was able to build a countercoalition that was directly attributable to the Hoover administration and the Great Depression. Franklin Roosevelt brought together a coalition of farmers, laborers, unemployed middle-class workers, Negroes, and national minorities which was to reelect Democrats to the presidency continuously from 1932 until 1968, except for the Eisenhower years, 1952-60. Would it now again be the Republicans' turn? Richard Nixon was able to assemble a coalition of middle-class voters, workers, suburbanites, various business elements, and southern conservatives. Neither Hubert Humphrey in 1968 nor George McGovern in 1972 could attract enough supporters to overcome Nixon's organization. It should be pointed out, however, that the Democratic party retained large majorities in Congress. To date, particularly since Watergate, it would appear that neither party has been able to put together a viable coalition strong enough to dominate American politics for years to come. This is perhaps attributable to the increase in the proportion of Independent party identifiers (see Table 2), individuals who reject either party label.

As our brief history emphasizes, political parties have always concerned themselves with the building of "grand coalitions." Since their creation, the major parties have been diversified and heterogeneous in composition. To succeed, a party must draw support from all the large elements of society. This was, in essence, the major cause of George McGovern's defeat in 1972; even though the Democratic party is broadly based, it could not avoid enervating factionalism.

Historically, the parties that have remained in power have been highly pragmatic and adapted themselves to changing times. Inflexibility in the face of change often assures losing a following to the opposition. In addition, to be successful a party must require that new majorities, upon assuming control, retain those parts of a predecessor's regime that have proved popular. The discussion thus far has argued for coalition building on the part of the two major parties, with little if any attention accorded third parties. Why is this the case? The two-party system at the national level is attributable in part to the Constitution. The election of the president through party slates of electors in each state has a bipolarizing effect. Third-party nominees are easily squeezed out. The single-member congressional districts with selection on the basis of a plurality vote make it difficult for third-party nominees to capture more votes than either of the major-party opponents. As pointed out earlier, state laws militate against third parties. Major parties receive the political patronage and select the election officials. A third-party candidate or an independent frequently encounters difficulty in placing his name on the ballot. In addition, the division of power between the national government and the states makes it very difficult for a third group to propose an adequate slate of candidates at all levels—national, state, and local, except for unusual temporary cases (such as Theodore Roosevelt's Progressive party in 1912 or George Wallace's American Independent party in 1968). Only the Republican party, founded in 1856 when the old parties could not reconcile their differences over the issue of slavery, has succeeded in becoming a major force.

Constitutional arrangements are buttressed by social psychological, economic, and political factors working in favor of a national two-party system. Historically, the nation began with a two-party grouping, and there is a tendency for parties to harden into "ins" and "outs." As one noted author observed, there is always a "duality of tendencies."[8] Practically speaking, third parties have never offered much hope of victory to ambitious and competent prospective candidates. Voters are creatures of habit, and tradition has it that voting for a third-party candidate is in essence throwing one's vote away. The great majority of Americans take a moderate and centrist position, which in turn has been embraced by both the Democratic and Republican parties.

As indicated previously, nationally the two major parties are loose configurations of local and sectional interests, whereas internally (organizationally) political parties are completely controlled by state regulation. Furthermore, all officials for the House of Representatives and state legislatures are elected in local constituencies. The president of the United States is the only official elected nationally, while governors and senators and at-large congressmen are elected on a statewide ballot. This makes it difficult for parties nationally to maintain centralized control and to formulate policy, especially when elected officials are locally elected and responsible. Yet nationally the parties and their leaders have centripetal pull while state and local parties function as decentralizers—the centrifugal pull of federalism. Although we may think we are operating under a two-party system, in reality each state has its own party system, and a basically autonomous one at that. We might go so far as to say that it is within the realm of possibility to have 50 Democratic and 50 Republican parties. More precisely, about half of the states have virtually a one-party system, although state party systems vary from monopolistic one-party to highly competitive two-party. All this is to say that state and local parties are entities unto themselves and not adjuncts invariably following the fortunes of a president or the lead of Congress.

## Voting Behavior and Party Linkages

American political parties are quite heterogeneous in structure, membership, and ideology. They play a dominant role in the selection of candidates for the voters to choose among, but more importantly they provide the citizen with an organized and legitimate means for exercising political power and influence. What actually is this relationship between parties and the individual voter? Who votes? For whom do they vote and why?

The subject of voting has produced many volumes and the promise of many more. Our attention must be limited to what the major variables are, what the data reveal about them, and what their implications are for the party system.

If you asked random voters why they voted for Nixon or Humphrey or Wallace in 1968, one might reply "Because I'm a Republican"; another, "Because Humphrey is for the little man"; yet another, "Because Wallace really says what he thinks."

There is no doubt that factors such as socioeconomic status, religion, family influence, and the state of national affairs affect our political attitudes; but our conscious feelings about parties, candidates, and issues are the immediate determinants of our voting behavior. These attitudes intervene between the more general and distant sociological and political forces that are exerted on the voter and his actual vote for Nixon, Humphrey, or Wallace, or for that matter the decision not to vote at all.

Since the first major study *(The Voter Decides)* was undertaken by Angus Campbell and his colleagues at the Survey Research Center of the University of Michigan in 1952, party identification has become a relatively uncomplicated psychological measure which arrays responses to the following questions:

"Generally speaking, do you usually think of yourself as a Republican, Democrat, Independent, or some other affiliation? Would you call yourself a strong (R) (D) or not very strong

(R) (D)? (If Independent) Do you think of yourself as closer to the Republican or Democratic party?"

> Strong Democrat
> Democrat
> Independent
> Republican
> Strong Republican

This psychological measure of self-identification of party loyalty is the best indicator of partisanship. Partisanship is the most important single influence on political opinions and voting behavior. No less than 65 percent of the American people express some degree of party preference, with almost 25 percent strongly attached to a particular party. They acquire this feeling of sympathy for and loyalty to a political party probably during childhood, and this preference usually endures throughout life. This self-image as a Democrat or a Republican is useful to that individual in a very special way. One who thinks of himself as a Democrat, for example, will respond to political information by using party identification to orient himself, and will react to new information in such a way that it fits within the ideals and feelings he already possesses.

Figure 1-2 shows that party identification is one of the most stable of all forces in American politics. The evidence drawn from history indicates that large masses of voters switch their basic loyalties only in rare instances of great crisis. One such time was the Civil War and the Reconstruction period, when the Republicans emerged as a majority party. The most recent was the Great Depression, the New Deal decade of the thirties, when the Democrats displaced the Republicans as the majority party and first achieved the dominance that Figure 1-2 shows they still enjoy.

A number of studies indicate that the most partisan people (the strong identifiers) are the ones most interested in election campaigns. They expose themselves to political discussions, they possess the most political information, they defect less to opposition candidates, they are the least prone to split their ticket, and they have the highest ratio of voters to nonvoters. The reverse is also true; the least partisan people (the weak identifiers) are the least interested, engage in the least political discussion, know the least about public affairs, and have the lowest ratio of voters to nonvoters.

Roughly one third of the voters can be classified as some type of independent—but "independent" is a tricky word. Some persons are called independents because they cross and recross party lines from election to election. Others are "ticket splitters"—in the same election they vote for candidates of different parties. Still others call themselves independents because they think it is socially more respectable, but actually they vote with some regularity for one party, as do others who are not so hesitant to admit party loyalty. Is the independent voter the more informed voter? There has been heated debate over this question, with much of it fruitless because it ultimately depends on what kind of independent one is talking about—a voter who fails to express a preference between candidates or a voter who switches parties between elections. The most nearly correct view of the independent voter is that he is not very interested in government or politics and certainly not concerned with partisan politics (he is not emotionally involved in party clashes). On the other hand, independents appear to have the information and the perspective on political affairs necessary for an evaluation of issues and candidates. The ideal independent may be a person of proud and free conscience, but the real-life independent is more likely to be one who couldn't care less about the whole process. Party identification colors one's attitudes toward issues and candidates. When a short-term force such as an overriding issue or an exciting charismatic candidate enters an election, party-label responses become less important.

As previously noted, the two major parties have fared very well in surveys of numbers of voters claiming party loyalty. It is not yet known precisely how party identification operates over a period of time, if at all. That is, if the Democrats or Republicans receive the majority of the total votes cast in a presidential election, does this then mean that most of the voters consider themselves Democrats or Republicans during the interim between elections? As already observed, many people today increasingly classify themselves as independents while casting votes for one of the two major parties. This perhaps suggests that the participation rate of 60 percent of eligible voters

Figure 1-2  **THE DISTRIBUTION OF PARTY IDENTIFICATION IN THE UNITED STATES**, 1952-74

Question: "Generally speaking, do you usually think of yourself as a Republican, a Democrat, an Independent, or what? (If Republican or Democrat) Would you call yourself a strong (R) (D) or a not very strong (R) (D)? (If Independent) Do you think of yourself as closer to the Republican or Democratic party?"

| | Oct. 1952 | Oct. 1954 | Oct. 1956 | Oct. 1958 | Oct. 1960 | Oct. 1962 | Oct. 1964 | Oct. 1966 | Oct. 1968 | Oct. 1970 | Oct. 1972 | Oct. 1973 | Oct. 1974 |
|---|---|---|---|---|---|---|---|---|---|---|---|---|---|
| **Democrat** | | | | | | | | | | | | | |
| Strong | 22% | 22% | 21% | 23% | 21% | 23% | 26% | 18% | 20% | 20% | 15% | 13% | 17% |
| Weak | 25 | 25 | 23 | 24 | 25 | 23 | 25 | 27 | 25 | 23 | 25 | 23 | 24 |
| **Independent** | | | | | | | | | | | | | |
| Democrat | 10% | 9% | 7% | 7% | 8% | 8% | 9% | 9% | 10% | 10% | 11% | 14% | 12% |
| Independent | 5 | 7 | 9 | 8 | 8 | 8 | 8 | 12 | 11 | 13 | 13 | 18 | 20 |
| Republican | 7 | 6 | 8 | 4 | 7 | 6 | 6 | 7 | 9 | 8 | 11 | 9 | 8 |
| **Republican** | | | | | | | | | | | | | |
| Weak | 14% | 14% | 14% | 16% | 13% | 16% | 13% | 15% | 14% | 15% | 13% | 13% | 12% |
| Strong | 13 | 13 | 15 | 13 ˙ | 14 | 12 | 11 | 10 | 10 | 10 | 10 | 8 | 7 |
| Apolitical, Don't Know | 4 | 4 | 3 | 5 | 4 | 4 | 2 | 2 | 1 | 1 | 2 | 2 | 0 |
| Total | 100% | 100% | 100% | 100% | 100% | 100% | 100% | 100% | 100% | 100% | 100% | 100% | 100% |
| Number of Cases | 1614 | 1139 | 1772 | 1269 | 3021 | 1289 | 1571 | 1291 | 1553 | 1802 | 2705 | 1444 | 1211 |

**Source:** The Center for Political Studies of the University of Michigan data made available through the Inter-University Consortium for Political Research, Ann Arbor, Mich.

in recent presidential elections is more indicative of interest in the office of the presidency and its aspirants, rather than an absolute and enduring loyalty to a party. Elections are not won simply on the basis of party identification; they are won by physically getting the supporters out to the polls.

A winning strategy for a candidate often requires that partisanship be de-emphasized. Candidates who direct their strongest campaign efforts toward their own party make a serious error (except in one-party states or districts) because these votes can generally be counted on anyway. The votes required to win lie in the uncommitted center (see Figure 1-2) and among the opposition party's weak identifiers—those with less intense party loyalties.

## Social Differentiation and the Vote

There is undoubtedly a link between psychological factors and sociological ones. The sociologist's conception of voting behavior tends to proceed from the importance of occupation and from diverse demographic characteristics such as socioeconomic status, religion, race, age, sex. However, there appears to be a gap in understanding and explaining the linkages between psychological and sociological influences. A major problem confronting one who studies the variables that affect voting behavior is the difficulty of isolating the impact of one variable from another. Beyond that, no social group acts unanimously; many have distinct central political tendencies that stem from their position in the society. There are two main types of groups with which the politician or campaign organizer should be concerned.

*Primary groups* are the face-to-face groups with which we are associated, such as family, friends, fellow workers, and colleagues. The most direct and most powerful social influences on voting behavior are those exerted by this group. All available evidence indicates that families and groups of friends are very likely to be homogeneous. These include initially one's parents and those living in the household; then friends, and later husbands or wives and co-workers. Most individuals are not overtly pressured by primary group members to conform or to change politically, at least not to the degree that they are influenced casually by the expression of the same ideas and values. It is

17

also most probable that members of any primary group are socially, economically, ethically, and racially alike because the same general social influences are at work on them. It is usually extremely painful for anyone to abandon the security and comfort of familiarity for the lonely and demanding posture of "standing on principle" at the cost of hurting family or angering friends.

*Secondary groups* may be defined as secondary organizations or collections of individuals with whom one identifies or is identified but which are too large to make contact with personally; e.g., social classes, labor union members, blacks, Jews, Japanese-Americans. The impact imparted by these nonprimary groups is based on the realization that one has an affinity with them. For example, college professors may join the American Association of University Professors; but even if they do not, they are conscious of an identity with other professors. Jews, Greeks, Catholics, farmers, policemen, truckdrivers, and persons in scores of other social and occupational categories may meet only a relatively few of their cohorts, yet they are conscious of common problems and outlook. Because of these shared interests, many of these groups form associations to advance the group's interests. As a result these kinds of groups become reference points for the individual. However, several psychological factors impinge upon the individual and the influence that a secondary group may have upon him. The first is the strength of the individual's identification with the group. The more conscious one is of being a Jew or a black, the stronger the group influence on him. Second, in turn, is related to the length of time one has been a member of the group. The longer the membership, the stronger one's psychological involvement with it. Third is the salience of politics for the group's leaders. The more important they perceive politics to be, the more they will insist that particular actions are marks of group loyalty, and the harder it will be for a group member to act otherwise. Finally, how important is politics to the individual? If one holds views deviant from the group and these views are salient, one will tend to disassociate from such a group. But if politics seems relatively unimportant, or at least less important than the relationship to the group, the individual is more likely to do as the leadership wishes.

The ways in which all of these factors affect individuals indicates that the political influence of any secondary group varies among its members. There will always be substantial differences between one group and another in the solidarity of the membership's preferences and the degrees of their activity.

## Social Class or Categorical Group Membership

Some of the leading hypotheses of social and political theory link social classes and political behavior. Generally speaking, the expectations surrounding social classes include the fact that there are differences in economic and social interests, and that these conflicting interests, which follow class lines, are translated into political action. Major political and sociological theories of social class have taken for granted the supreme importance of class interests, but all evidence indicates that this assumption is somewhat unrealistic in American society. About one third of all American adults say they never think of themselves as members of a social class.

A majority of Americans, however, are able to place themselves in a general position if given a choice between "middle class" and "working class" and, to some extent, "upper" and "lower" within a particular class. These individual self-ratings are not perfectly congruent with the ratings that a social analyst might assign on the basis of characteristics such as income, education, and occupation, but a social class structure does exist. Studies indicate, for example, that in the 1948 presidential election there was a much stronger relationship between vote choice and social class than in the elections of 1944, 1952, and 1956. In other words, those who supported Roosevelt and Eisenhower were from both the middle and working classes. These patterns of low relationships have continued through the 1972 election. Such voting patterns of low association reflect in great part the tendency of political leaders to de-emphasize highly divisive social class issues. Furthermore, there is a conscious effort by American politicians to make broad appeals intended to cross and disrupt class lines. Not all groups of Americans are equally likely to vote. In general, those groups that are socially disadvantaged tend to be nonvoters, while the socially advantaged are the ones who regularly show up at the polls to cast their vote.

The following are the factors that influence voting behavior (see Figure 1-3).

*Income.* The more money a person makes, the more likely he or she is to vote. Recently, however, there are signs that income alone is not an adequate indicator of whether a person will participate in politics. Younger people without regular incomes took part in large numbers in the Robert Kennedy, McCarthy, McGovern, and Wallace campaigns.

*Sex.* Men are more likely to vote than women, although in recent elections the voting gap between men and women has narrowed. Despite these general differences, men and women of approximately the same educational level take part in politics in almost equal proportions. Neither sex favors either political party. If there are differences, they could reflect other social characteristics rather than intrinsic political differences.

*Education.* The higher a person's educational level, the more likely he or she is to vote. Also, studies indicate that persons with college educations are more likely to be active in politics than those with high school and grade school educations.

Many consistently Republican voters tend to have more formal education than Democratic voters; and because education is part of class status, many Republicans are from the upper class.

Although many Republicans are college graduates, not all college graduates are Republicans.

*Age.* People between the ages of thirty-five and sixty are more likely to vote than are younger or older persons. It would appear that people do not establish regular voting habits until they have established some sort of life-style. The decline in voting among the elderly seems to be due to physical infirmities. No age group shows consistent partisan preferences, but age does influence political choice.

*Race.* Whites are more likely to vote than are nonwhites. In American elections, blacks register and vote in smaller proportions than whites; whites also tend to know more often who their congressmen and senators are and what political party they represent. But these differences are attributable to low social standing (education and income) of blacks rather than mere color. Minority voter turnout rises greatly when a member of a minority is a candidate for office. As to party preference, since before 1936 blacks have tended to vote Democratic.

On the other hand, voting studies indicate that the Democratic party also draws electoral support from voters of Irish, Italian, and Slavic descent. Republicans still appeal to Americans of English, Scottish, German, and Scandinavian ancestry.

*Religion.* Another characteristic of political participation closely related to social class is association with a religious group. Generally, Protestants tend to be the least active (with Episcopalians and Presbyterians slightly more active than Baptists). Catholics are more active than Protestants, with Jews the most active proportionally. One should keep in mind that the lower participation by Protestants does not alter the fact that they make up two-thirds of the American electorate. To some extent these differences in participation are attributable to the use of politics by Catholics and Jews to combat religious and ethnic discrimination.

Although there are both Catholic Republicans and Protestent Democrats, Protestants are more often affiliated with the Republican party, Jews most often vote Democratic, and while Catholics support Democratic candidates less often than Jews, they still will remain a major source of Democratic voting strength.

A major reason for these differences in voting patterns is the degree to which people believe they can influence political decisions, to the "political efficacy" of the electorate—the extent to which the public believes "the affairs of government can be understood and influenced by individual citizens."[9]

Neither of the two major parties has a secure base of support in any of these social characteristics. Neither is in a position to appeal to deep-seated animosities between category groups—rich and poor, educated and uneducated, Protestant and Catholic—as might occur in many countries outside of the United States. Instead, as indicated elsewhere, both parties must help mold a consensus among people of different social backgrounds by blunting the conflicts between diverse interests.

## The Voter's Decision

It has been argued that relatively stable party identification conditions one's voting behavior, that is, the way in which the

21

voter looks at the candidates, parties, and issues in political campaigns. Voter evaluation of these forces is consistent with party loyalties, particularly if they are "strong Democrats or strong Republicans." If all voting choices depended upon strong partisanship and the tendency to act consistent with it, the winners and losers would be determined simply by how many voters of

Figure 1-3

## PARTICIPATION IN NATIONAL ELECTIONS
## BY POPULATION CHARACTERISTICS
### 1968 and 1972

| Characteristics | Percentage Voting | |
|---|---|---|
| | 1968 | 1972 |
| Male | 69.8 | 64.1 |
| Female | 66.0 | 62.0 |
| White | 69.1 | 64.5 |
| Negro | 57.6 | 52.1 |
| **Age** | | |
| 18 to 20 years | 33.3 | 48.3 |
| 21 to 24 years | 51.1 | 50.7 |
| 24 to 34 years | 62.5 | 59.7 |
| 35 to 44 years | 70.8 | 66.3 |
| 45 to 64 years | 74.9 | 70.8 |
| 65 and over | 65.8 | 63.5 |
| **Education** | | |
| 8 years or less | 54.5 | 47.4 |
| 9 to 11 years | 61.3 | 52.0 |
| 12 years | 72.5 | 65.4 |
| More than 12 years | 81.2 | 78.8 |
| **Employment** | | |
| Employed | 71.1 | 66.0 |
| Unemployed | 52.1 | 49.0 |

Source: *Statistical Abstract of the United States*, p. 437.

each party went to the polls to express their loyalties. Campaigns then would be designed not to build winning coalitions but to retain the support and increase the turnout of those who had already made up their minds.

During a campaign, voters may learn that their party's candidate has a quality or a position that they find disagreeable, as was the case in the 1960 presidential election. Voters were torn between Kennedy, the Catholic and Democratic candidate, and Nixon, the Protestant but Republican contender. On what basis do voters decide when faced with such a conflict?

People who are confronted by these contradictory influences (cross-pressures) try to order their personal attitudes and perceptions of reality, thus composing a consistent outlook. Social psychologists call this effort a "strain toward consistency," a "drive toward congruity," or a "reduction of dissonance." The cross-pressured voter will attempt to achieve consistency by changing a previous attitude. If, however, the voter finds it impossible to resolve this conflict between his attitudes and the contradictory views of the political leaders or party policy position, he may split his vote, make a late decision on voting, or simply not vote at all. In the last resort he will seek not to distort his perceptions of what is going on nor change his personal views, thus relieving himself of the need to settle this inner conflict.

The discussion of political parties and voting has thus come full circle. The fact that both political parties must build "grand coalitions" and attempt to gain significant support from all major groups keeps the Democratic and Republican parties anchored in the middle of the left-right political spectrum. Victory in elections depends upon gaining the support of independents and weak identifiers of the opposition party. Yet, there is another way of looking at this situation: American voters tend to be concentrated in the middle of the political spectrum because therein lies the only range of plausible political alternatives available to them.

As long as the two-party system endures, clearly differentiated political choices will be uncommon in American politics. In light of the structure of the American electoral system and of the nation's traditions, the two-party system is apt to be around for a long time, and American party politics will remain a politics of the center, appealing to the majority of voters. Two-party systems tend to compromise differences within parties prior to election, rather than compromising differences between parties after election as is the case with Western European parties.

Parties nominate candidates, provide the machinery in organizing government, promote continuity in the political struggle, and play a role in shaping policies and programs. Yet because of their diverse bases of support and the fact that they are organized from the bottom up, parties are prevented from exercising much control over candidates once they are in office.

Because of voter apathy, lack of a sense of political efficacy, and residency requirements, only a bare majority of the American public votes. Political affiliation and voter turnout are strongly related to income and educational levels. And yet voter loyalty to party tends to be high in spite of the coalitional nature of American political parties that makes them virtually indistinguishable on many issues.

## NOTES

1. Property-holding requirements for certain types of elections, e.g., bond elections, survived until very recently.

2. Guinn v. United States, 238 U.S. 357 (1915).

3. Smith v. Allwright, 321 U.S. 659 (1944).

4. The Twenty-fourth Amendment to the United States Constitution in 1964 ended the use of the poll tax in federal elections. In 1966 the Supreme Court forbade the poll tax as a condition in any election (Harper v. Virginia).

5. See the following decisions of the United States Supreme Court regarding political parties: Nixon v. Herndon, 273 U.S. 536 (1927), Nixon v. Condon, 286 U.S. 73 (1932), Grovey v. Townsend, 295 U.S. 45 (1935), United States v. Classic, 61 Sup. Ct. 1031 (1941), and Elmore v. Rice, 72 F. Supp. 516 (1947).

6. Herbert Alexander, *Political Financing* (Minneapolis: Burgess Publishing, 1972); *Congressional Quarterly* 33, no. 16 787–94.

7. *The Book of States* (Lexington: Council of State Governments, 1975), pp. 28–30.

8. Maurice Duverger, *Political Parties: Their Organization and Activities in Modern States* (New York: John Wiley & Sons, 1967).

9. Angus Campbell et al., *The American Voter* (New York: John Wiley & Sons, 1960), p. 473ff.

# 2
# Getting Started in Politics

It is not particularly difficult for any concerned person to become an active participant in politics. Political parties and related organizations (such as citizens' pressure groups espousing given causes) are increasingly eager to broaden their participatory bases through recruitment of "new blood." With a wide variety of avenues for involvement open to the newcomer, the task becomes one of judging among such factors as:

——Where can I be most effective?

——Where will I feel most comfortable with regard to ideology and method of operation?

——Where will I be most likely to advance any long-range goals and ambitions?

To find the answers to such questions, it is necessary to consider the various modes of entry into the political system.

## Affiliating with a Party

Although many people are wary of being swallowed up by a vast, insensitive party apparatus and although party politics is no longer the "only game in town," it would be a mistake to dismiss participation in party activities without first carefully examining the pros and cons of this kind of involvement.

In recent years both the Democratic and Republican parties have engaged in considerable soul-searching in an attempt to find ways in which party politics might be made more attractive to an increasingly disenchanted electorate. One of the Democratic party's reform commissions noted that it had proceeded in its work "against a backdrop of genuine unhappiness and mistrust of millions of Americans with our political system. We are aware that political parties are not the only way of organizing political life. Political parties will survive only if they respond to the needs and concerns of their members." The basic thrust of the response of the parties has been to provide a clear channel for involvement in delegate selection and the nomination process. A by-product of specific reforms in delegate selection procedures has been a de facto reform of party organization as a whole. In other words, requirements of the reformed nomination process could not be met unless the day-to-day operations were likewise made more open with regard to who can participate and how the party is to conduct all its internal business.

What does all this mean to the individual who is considering political action? Perhaps most importantly it connotes the removal of ceilings on advancement within the party. Positions still must be earned through hard work, but there is no longer an imposed cutoff point in party organization (be it national, state, or local) beyond which the newcomer cannot advance. Therefore, in appraising local party organizations, one must consider their degree of commitment to reform. One may find that the party structure is tailor-made for what the individual wishes to accomplish as a candidate, issue advocate, election worker, or anything else.

This consideration of what it is one desires to accomplish should be an integral part in judging the value of involvement in a party. If someone wants to have a voice in choosing who will be on the ballot or in developing via the party platform the policies that will be advocated in the course of a campaign, then participation in party politics is essential. It is unrealistic to hope to have much effect on the course a party takes if the attempt to wield influence is made from outside the party machinery. An individual's political power and influence generally will be in direct proportion to the extent of his active, internal participation.

Another factor that should be considered in evaluating party activity is the potential for long-term involvement and effectiveness. Like them or not, political parties are going to be with us for a long time and will probably outlast most non-party political organizations. If a person is thinking in terms of a career in politics or if his reason for political involvement is based on an issue that requires development over a considerable period of time, the permanency of a political party might be particularly attractive. The transient nature of most ad hoc organizations is sometimes a serious flaw in their effectiveness—the entrenched "establishment" can weather most challenges if it knows it can outlast the challenger. Therefore it might be more effective to try to change the "establishment" from within. Some people spend considerable time moving from "committee" to "movement" to "council" in an unending cycle that encompasses some lost causes and some successful ones. The participant should ask himself: How can my time best be spent? If he is thinking of long-range goals and long-term involvement, he might find that effectiveness can be heightened by working within a structure that has a degree of permanence. /

The same factors that make party activity seem the best means of political action must be considered in a negative light as well. The stability and permanence that can prove so useful to long-term activities may also lead to organizational stagnation. A lazy party organization concerned only with self-perpetuation not only will accomplish little or nothing, but it will also tend to smother the efforts of well-meaning newcomers who lack the strength or expertise to struggle with the party structure. Even a "reformed" party organization can be so controlled that new arrivals find themselves pressed into old molds. This lack of dynamism usually can be overcome, but it might require waging a campaign *within* the organization. The often devil-may-care political approach of many nonparty organizations may be lacking in some aspects of party politics, but with a proper dosage of ingenuity the situation can be enlivened. Politics can and should be fun; occasionally, politicians must be reminded of this.

Perhaps a more substantive problem with party involvement is the existence of a discrepancy between the ideology and basic principles of the party and the individual. The parties seem to be pursuing a "great umbrella" approach by claiming that there is room for everyone and every idea in each party. These claims understandably have a hollow sound to the person who is deeply committed to a specific issue position. In order to match his ideas to an acceptable form of political participation, he might well have to look outside the party system. The parties seem to offer the most comfortable home to the generalist or the person who is interested in taking his ideas and jointly shaping both those ideas and the political mechanism with which he is working. In the parties, one must be prepared for considerable give-and-take. But if a person has refined his position as far as possible and feels that it is neither morally nor pragmatically proper to undergo any further modification, there is no need for him to have to choose between submitting to the inherent constraints of a party or dropping out of politics altogether; he must be prepared to look beyond the offerings of the parties. The options open to this person will be discussed later in this chapter.

Successful participation in political parties is a demanding proposition. Those who make only a half-hearted commitment will find their effectiveness limited accordingly. Internal competition is endemic to party politics, and to at least a certain extent, one must play the game or be left behind. There are many deeply committed individuals who have neither the time nor the inclination to master the practice of party politics. Because their personal perspectives are sufficiently broad to allow them the realization that there are other things in life besides politics, their input into the political system is highly valuable. They will not—nor should they—fully conform to the demands of party participation, and yet the political system cannot afford to lose them. They should recognize that a party might not be their best mode of activity and they should likewise recognize that they might have to search a little harder to find a political mechanism suitable for themselves.

Political parties clearly have both advantages and disadvantages for those seeking to become active in politics. The decision as to approaching politics via a party or by some other method must be made on a highly individualized basis: consider *all* the factors involved as they apply to *you*. If one decides against entering party affairs as his first step into politics, he should remember that there are ample substitute courses of action.

## Alternative Avenues for Involvement

Throughout the history of American politics, there have been occasions when the parties have been judged by individuals or groups to be incapable of properly responding to given political situations. In response to these perceived failures, a wide variety of alternative political mechanisms have been created. Some of these creations (such as the Americans for Democratic Action) have performed effectively and have achieved a degree of respectable permanence. Others, such as the antiwar groups of the late 1960s, have relatively quickly served their designated function and then faded away. Still others have fizzled ignominiously. The relationship of nonparty groups to the parties varies. An organization such as Common Cause tries to keep its distance from the Democrats and the Republicans, but some of the Vietnam peace organizations of the 1960s saw themselves as a staging ground for entry into the internal politics of the Democratic party. It often seems that for any given position on any given issue, an ad hoc political group exists (and if one does not, one probably can promptly be formed). The functions of these groups vary: some are engaged in sophisticated lobbying efforts, others in voter education, still others in civil disobedience.

Some of the advantages of nonparty politics coincide with the disadvantages of party activities. With the vast array of special interest organizations, it is likely that a comfortable ideological match-up can be found between individual and organization. Activity is immediate and intense and yet the organizational structure is likely to be of the flexible type that allows participants to determine how, what, and when activities are to be undertaken. But there is a price that must be paid for any such political malleability—lack of permanence and perhaps limits on effectiveness. The same open-ended approach that makes ad hoc politics attractive also creates a serious vulnerability—the organization is highly dependent for its very existence on the rise and fall of public passions and events beyond its

31

control. For example, a court order might overcome the main impetus behind an antibusing crusade, and the organization might quickly lose many of its supporters even though the issue in question has not been solved but only become dormant. In other words, many ad hoc political groups find it difficult to sustain their operations when the excitement surrounding an issue dies down. As noted above, more permanent organizations such as political parties might seem bland and slow-moving but generally their continued existence is likely, and when the ad hoc groups fade away, the residual power of long-lasting organizations will be all the more evident.

Choosing the mode of participation may be the first difficult decision for the emerging political activist. The choice, however, is only of limited finality. There has always been considerable movement from ad hoc groups into party politics and vice versa. This should be kept in mind when evaluating such matters as the likelihood of immediate results from one's efforts and the possibility of gaining valuable experience. What matters most is that the individual consider all the options before choosing the course of action most suited to his talents and interests.

### Entering the Political Structure

Once someone has an idea as to whether he wants to try party or nonparty politics, the next questions to which he should address himself are: How should I begin my involvement? How can I gain entry to the political entity in which I am interested?

The most visible and intensive political activity generally occurs during an election campaign. As a rule, a campaign never has enough workers, so anyone is likely to be well received. Once involved, though, the participant must keep alert to avoid being lost in the frantic shuffle that is part of every campaign. Here are some basic pointers for successfully becoming involved in a campaign:

——If possible, one should try to join the campaign effort in its early stages. The person who does so not only will be able to participate in the full spectrum of campaign activities, but he will also gain some seniority, making it more likely that he will be assigned tasks of greater responsibility. Being in the right place at the right time is often the key to initiating a successful political career.

——One should be flexible as to his duties in the campaign. It is rare for a neophyte to be engaged immediately in making policy or mapping grand strategies. Tasks that at first glance might seem menial are absolutely essential to the smooth operation of the campaign. It is important that the newcomer establish a reputation as a willing worker; anyone who thinks he can always pick and choose is likely soon to find himself with nothing at all to do.

——As with a willingness to assume various responsibilities, one should try to maintain flexibility in his time commitment to the campaign. Almost everyone will have some limits on the amount of time available, but one should try to go to the limit and devote every spare hour to the task. Those who merely "dabble" in politics limit their effectiveness and their expertise. Politics is a time-consuming business, and one soon learns that giving up hours of sleep is one of the sacrifices that must be made.

These suggestions are applicable to the normal candidate-oriented campaign as well as to political activity of other sorts, such as petition drives or referendum questions centering on an issue rather than a candidate. An additional suggestion that is particularly pertinent to "noncandidate" campaigns is that the worker turn himself into a valuable resource as an expert on whatever issue is of concern to the campaign. Even with limited political experience, this campaign worker will have a good chance of being a sought-after commodity if he can master the nuances of a given issue. A good politician knows that he needs more than just an understanding of political technique. From the outset of involvement, one can provide candidate or campaign manager with a supplemental strength he will be seeking.

The kind of excitement inherent in campaigning may not be readily apparent in the ongoing business of politics that quietly proceeds between campaigns. This continuing operation is normally a function of a party or other permanent organization. Beginning one's involvement during a slack period has its advantages:

——One can learn how things work at a less frantic pace and without being subjected to the intense pressures of a campaign;

——When a campaign begins, the "veteran" will be able to step into a more active role, as something of an "insider";

——Early involvement fosters a better perspective of politics, seeing it in its cohesive and changing aspects.

Getting one's foot in the door is not as hard as it might seem. Just as campaigns always need volunteers, so also do most other political activities welcome new participants. Money is usually in short supply, so at the start the newcomer may have to offer his services gratis or for a very nominal amount. But what the novice should be most concerned with is gaining experience. If the organization for which the new participant wishes to work does not have some sort of internship or training program, he should devise one himself—such a suggestion probably will be well received. The "rookie" will often face masses of envelopes that need to be stuffed or index cards that need to be filed. He should accept these jobs, while trying to create a program that will let him have a look at everything with which the organization is involved. From the first day in politics, one should be the constant observer, noting (mentally or on paper) everything being done, whether properly or improperly, and considering how it might be done better.

Another early task for the newcomer to pursue largely on his own is to learn any formal and informal "rules of the game" that might exist. Party organizations in particular seem to delight in bylaws and regulations that sometimes are so complex that no one ever really masters them. Understanding of the internal organizational machinery will be enhanced if one familiarizes oneself with such procedures. There have been frequent occasions in politics when newcomers have learned party rules ignored by "oldtimers" and quickly established themselves as the real power in the party. (A good example of this may be found in the efforts of George McGovern's supporters in 1972 who so successfully challenged party "regulars" in a number of states.) Even if one is not thinking in terms of a "takeover" of party apparatus, any knowledge of this type is certain to prove helpful in the long run.

Actual access to the system is not difficult to gain, but it is almost entirely up to the individual as to what he makes of it. One should enter politics with some general plan in mind—what one wants to see, what one wants to learn—and be prepared to work diligently to adhere to that plan.

### Learning through Campaigning

The maxim that there is nothing more educational than practical experience is particularly applicable to the practice of politics. No matter how many books one might have read or how long one has studied, there is a "feel" for politics that can be developed only in the field.

This book offers some suggestions on how to organize and run a campaign, but since every campaign is to a large degree unique, there are certain things each individual should look for whenever he works on a campaign for purposes of comparison with practices in other campaigns:

——Does the campaign have a dominant theme (such as an issue or a personality)? How is this theme developed?

——How is the campaign organized? Along what patterns are responsibilities assigned?

——What aspect of campaigning is most emphasized (e.g., personal appearances by the candidate, canvassing, media use)? Is this emphasis in proper balance with the rest of the campaign or are some parts being neglected?

By considering these and similar matters, the campaign worker will be able to develop a reservoir of political knowledge that will stand him good stead in any future political activities.

Underlying all of these considerations is the basic question of the level of politics at which one wishes to become involved. Some have begun their political activity by successfully running for office. Most, however, go through a self-imposed apprenticeship in order to develop competence and, thus, self-reliance. Probably the best advice in reaching a decision is that each person should keep as many options open for himself as possible. One should not try to rush things, but rather take the time to learn as much as one can about a variety of political techniques. Before anyone makes a decision about politics as a career or as some lesser aspect of his life, he should try to

35

consider all the factors involved so his decision will have a firm basis. Chapter 3 will suggest the great variety of matters a potential candidate must consider before beginning a campaign. Since politics definitely is not a business, at any level, for the fainthearted, even a potential political activist who does not plan on becoming a candidate himself should weigh these same (or slightly modified) factors.

Once political involvement is under way, introspection should not halt. Not only should the participant be able to adapt his political plans to changing events, but he should also think about his political motivation and the basic moral reference point from which he operates. His personal commitment to political participation should be such that he can always reexamine and expand it. There is always the danger that one will find oneself caught up in the political whirlwind and begin behaving like something of an automaton—events controlling the individual rather than the individual controlling events. Politicians at every level have been known to succumb to this malady, and it is their resultant behavior that has done much to give politics a bad name.

If someone puts his mind to it, he can be the kind of politician he really wants to be; there is no need to surrender ideals or principles. However, one must keep the potential pitfalls in mind from the outset of his involvement. This aspect of getting started in politics goes hand in hand with the more mechanical matters. If the political worker knows what he is getting into and what he wants to get out of it, his entry into politics is likely to be auspicious and he can proceed to make the most of his participation.

# 3

# The Making of a Candidate

Although the visibility of a candidate for office might grow with great speed, leaving the observer with the impression that an overnight sensation has arrived on the scene, in truth almost every serious candidacy is the product of much thought and intensive labor. What makes a candidate subject himself to the grueling demands of a campaign? How does he transform vague ideas and desires into a comprehensive plan upon which a campaign may be based? To what extent will precampaign planning determine the success or failure of the effort? In searching for the answers to such questions, one begins to develop an appreciation for the many factors that comprise the foundation of any campaign.

**Rationale for Running**

Many candidates claim to be—and most actually are—motivated in their political involvement by a given issue or other unselfish purpose. Strong feelings about a single policy matter might seem to be sufficient reason in itself to justify entering a campaign. For example, in the 1970 congressional campaigns, there were numerous "peace candidates" whose sole purpose was to direct public attention to the conduct of the war in Southeast Asia and thus to serve as a channel for public opinion that might be mustered against the Nixon administration's general Vietnam policies. Many of these candidates were new-comers to politics, and some entered their respective races knowing full well that their chances of winning were slight. Nevertheless, they became candidates on the strength of their beliefs pertaining to a single issue. The advantages in such mo-tivation are found mainly in the clarity of the candidate's po-sition. He is sure (in his own mind) and the voting public may be similarly certain of why he is running. The obvious dis-advantage is that such a candidate may be labeled as a "one-issue" politician who might not be able to handle the diverse responsibilities of office. How the advantages and disadvantages balance each other will depend largely upon the circumstances surrounding the election.

Often the issue orientation of a campaign will be more subtle, based on a general political philosophy rather than on one or two highly controversial matters. Such concerns might be an overall approach to economic or foreign policy or the need to have the government develop a more conservative or liberal outlook. This strategy provides ample concentra-tion on issue questions while allowing appeals to a broad-based constituency.

The candidate's own outlook toward the relationship be-tween his views on an issue and the desirability of running for office is a matter requiring difficult decision making. Among the factors to be considered are:

——How crucial is the issue?

——How well defined is the particular viewpoint that the candidate will be espousing?

——Is running for office the best way to accomplish the given goals related to the issue?

——Could some other candidate or official do a better job of reaching the goals?

——How do the voters perceive the issue; how will the voters respond; to what degree do they need to be educated about the issue?

Questions such as these defy simplistic answers, but a can-didate would be derelict if he failed to attempt to deal with them. The first step is to appraise objectively the true impor-tance of the issue. The candidate must ask himself if the issue

is truly significant or if it just seems so to him; personal pre-
judices must be put into proper perspective. Unless the voting
public shares (or can be convinced to support) the candidate's
perspective on the crucial issue, it is unlikely that his campaign
will be a success. Not only must the issue be generally viewed
as a matter of importance, but also the candidate's particular
viewpoint must be so well-developed and finely honed that it
can be put to use in a campaign. Complex philosophical theories
have their uses, and the candidate should utilize such as he develops his position, but in the task of winning popular support
and votes, theories must be distilled to the point at which they
may be easily grasped by the average voter. Again, failure to
modify personal predilections can greatly impair the efficacy of
a campaign. Examples of this problem may even be found in
national campaigns. Some critics of Barry Goldwater's 1964
presidential race contend that he crippled his own campaign
by refusing to put his basic proposals into terms that could
be understood and perhaps found acceptable by the voters.
Instead, his opponents were able to label him as a "shoot-from-
the-hip" candidate whose platform was irresponsible and
lacking in substance. In 1968 Eugene McCarthy was running for
a presidential office that he perceived in a different light than
did many voters. The failure to attempt to reconcile this dichot-
omy was a significant flaw in the McCarthy campaign.

Once the important issues are determined and properly
defined and basic goals with regard to such issues are understood, a slightly different sort of analysis must be undertaken
by the potential candidate. He must ponder to what extent running for, and perhaps being elected to, office will serve to advance his goals. Election to office is not always the ultimate
political accomplishment. There are instances in which political
goals are more effectively furthered by nonelectoral participation. An example is to be found in the work of Ralph Nader.
Nader has been quite successful in drawing public attention to
the field of consumer affairs. He has advocated specific legislation as well as general principles and been quick to point out
alleged failings on the parts of various officeholders. Rather
than running for office himself, he prefers to raise public consciousness and thus indirectly affect voting behavior. Nader's

efforts certainly have led to voters demanding more of their representatives in a variety of fields. This orchestration of public sentiment might be more important than the winning of a single elective office for himself. This example should be kept in mind by anyone whose concern over an issue is so great that he is considering running for office. A further, related question is: Even if the issue of concern is of such a nature that it can be best affected by someone holding public office, who is truly the best person to undertake the necessary efforts? Answering this requires a degree of selflessness that is rather rare, but it is certainly relevant to the question of motivation. If it appears that another candidate could run a better campaign with greater chance of success, or if someone already holding office is likely to accomplish what needs to be done, it might be best to forgo an active candidacy. If it is truly an issue, rather than self-interest, that motivates one's political activism, it would seem logical that this sort of decision will have to be made.

After the nature of the campaign issue has been defined, and after the general advisability of a candidacy has been considered, a final question concerning basing a campaign on an issue arises: Do the voters really care about the matter? This is another instance when the potential candidate must assume a detached view, setting aside his own feelings—however strong—and appraising the importance of the issue to the people who cast the votes. It may be that however incensed people "should" be about a matter, they simply are not at all concerned and show no inclination to become properly aroused. It may be that the campaign should proceed nevertheless, serving at least as an educative influence. But any candidate undertaking such an enterprise should know where he stands before he starts. Even a campaign that ends in electoral defeat can be valuable in drawing attention to an issue and making the voters more conscious of their political environment. However, any campaign will have considerable effect on its participants, and the candidate should beware of raising unrealizable expectations. Very few campaign workers are striving for anything less than victory. The candidate has the obligation of recognizing this and doing all that he can to maintain the intellectual honesty of his approach to the campaign.

Concerns over issues are not only motivating factors behind candidacies. A politician's ego is a complex maze of often conflicting goals and values. Somewhere within this maze, the decision to run for office takes shape. Although a campaign may center on a "cause," it cannot be forgotten that it is a person— not an impersonaiized principle alone— that is the subject of the voters' consideration. A bit of amateur psychology is called for in evaluating a candidacy, in seeking to determine, "Why does this person really want the job?" Personal ambition is, to some degree, a necessary characteristic of anyone running for office. The demanding nature of campaigning and public service is such that recompense is naturally sought through self-aggrandizement. It is perhaps too cynical to believe that only the overly ambitious can succeed in politics, but there are certain stereotypes that voters, campaign workers, and potential candidates should be wary of supporting or becoming. These include:

——The "stepping-stone" candidate, who clearly is running for his current office solely to establish a base from which he can run for something else (e.g., running for state legislature only to prepare to run for governor or Congress). When such people are elected, they generally do a poor job in their "transition" position, providing no better than minimal service to the constituency. Candidates of this type often are easy to spot, and the voters who elect them usually deserve what they get— inadequate representation.

——The "run anywhere at anytime for anything" candidate, who seems to feel that his civil rights are being violated if he is not perpetually engaged in campaigning. Some candidates of this species are actually devoted public servants with a genuine desire to be useful, while others have allowed themselves to be so caught up in the frenetic whirl of politics that they have suffered a diminution of perspective. After enough time has passed and enough races have been run, there arises the danger that if the candidate finally does win an election, he will not know what to do when he is in office. Such candidates have been known to appear anywhere from the local to the national level. A candidate who seems enraptured with campaigning just for the sake of campaigning probably deserves close scrutiny.

41

——The "glory hound" candidate, who is intent upon basking in the public attention that is part of every campaign. The desire for public exposure is natural for—and essential to—any politician, but when carried to extremes it seems logical to wonder whether the candidate is interested in representing anyone other than himself.

Almost every campaign situation produces its own variation of the role of personal interest in motivating a candidacy. This matter is not a "problem" that needs to be solved, but rather something of which all parties to a campaign—candidates, supporters, workers, voters—should be aware. Public interest and personal interest are not mutually exclusive, but proper balance between the two is often difficult to maintain.

Determining the "Why" of a candidacy is a task that can involve mental gymnastics and sometimes nebulous concepts. When these matters are satisfactorily dealt with, the process of the making of a candidate moves into areas that, although speculative at an early stage of a campaign, at least make use of more concrete factors for consideration.

## Feasibility of Running

Whatever one's motivation for entering a campaign, a final decision as to whether or not to become a candidate should be based in part on a preliminary feasibility study. Such a study should not be directed at determining *how* the campaign should be run (that will come later) but rather at gaining a rough idea of the chances for success of such a venture.

The first step is to arrive at an approximation of the resources available to the campaign. The most important resource at this early planning stage is people—friends and political allies who can provide an initial core of personal support and financial backing. Does such support exist? Can the candidate count on some hours of volunteer labor and perhaps some seed money to launch the campaign? If the candidate must answer "No" to these questions, the viability of his running for office becomes suspect. If no one cares enough about the candidacy to help it get started, perhaps there is no reason for the candidacy to exist. If the answers to the above questions are affirmative, more specific questions must follow. Is a competent campaign manager available? Are volunteer workers at hand who will perform consistently throughout the campaign? Can the candidate's supporters spare the time to become actively involved in the campaign? Can the candidate himself devote the substantial part of his time and energies to campaigning? As these questions are answered, the candidate should be developing a mental picture of the shape of his campaign organization: Will the staff be paid or volunteer? large or small? Who will do what? When this picture is completed, the candidate can decide if the organization meets the requirements of his particular race.

Related questions should be raised concerning financial aspects of the campaign. How much money is needed? How much is likely to become available? The candidate must evaluate the discrepancy in the answers to these two questions. The greater the difference between the two sums, the more difficult the campaign is likely to be. These considerations may necessitate a wholly new approach to the campaign's strategy or even a reconsideration of the proposed candidacy.

However the questions are phrased in these matters, the underlying realization must be that it is not feasible to begin an active campaign without first determining what resources are needed and which among these are actually available. A candidate possessing knowledge about his campaign resources is more likely to be able to mount a balanced, coherent, and effective campaign effort.

The early feasibility study should also include a realistic (although necessarily speculative) prognosis of the campaign's likely results. Is the election truly achievable or is the political situation such that victory is virtually impossible? Although it is close elections that usually come to the public's attention, in most races there are factors such as the nature of the constituency or the status of the incumbent (if any) that will allow an experienced political observer to predict with fairly consistent accuracy what the election results are likely to be. Naïveté is a luxury no candidate can afford. If chances of victory are minimal, the candidate should make his plans accordingly. He may decide to run anyway to call attention to a given issue, to provide at least some opposition to the other candidate, or to lay groundwork for another race under better circumstances.

These may be perfectly valid rationales, but they are reasonable only to the extent that they are considered in a politically realistic context. A basic understanding of the demographic characteristics of the electorate (discussed in detail in Chapter 14) is essential in making these judgments.

If, on the basis of the feasibility study and any other grounds for judgment, the candidate decides to proceed, organization of the campaign structure must be moved from the realm of the speculative to that of the operational. The candidate must commit himself to the idea of running as he begins to construct the basic framework for his campaign strategy.

### The Important Decisions

The development and implementation of a campaign strategy require careful planning and a continually arduous decision-making process. Matters that were mere abstractions in preliminary evaluations of the campaign now must assume the shape of integral aspects of campaigning. Among the first of these elements is the candidate's rationale for running. Not only must this reasoning be clear and acceptable in his own mind, but he must also articulate it in such a way as to be able to win electoral (and financial) support. Whether the motivation behind the campaign is interest in a complex issue or just general self-confidence in being able to do a good job, such must be communicated to the voters. A statement of principles in the form of "Why I am running" can prove of great use both in winning new supporters and in providing an ideological base for those already supporting the campaign. This does not have to be a massive dissertation; a concise outline of operating principles usually will suffice. From such a document the basic themes of the campaign may be developed.

Another aspect of precampaign planning that must be put quickly into definitive form is an evaluation of the financial needs both for launching the campaign and for carrying it to its conclusion. Three budgetary outlines should be prepared: an optimal budget, providing for every contingency and every desired campaign tactic; a minimal budget, dealing only with the absolute essentials; and an operational budget, evolving from a realistic combination of the optimal and minimal projections. To compile such budgets, it is necessary to develop plans in the following areas:

——*Staff*: how many salaried employees and how many volunteers will be involved;

——*Logistics*: how many campaign headquaters will be opened, what sort of office equipment will be needed (e.g., telephones, typewriters, mimeograph machines, etc.), what general operating expenses (e.g., utilities, postage) will be required;

——*Support functions*: will outside consultants be required to aid in media work, polling, etc; will it be necessary to hire legal counsel to advise on election law matters;

——*Media usage*: how much advertising space and broadcast time will be required in the course of the campaign, what production costs are involved;

——*Voter contact*: what canvassing costs will arise, what propaganda items (e.g., pamphlets, buttons, bumper stickers) will be used, what actual contact costs (such as postage or telephone) will be essential;

——*Fund raising*: how much capital will be required to undertake a direct mail program or some other type of solicitation;

——*Candidate activity*: what kind of advance work will be required, what costs will be involved in providing opportunities for the candidate's campaigning;

——*Special activities*: what types of budgets should be allocated for voter registration, get-out-the-vote, polling, media, and other such projects.

\ To a considerable extent, the tempo of the campaign once under way will dictate if and how these various activities will be utilized. The budget planning should cover as many contingencies as possible; it is far easier to drop an unnecessary activity than it is to find the money to meet an unforeseen need. This sort of planning is rendered even more difficult by the fact that cash income and expenditures do not proceed at a consistent pace during a campaign. In the early months before public interest in political activity reaches its peak, contributions may accrue at a very slow rate. And yet it is during these early days when it is necessary to make financial commitments for the duration of the campaign. For example, the best broadcast time spots for political advertising must be bought months in advance. If a finance chairman has not devised proper budgetary projections and decides to wait for contributions to catch up with expenditures, he might find that the opposition or other advertisers have procured the desired time slots. There is a considerable amount of risk involved, but careful, comprehensive planning can minimize the risks and maximize the results.

Related to the financial planning of a campaign is the need to study the legal aspects of political finance as well as facets of campaigning. Election laws are increasingly becoming more pervasive and complex. The voting public is likewise more concerned than ever with adherence to these regulations. Most infractions of election laws occur as a result of oversight or honest mistake, but this is not a valid excuse, and the electorate rightfully may guarantee that the candidate who makes such errors will be defeated at the polls. A basic question related to campaign finance is: What is a contribution that must be reported? Obviously a cash donation of $100 is one such contribution, but what about the loan of a mimeograph machine by a supporter? Is the value of the use of the machine a financial contribution? There is an almost infinite variety of questions such as these. They are best answered at the earliest possible time in order to avoid inconvenience, embarrassment, or a potential political disaster. Every campaign staff should include a legal counsel who will monitor the opposition as well as supervise any aspects of the campaign that may be controlled by election laws. He is a staff member who should be put to work at the earliest possible time.

An effective campaign is usually one with a basic theme and style that give it a unique identity which, in turn, serves to provide candidate and supporters alike with an intangible feeling of unity in their efforts. In large part this theme evolves from the candidate's rationale for undertaking the campaign. The thematic idea develops as the candidate discovers the sort of appeal he feels most comfortable with as well as voter response to his appeals. Although it takes time for a theme to evolve fully, the candidate should set his basic course at the outset, thus providing some measure of consistency to a venture that is to a large extent unavoidably unpredictable.

The style of campaigning utilized by a candidate is one manifestation of the campaign theme. The nature of the constituency, the strength of the opposition, the types of issues that are most salient—all these factors influence such decisions as how much television and radio campaigning is to be utilized, how much direct (in-person) voter contact is desired, and how strident or low-key the candidate's appeal should be. For example, a candidate who does not have substantial funding but believes that voters are tired of slick, expensive campaigns may decide to walk across his state or district and thus personally reach as many voters as possible on a one-to-one basis. (In 1970 Lawton Chiles in Florida and in 1972 Dan Walker in Illinois walked across their states and were well received by the voters. They were elected United States senator and governor respectively.) Most campaigns will feature a mixture of in-person and media campaigning, but it is helpful for the campaign to develop a distinctive character that the voters will easily recognize and with which they will identify. Most election years feature more races than the average voter can keep track of. A distinguishable element of style might keep a campaign from becoming "lost in the shuffle."

As discussed above with regard to financial planning, it is desirable to prepare a timetable covering the entire campaign. Strategies developed well in advance of implementation can be refined to reach their greatest effectiveness. Canvassing, media exposure, fund raising, and just about any other campaign activities are great'y diminished in value if utilized in a hit-or-miss fashion. Every aspect of a campaign is related in some way to the rest of the campaign, and it is the strength of these interrelationships that determines the strength of the campaign as a whole. Beyond a generalized schedule of what campaign efforts are to take place at what times, a more specific schedule for each campaign activity must be devised. For example, the overall schedule might indicate that voter registration is to begin in August, reach its peak in early September, and terminate at the beginning of October. The subschedule would break this down to a specific week-by-week or day-by-day basis. (*NB*: In later chapters, where pertinent to the discussion of various campaign activities, model subschedules are included.) The decisions as to tactical timing will determine the pace of the campaign; they should be made with full recognition of their importance and only after careful consideration.

Depending on the political context in which the campaign is being run, it may be necessary to decide on relationships with the regular party apparatus and with other candidates of the same party. Such decisions range from virtually becoming part of a slate of candidates in areas of strong party organization to running as something of an independent where the individual candidacy is stronger than the party. Such matters must be handled with great care or the candidate will find himself fighting two battles—one against his nominal opposition and one against irritated members of his own party.

Working with the party organization usually has certain advantages. Lists that have been compiled over the years of friendly voters and contributors may be made available. Particularly if the candidate is a political newcomer, valuable contacts with party regulars may be made easily. From close contact with other candidates, much can be learned from a common reservoir of knowledge of past tactics that have succeeded or failed. Particularly strong candidates may be able to transfer some of their strength to struggling compatriots. The main disadvantage of close association with the party's candidates and organization is that some independence is necessarily surrendered. If the party organization happens to be inefficient, it can be a serious impediment to efficient campaigning. This decision for the candidate must be based on his ability to judge the balance between such advantages and disadvantages.

When all these questions have been answered and decisions made with as much finality as circumstances will allow, the candidate will find himself on the brink of the intensive part of his campaign. The "preliminaries" are over; it becomes time for the main event.

## Getting Under Way

Having finalized the commitment to run and with the initiating of an active candidacy, the candidate will find that the pace of events will increase drastically. Although important decisions will have to be made quickly and frequently, it is essential that a proper perspective be maintained. To be successful, a politician must be able to see how each decision and each political event fits into the grand scheme of the campaign.

The basic campaign approach and the strategic timetable are matters that always can be refined to points of greater specificity and accuracy. One way to do this is by upgrading the quality of any demographic analysis that may have been used when making the decision to run. The basic items included in such an analysis (which someone with skills in political research should be updating and expanding throughout the campaign) are:

——Mapping of voting strength, based on voter registration lists of where the voters are. If voters in a given state register by party, so much the better; the map will then indicate where potential strengths and weaknesses exist (see Figures 3-1 and 3-2).

——Charting of general population characteristics, such as race, age, type of housing, and income level. This information will aid in development of specialized appeals to identifiable constituent groups such as black voters, lower-income voters, etc. (see Figures 3-3 and 3-4).

——Interpreting of any available polling data, particularly that which relates to party preference, name recognition of candidate, and issue salience.

The information gleaned from this analysis will enable the candidate to target areas for intensive or only cursory campaigning. For example, a Democratic candidate will want to know if 80 percent of an area's registered voters are Republicans; if so, it might be a waste of time to devote much energy there. Similarly, if the data indicate a high percentage of unregistered blacks, special voter registration efforts may be desirable.

While planning progresses in accord with available information, the candidate should seek to increase his visibility, thus increasing the credibility of his candidacy. Those persons who are friends of the candidate or otherwise can be counted on as supporters may be sent a mailing just to let them know that the campaign is beginning. This stratagem, rather than being an effort to win new supporters, is designed to build some early momentum and increase the visibility of the campaign. More public exposure can come through appearances before civic groups,

Figure 3-1

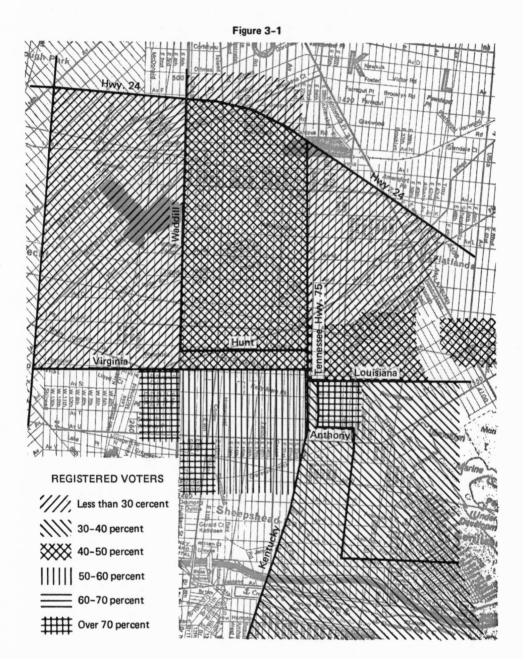

REGISTERED VOTERS

///// Less than 30 cercent

\\\\\ 30–40 percent

XXXX 40–50 percent

|||||| 50–60 percent

≡≡≡ 60–70 percent

▦▦ Over 70 percent

**Figure 3-2**

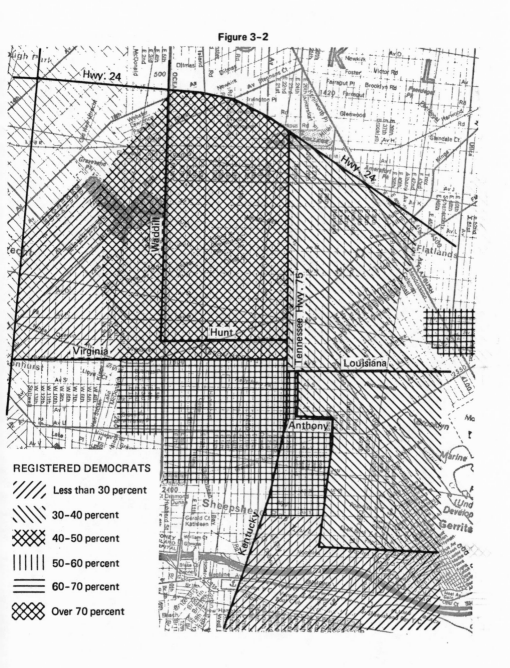

REGISTERED DEMOCRATS

/////  Less than 30 percent

\\\\\  30-40 percent

XXXXX  40-50 percent

||||||  50-60 percent

=====  60-70 percent

XXXX  Over 70 percent

51

Figure 3-3

## 1970 CENSUS STATISTICS FOR 5th CONGRESSIONAL DISTRICT, DALLAS, TEXAS BY AREA AND CENSUS TRACT

AREA — W DALLAS

| Census Tract | Total Population | White | Black | Spanish | Median Income | Mean Income | Population Household | Total Families | Families With Children Under 18 | Median Education | Total Housing Units | Owner Occupied |
|---|---|---|---|---|---|---|---|---|---|---|---|---|
| 4.01 | 2893. | 1017. | 0. | 1808. | 7830. | 8172. | 3.29 | 588. | 326. | 8.1 | 1091. | 253. |
| 4.02 | 5647. | 4247. | 121. | 1222. | 9548. | 11201. | 2.08 | 1158. | 438. | 12.5 | 2964. | 424. |
| 4.03 | 6509. | 4282. | 129. | 1910. | 8213. | 9473. | 2.91 | 1718. | 870. | 10.5 | 2362. | 1008. |
| 5.00 | 4582. | 3885. | 58. | 613. | 10102. | 12756. | 1.79 | 875. | 225. | 13.3 | 3723. | 231. |
| 6.02 | 7897. | 6983. | 49. | 807. | 10772. | 14638. | 1.74 | 1850. | 454. | 12.9 | 4951. | 694. |
| 7.01 | 3363. | 2300. | 8. | 998. | 8942. | 9791. | 2.08 | 745. | 281. | 12.6 | 1763. | 117. |
| 18.00 | 2657. | 1167. | 17. | 1411. | 8974. | 15632. | 2.17 | 488. | 202. | 12.5 | 1370. | 98. |
| 19.00 | 1447. | 112. | 28. | 1278. | 5635. | 6665. | 3.85 | 300. | 168. | 5.3 | 369. | 90. |
| 71.02 | 7662. | 1510. | 5861. | 253. | 7969. | 9333. | 3.03 | 1900. | 941. | 11.9 | 2574. | 1219. |
| 148.00 | 3366. | 3299. | 7. | 27. | 9075. | 9711. | 3.20 | 917. | 502. | 10.4 | 1097. | 609. |
| 149.00 | 2564. | 2304. | 0. | 244. | 8766. | 10879. | 2.71 | 729. | 371. | 11.0 | 1002. | 322. |
| 150.00 | 5424. | 4894. | 1. | 489. | 10191. | 1156. | 3.15 | 1463. | 845. | 10.8 | 1817. | 984. |

Figure 3-4

## 1970 CENSUS STATISTICS FOR 5th CONGRESSIONAL DISTRICT, DALLAS, TEXAS

| Area | Total Population | Percent White | Percent Black | Percent Spanish | Median Income | Mean Income | Population Household | Total Families | Percent Families With Children Under 18 | Median Education | Total Housing Units | Percent Owner Occupied |
|---|---|---|---|---|---|---|---|---|---|---|---|---|
| 1 North Dallas | 99882. | 93.4 | .5 | 5.3 | 12766. | 15612. | 2.46 | 26770. | 41.1 | 13.3 | 42186. | 51.5 |
| 2 Garland | 53994. | 95.7 | .3 | 3.5 | 11696. | 12644. | 3.38 | 14354. | 66.7 | 11.9 | 16784. | 67.6 |
| 3 South Dallas | 122039. | 27.6 | 63.6 | 7.5 | 6374. | 6853. | 2.66 | 28104. | 49.6 | 9.9 | 46968. | 21.1 |
| 4 Casa View | 54726. | 94.3 | .4 | 4.8 | 11836. | 13125. | 3.26 | 14527. | 48.1 | 12.1 | 17332. | 69.3 |
| 5 Pleasant Grove | 59938. | 94.3 | .1 | 5.0 | 10046. | 11319. | 3.23 | 16381. | 56.0 | 10.7 | 19297. | 71.9 |
| 6 Mesquite | 53495. | 95.2 | .0 | 4.3 | 10861. | 11423. | 3.71 | 13379. | 75.8 | 11.9 | 14887. | 84.7 |
| 7 Seagoville | 17884. | 87.7 | 7.1 | 4.5 | 9799. | 10055. | 3.76 | 4297. | 66.8 | 10.7 | 4900. | 77.0 |
| 8 West Dallas | 54011. | 66.7 | 11.6 | 20.5 | 8835. | 9856. | 2.67 | 12731. | 44.2 | 11.0 | 25083. | 24.1 |
| 9 Kleburg | 20198. | 94.3 | .3 | 4.8 | 8866. | 9505. | 3.53 | 5105. | 64.1 | 9.7 | 5945. | 73.7 |
| 10 Rowlett | 26679. | 82.3 | 12.3 | 4.9 | 10239. | 11037. | 3.65 | 6605. | 72.9 | 11.3 | 7496. | 77.2 |
| Total for 72 Boundaries | 461958. | 76.5 | 17.3 | 5.4 | 9459. | 11576. | 2.91 | 117812. | 54.1 | 11.2 | 162354. | 52.5 |
| Total for 74 Boundaries | 462964. | 72.8 | 19.2 | 7.2 | 8746. | 10329. | 3.07 | 115483. | 57.5 | 10.8 | 158692. | 50.2 |

participation on television or radio talk shows, and letters to the editors of local newspapers. These early appearances allow some trial-and-error efforts to develop issues and gauge audience response. But this is not to say that the candidate can be anything less than fully prepared when he makes these forays into public view. If he appears inept at the outset of his campaign, it may be difficult for him to dispel such an image.

These preliminary efforts should be capped with a formal announcement of candidacy that in itself is sufficiently newsworthy to draw some attention from the media. The announcement does not require too much showmanship. A very brief statement of intent is far more likely to receive broadcast coverage than a lengthy philosophical discourse. Time should be allowed for answering reporters' questions. This can be an important exchange since it will be the first public appearance of "the candidate" and might be the first look reporters will have at a person who will be receiving their attention for some time to come. Tough questions (such as "Why are you really running?" or "Why do you think you have a chance of winning?") should be expected. Aside from news media representatives, the audience for the announcement probably will be a friendly mixture of family and supporters—the more the merrier. It is good to be able to start a campaign on an emotional upbeat.

With the announcement of candidacy, the campaign is under way. All the preliminary preparations now must be directed at generating votes. Voters must be identified, registered, presented with the candidate's views, and wooed in every way. On election day the success or failure of the efforts will become evident.

# 4

# Campaign Personnel

It is often said that a politician is only as good as the people he has around him. In large part this is true, because a wise candidate or elected official will recognize that he cannot do everything by himself and, therefore, must find a staff of talented assistants who can aid in the development of ideas and in the effectuation of policies. The politician's ability to recruit from among "the best and the brightest" is a test of his talent as an administrator and as a leader able to inspire people to work with him.

The hectic nature of a campaign, with every day presenting numerous occasions for critical decision making, requires a skilled and well-coordinated staff operation. Many candidates begin a campaign with the desire to be their own campaign managers. The smart candidate will abandon such an idea promptly. The role of the candidate and the role of the campaign manager are full-time jobs; it is virtually impossible for one person to do both except in the smallest of campaigns. (In fact, the candidate who attempts such a feat is likely to prove to be both a poor candidate and a poor manager.) Responsibilities must be delegated and clearly defined.

The structure of the campaign staff will vary according to the exigencies of the given campaign. Both size of staff and working time required of staff members depend on the intensity of the race and factors such as the amount of money available for salaries. The positions here discussed are those which, in some shape or form, are useful to most campaigns. Figure 4-1 shows a general outline of the organization of campaign personnel.

Figure 4-1 BASIC ORGANIZATIONAL CHART OF CAMPAIGN PERSONNEL

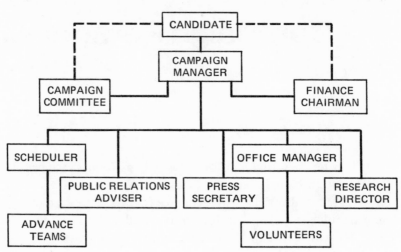

## The Manager

The campaign manager (sometimes called a campaign director) is the candidate's organizational alter ego. While the candidate concentrates on publicly winning the support of the voters, the manager must ensure that such efforts produce maximal results. Every aspect of the campaign is within the manager's purview. Coordination is his primary responsibility—assigning tasks to various members of the campaign staff and then putting results of these labors together so as to fashion a cohesive product. For example, if a voter registration drive is deemed important to the campaign, the manager must assign the volunteer coordinator the task of finding the manpower to conduct the drive, the political research specialist must analyze his information to determine where the drive should be concentrated, the press secretary must see that the drive is properly publicized in the news media, the finance chairman must find needed funding, the legal counsel must investigate the intricacies of registration procedures, and so on. The manager will tie together the contributions of these staff members and, with appropriate "cracking of the whip," will see to it that a voter registration drive takes place.

The authority of the manager must be unquestioned. He is the voice of the candidate and as such must maintain firm control or risk having the campaign plunge into organizational chaos. (The 1972 McGovern campaign for the presidency provides an example of this sort of chaos. Among many major problems was the fact that no one really knew who was running the campaign.) The manager must have control over the budget and must divert unnecessary matters away from the candidate. Access to the candidate by staff members must be limited, and the staff should be able to realize why this is necessary. Every campaign is plagued by a shortage of time; there simply are not enough hours in the day for anyone, particularly the candidate. Suggestions and complaints for the candidate's attention must be filtered through the manager and presented by him, if necessary, in concise form for the candidate to consider. Meetings of the upper echelon of the staff (such as the press secretary, finance chairman, etc.) are useful to discuss current endeavors, to seek suggestions, and basically to ensure that everyone knows what everyone else is doing, but even these may be directed more often by the manager than by the candidate. Undoubtedly, the candidate will want to meet at times with individual members of the staff, but the frequency of such consultations probably will be erratic.

Major strategy decisions must be made or at least approved by the candidate. The manager can expect to spend considerable time (usually long after the "working day" has ended) with the candidate, providing him with progress reports, reviewing the status of the campaign, and planning for the days ahead. The relationship between the candidate and the campaign manager must be exceptionally close. If they are not on the same mental "wavelength" and if they do not have faith in each other's abilities, it is unlikely that the campaign will be able to proceed smoothly. A well-known example of such a close

57

relationship was that of John and Robert Kennedy in the 1960 presidential campaign.

As he orchestrates the performance of the campaign organization, the manager must draw on all possible sources of information, avoiding the fatal mistake of trying to make decisions in a vacuum. The creation of an advisory campaign committee can help to provide a balanced input of political information.

## The Committee

The campaign committee is not a part of the day-to-day campaign organization. Its role is advisory, providing assistance when summoned by the candidate or manager. The composition of such a committee should reflect all major elements of the candidate's constituency. Minority group members, professional people, businessmen, union representatives, leaders of women's organizations, and representatives of any other groups of significant political status should be recruited. Such a committee can serve a two-way communications role: it can report on the political attitudes and activities of the respective constituencies and it can provide a direct channel from the candidate to the identifiable groupings of voters for purposes of specialized campaign appeals. A representative on the committee can provide information on what issues certain voters consider most important, how they view the campaign at any given time, and how the candidate might do a better job of reaching these voters. In turn, this committee member may perform an ambassadorial function by clarifying the views of the candidate for his constituents, thus serving as a campaign spokesman who is likely to be trusted by his peer group within the electorate. For example, a labor union representative might suggest that union members are greatly concerned about the need for an increase in the minimum wage law and, therefore, a statement by the candidate on this issue (assuming he agrees with the union position) might well win him some votes. The same committee member might also report that too few union members are aware of the candidacy, and suggest that the campaign manager schedule handshaking appearances by the candidate at local factories. When the candidate does make personal appearances before union audiences, this committee member might be requested to supply the candidate's introduction or provide other assistance.

Especially for a candidate who is a newcomer to campaigning, such a committee can be of great value, not only for the reasons stated above, but also because a campaign committee composed of respected members of the community can provide the campaign with an aura of credibility. For this reason it is essential that the membership of the committee be carefully chosen. Members should represent the mainstream of thought of their constituencies. When such is the case, the campaign committee can prove to be a great asset to the candidate from the earliest planning stages to the final days of the campaign.

**The Finance Chairman**

Perhaps the most thankless job in a campaign is that of the finance chairman. Rarely does a campaign fail to require readjustments of its original budget and likewise rare are the campaigns that are funded adequately to meet all the financial demands that arise. The finance chairman must supervise both fund raising and disbursements and must develop an operable balance between these two functions.

The finance chairman should be appointed during the earliest stages of precampaign planning so that he will be available to inject a note of fiscal realism into the process of developing the alternative budget outlines of campaign priorities. Even the optimal budget—that setting forth all the plans the candidate would *like* to utilize during the campaign—should be devised with an eye to how much money realistically (if optimistically) can be expected to be available. Not only must the finance chairman try to determine how much money will be raised for the campaign, but he must also know when such sums will become available. Money contributed the day before the election is of little use unless such a contribution was foreseen far enough in advance to allow the funds to be committed on the reasonable expectation of their arrival. This is an inherently risky business and many campaigns reach election day in a pool of red ink. But the finance chairman who is unable to anticipate the ebb and flow of campaign income may *under*spend, thus depriving the campaign of needed services.

Once the budget for the campaign has been established, the finance chairman must supervise fund-raising operations. Initial seed money usually may be procured from a small number of persons, perhaps personal friends of the candidate. Soon, however, a far broader base of support will be required. Direct-mail solicitation, fund-raising events, advertising, and many other techniques should be utilized to build a campaign treasury. (See Chapter 10 for discussion of some of these techniques.) Because of changes in public sentiment and laws regulating campaign contributions, the heyday of the large individual contributor seems to be fading away, to be replaced by a greater number of small contributors that the candidates are able to attract. Several large-scale campaigns (including those for United States Senate) have put a $100 limit on individual contributions and at the same time have managed to find enough small contributors (often by using direct-mail programs) to allow the campaigns to be adequately financed.

Once the money has been raised, how it is to be spent poses a different set of problems. The campaign manager and the finance chairman must determine, with as little acrimony as possible, the priorities for spending. At some point in most campaigns, a battle will rage between a manager who says he *must* have a certain number of dollars to rent another billboard and a finance chairman who claims that there is no money available for such an expenditure. The candidate may find himself in the unfortunate role of referee on occasion, but for the most part financial solvency (of sorts) must be maintained by compromise shuffling of budget items. Scrupulous accounting procedures are needed so that every contribution can be put to best use and to eliminate any possiblities of waste. A well-run campaign can exist on surprisingly little money *if* the money that is available is handled wisely.

## The Legal Counsel

The work of a campaign's legal counsel begins during the earliest discussions concerning a potential candidacy. Election laws are often a maze of details from which must be extracted crucial information concerning when and how money may be raised and, generally, how campaigns may be conducted. These matters should be fully considered before planning for a campaign goes too far. The candidate, campaign manager, and finance chairman should be provided with a concise but thorough summary of pertinent election law provisions.

In the course of the campaign, the legal counsel's duties will include:

——Reviewing all contracts for goods (such as campaign buttons) and services (such as media consultants) that are authorized by the campaign manager and/or finance chairman.

——Reading all campaign materials (such as brochures and advertisements) to ensure compliance with laws relating to attribution of sources of campaign documents, to potentially libelous material, and to material that might be held under copyright.

——Examining public statements and campaign materials issued by the opposing candidate. This will help safeguard campaign fairness. If the opposition violates the law or ethical standards, this might prove to be a useful campaign issue.

——Preparing contingency plans for violations of any laws by the opposition on election day. (See Chapter 13 on election day activities.)

——Paying particularly close attention to all fund-raising activities. A campaign can be quickly crippled if the public detects financial dealings that are improper, even if not truly illegal. There may be times when contributions will have to be refused. When such situations arise, the refusals must be prompt and politely forceful.

——Keeping track of media coverage of the candidate. Statutory guidelines may exist that will ensure redress for a candidate who is unfairly treated by unbalanced news coverage (particularly with regard to such events as television or radio "talk shows.")

To ensure the most objective possible performance of these tasks, the legal counsel should be, whenever possible, someone who is not burdened with other campaign duties. This is a good position for an attorney who wants to help the campaign but cannot afford to be a full-time volunteer. By being on call for legal advice, he will be performing an invaluable service to the campaign.

## The Press Secretary

The nature of the press coverage accorded a candidate can be an important factor in determining the success or failure of a campaign. Hostile coverage can create a negative image of the candidate in the minds of the voters, while too little coverage can leave many voters wholly unaware of the existence of a given candidate. The press cannot be told what or how much to write, but it is the job of the press secretary to work on the candidate's behalf with the press, making them aware of the candidate's positions and activities. This working relationship is a fragile arrangement; both press secretary and press have their own interests and professionalism with which to be concerned. The best press secretary is one who earns a reputation for honesty, providing reporters with information when he has it, admitting when he does not know an answer, and never engaging in deceptive gamesmanship to seek advantage for his candidate at the expense of journalists. Reporters can be fooled on occasion, but the odds are that in the long run they will find out all they wish to know, and the campaign that has tried to deceive the press—and thus the public—will undoubtedly suffer in the end. Many candidates choose as their press secretaries former journalists who are likely to be able to establish a proper rapport with newspeople covering the campaign.

In addition to his general "diplomatic" duties, the press secretary's job includes the following:

——Conducting briefings for the press, specifically outlining the candidate's schedule and his positions on any issues related to the campaign. The press secretary is the official spokesman for the candidate, so he must proceed with great caution when he has not been briefed fully by the candidate. When in doubt as to an answer, the press secretary should defer responding until he has discussed the matter with the candidate or the campaign manager.

——Preparing press releases to provide reporters with substantive material for news stories. Such releases should be frequent enough to facilitate comprehensive coverage of the candidate, but they should not be issued in such a constant flood that they are disregarded.

——Assisting press coverage of campaign events involving the candidate. This may require solving a myriad of logistical problems including submission of a detailed, accurate schedule, provision of transportation for the press (usually the infamous press bus), allowance of time on the schedule for reporters to call in stories to their offices, and general supervision of the care and treatment of the campaign's press entourage.

Special note should be taken of the relationship between candidate and press secretary necessitated by the press secretary's role as the "voice" of the candidate. Since the press secretary cannot put his own words into the candidate's mouth, he must develop a comprehensive understanding of the candidate's attitude toward virtually every issue in the campaign. This in turn requires that the press secretary have almost unlimited access to the candidate and that he be able to spend adequate time with him to become a truly authoritative spokesman. Failure to provide for this sort of relationship can severely limit the effectiveness of the campaign's press operation.

The press secretary should keep track of his success or failure in dealings with the news media. To a limited extent, he may gently prod reporters whose coverage of his candidate is weak or who may be according better treatment to the opposition. This is where the subtle diplomacy of the press secretary is put to the test. If he has established a proper but comfortable working relationship with the media, the press secretary may be able to serve as one of the campaign's most important assets.

## The Research Director

The research requirements of a campaign may be divided into two categories: issues research and political research. Depending upon the work load of a given campaign and the availability of qualified personnel, directors might be appointed for each of these areas.

The issues research director is charged with the responsibility of developing the policy views espoused by the candidate into substantive positions that will withstand the scrutiny of voters, press, and opposition. No matter how good an idea is that a candidate may generate, it will not help his election chances unless it is virtually impregnable to attack. The research director must supply the candidate with background information, supportive (and contradicting) facts and figures, and any other relevant data or observations that might strengthen the position on the issue. To the surprise of some politicians, voters are able to distinguish between well-reasoned, carefully prepared approaches to issues and those positions that a candidate adopts for no reason other than political expediency.

It is important that all available resources be utilized fully in the process of researching issues. The campaign committee, as noted above, may prove helpful in pointing out potential issues and suggesting possible approaches to them. Newspaper and magazine articles may provide further background information. From the earliest days of the campaign, articles that might in any way eventually prove useful should be clipped and filed according to subject matter classification. This private filing system plus materials normally available from libraries will provide the basic resources for the research operation. The director must see to it that the materials are properly distilled for the candidate's use. The candidate will not have the time to digest voluminous information; he must be provided with concise (but not superficial) summaries with ample material in reserve if difficult questions arise.

One method of candidate preparation that has proved successful in many campaigns is the use of a "briefing book." This is a loose-leaf notebook providing the candidate with constantly updated information on a variety of subjects, with sections prepared for use for special events on the candidate's schedule. For example, if the candidate is scheduled to speak at a Chamber of Commerce luncheon on economic issues, he would want the briefing book's economic section to contain the most recent figures relating to inflation, unemployment, and other economic indicators. The book would also contain information likely to be of help in answering questions put to the candidate by such an audience. Further, a section devoted to background information on this Chamber of Commerce might be included—past political activities, the names and pertinent facts on the officers to whom the candidate is likely to be introduced, and so forth. A candidate who obviously is well prepared campaigns from a position of strength. Even voters who disagree with certain of the candidate's views might not be indisposed toward seeing him in office if he seems particularly competent, especially if his opponent suffers by comparison. The candidate and his entire staff must be properly appreciative of the value of doing one's political homework.

Another job for issues research personnel is to maintain information on the record and campaign activities of the opposition. If an opponent has ever held office before, his complete voting record should be thoroughly analyzed and any inconsistencies or failures of performance noted as possible issues for the current campaign. A clipping file should be maintained on the opponent during the campaign, again as a means of detecting inconsistent statements or any other vulnerabilities. If an opponent is vulnerable in any way, the public record generally will contain all the necessary information for making his performance an issue. A campaign should not be based merely on responding to what the opponent has done or is doing, but it would be foolish to ignore the activities of the opposition.

The field of political research has the potential to provide a campaign with information invaluable to the development of campaign strategy. The job of the research director in this area is to gather as much political information as possible about the district in which the campaign is taking place and then interpret this information for the benefit of the candidate's planning. The goal of these endeavors is to be able to predict how voters will react to stimuli that can be applied in the course of a campaign. This research is based on three types of information:

——Demographic, portraying the population by means of statistics on race, age, educational attainment, size of household, employment, income level, and any other information that might have a causal positive relationship with political behavior.

——Historical, representing past electoral history in terms of numbers of registered voters, turnout, votes by party, and comparisons among past races.

——Polling, utilizing all relevant information obtained by the candidate's own polls, published polls (those commissioned by newspapers), marketing surveys, and any other methods used to determine current public sentiment.

As the candidate and campaign manager develop their plans in the course of the campaign, they will regularly draw upon the storehouse of information amassed by the research director. Polls and demographic data will give indications of how receptive certain voters might be to a new issue or approach the candidate may wish to utilize, and historical information might indicate how similar tactics have fared in the past. With this sort of information at hand, political strategy becomes less a matter of gambling and more a matter of reasonable predictions. Political strength is a direct product of political knowledge.

## The Public Relations Adviser

In almost any campaign that makes use of broadcast or other advertising, the public relations adviser is more of a necessity than a luxury. Any media usage is expensive, so careful professional planning should be utilized to make sure that the candidate receives the most exposure for the money spent. The public relations adviser also may be able to assist the press secretary in maximizing the effectiveness of press releases and other contact with the news media.

The first task for the adviser is to determine that aspect of the campaign that can best be conveyed to the voters as epitomizing the candidate himself. This must be an important, but not an overly complex, facet of the campaign; furthermore, it must be "digestible" by the public. If the campaign is keyed to a particular issue or theme (e.g., "Elect John Smith, the law-and-order candidate"), the choice of the message for communication is simplified. The information compiled by political research workers also is helpful in this process.

Once the message is chosen, the question becomes, How is it to be communicated? Market research must be undertaken to determine—in terms as specific as possible—the best medium for the message. (See Chapter 8 on how to implement a media campaign.) The adviser then must analyze both the candidate and the message to determine the best format for communication. For example, if a candidate is particularly lacking in his ability to master the techniques of television, perhaps a "voice-over" by the candidate accompanying film illustrating aspects of an important campaign issue would be most effective. On the other hand, a telegenic candidate should take full advantage of his skills. The public relations adviser should possess the expertise necessary to consider all the possible options and then present his recommendations to the campaign manager. The adviser may want to work directly with the candidate to improve his talents as a media performer. When the final decisions have been made as to the type of media campaign to be utilized, the adviser should take charge of the technical aspects of producing the material.

In addition to electronic media, advertising in newspapers, on billboards, and through any other devices should first be considered by the public·relations adviser in consultation with the campaign manager, who often must keep a fairly tight rein on public relations efforts that might tend to create a "Madison Avenue" image. Voters react negatively to campaigns that are too slick. The secret of effective public relations work in politics is subtlety. After all, a political campaign is an effort to "sell" a candidate or a position to the voters, but public skepticism about politicians makes it far more difficult to market a political product as opposed to a box of detergent. In the course of the campaign, polling should be done to determine the public's reaction to the candidate's media efforts. It may be necessary to tone down advertisements if voters are finding them too strident, or, if no one is paying attention to the media work, a stronger approach might be desirable. The public relations adviser should constantly be monitoring all the public exposure the campaign receives, and should continually supply suggestions to the campaign manager on how the public image of the campaign might be improved.

### The Scheduling and Advance-Work Coordinator

Time is a valuable commodity in a campaign. The candidate must be programed so that his every moment is being utilized in a way that will win votes. Every personal contact with a voter increases the chances of winning that voter's support. Every public gathering attended or media appearance made leaves the candidate's name and message with an ever-growing portion of

67

the electorate. It might be possible to devise a formula establishing the relationship between minutes of campaigning and votes. The candidate's regimen is grueling and tedious, and always there is the pressure to find time for one more campaign appearance, perhaps reaching that one vote that might prove to be crucial.

In this pressurized environment, it is the coordinator of the campaign's day-to-day schedule who has the responsibility of ensuring that the candidate's time is put to best use. His basic precept is that there are no wasted moments. When one reads about candidates who have lost elections, there are often a few accompanying paragraphs describing the candidate waiting at the airport for someone to meet him or spending an hour in small talk at a reception when a ten-minute appearance would have sufficed. This waste of time probably was not, in and of itself, the cause of the candidate's defeat, but such often is symptomatic of a campaign so poorly organized that victory is impossible.

The scheduler must have every minute of the day planned and charted. Even when the candidate is to be granted a brief rest at some point, such a block of time must be precisely included in the schedule. Not only must the day's activities be planned carefully, but so too must the transition periods between events. If the candidate has to make a speech at ten o'clock and attend a meeting across town at eleven o'clock, how will he get there and how long will it take? Again, the emphasis is on precision.

The scheduler must assemble all pertinent logistical and background information (such as travel times and anticipated crowd sizes) and then meet with the campaign manager to shuffle activities so that the campaign's interests are best served. The result of the scheduler's work should be a daily plan in which the candidate's vote-getting talents are put to their most efficient use.

The implementation of the schedule presents related, often more complex, problems. Logistical matters considered by the scheduler must be made the responsibility of a staff member who will ensure that the events planned for the candidate actually. take place. It is to the advance person that the campaign manager and scheduler assign this task. Before the candidate makes an appearance, arrangements such as organizing a press conference, checking physical facilities for speaking, ensuring an audience of proper magnitude, contacting political and community leaders—all these and any other details no matter how infinitesimal must be so thoroughly handled that the candidate's day goes without a hitch. The attribute most valued in this area is efficiency, on the theory that the campaign that runs smoothly in the field is bound to be winning more votes than would a less organized effort. Advance persons are artists of a sort, nimbly staying a step ahead of the candidate, taking great pride in their ability to foresee every possible circumstance. Good, experienced advance people are generally in scarce supply, and a campaign blessed with skilled advance workers tends to guard them jealously.

### The Office Manager and Volunteer Coordinator

Just as the field operations surrounding the campaigning candidate must run smoothly, so too must the basic support functions of the campaign headquarters be performed at a level of consistent efficiency. This is the responsibility of the office manager, who serves as an administrative assistant to the campaign manager, relieving him of the burden of overseeing clerical matters. The "invisible" work of a campaign must be performed perfectly. This is an area which can be fully controlled, since it is primarily an internal organizational matter and may be sheltered to some extent from the political exigencies that affect "in-the-field" campaign work.

The office manager must supervise a working headquarters in terms of maintaining the physical necessities of the campaign and overseeing the performance of clerical duties. The former matter is no easy task during an active campaign. It requires an ability to foresee needs before they arise—to have ten thousand envelopes on hand when a mass mailing is necessary, to have enough stencils for the mimeograph machine, to have ample coffee in supply to keep the staff awake. A campaign can come to a grinding halt if such matters are neglected. Although it usually is not necessary to "crack the whip" to make campaign workers perform their tasks, the volume of work may be such (especially in the latter period of the campaign) that a well-defined system of assigning responsibilities may be necessary to ensure that all essential functions are performed. The office manager should maintain firm control over this assignment process, making sure that everyone knows what to do and is kept busy. The only alternative is some form of chaos.

In most campaigns the office manager will also assume the role of volunteer coordinator. Since no campaign can afford to pay all the people whose assistance is necessary, a highly motivated volunteer worker is one of a campaign's most valuable assets. This high motivation should be matched with proper training and supervision. The volunteer coordinator must determine any special skills a volunteer has, assign him to a needed function for which he seems qualified, provide any necessary training in basic techniques required, and maintain some degree of supervision. Perhaps the most important job of the coordinator is to make sure that all volunteers are kept busy all the time, using rare slack periods to do work in advance of when it will be needed. A volunteer who finds himself with nothing to do is unlikely to maintain his involvement in the campaign. (A famous example of how to keep volunteers busy arose in one of John Kennedy's early campaigns when volunteers were kept busy preparing handwritten notes thanking other volunteers for volunteering. This made everybody happy; the writers were kept busy on a worthwhile project and the recipients were pleased to know that their efforts were appreciated.)

A simple records system should be used to keep track of campaign volunteers, particularly with regard to any special skills they might possess for which a need could arise at some future point. Win or lose, the candidate must be certain to thank properly all those who donated their time and energy to promoting his efforts.

This chapter has outlined the duties of the basic nucleus of a campaign staff. Depending upon the nature of the race, the staff structure might assume any form that will meet both the essential needs of the campaign and any special requirements of the particular election. Many campaigns utilize the services of advisers in such areas as minority or youth affairs, or establish special liaison with labor unions or other groups that comprise an important part of the electorate. Most of the candidates who win elections are properly appreciative of their staffs. They know that the invisible quality of motivation can make a tremendous difference in staff performance and thus in the effectiveness of the campaign as a whole.

Properly structuring a staff is not enough in itself; the various functions must supplement and complement each other, creating a unified entity that is solid enough to endure a long campaign and at the same time flexible enough to adapt to the dynamism of events.

One question that must be kept fully in mind at every stage of campaign planning is: Can the transition be made from drawing board to actual operation? As the staff begins to increase the pace of the campaign, concentrating more and more on reaching the general public and finding every potential voter, the quality of the campaign organization quickly will become evident.

# 5

# Canvassing

The ultimate task of a political campaign is to reach the voters in order to present them with an appeal that will garner their support. There are various ways of doing this, including personal appearances by the candidate, media campaigning, and canvassing. Most campaigns should feature a combination of these approaches. Canvassing—personal contact with individual voters—deserves special attention because:

——It can (and should) be used in campaigns at every level, particularly those in which media campaigning is not feasible or appropriate.

——Since the candidate probably will be able to reach only a small percentage of the electorate through personal appearances, canvassing provides a means of directly contacting targeted voters.

——It is a highly flexible type of campaigning, lending itself to practically any budget situation and any campaign style. Canvassing is effective "person-to-person" contact at a time when voters are growing weary of super-slick political techniques.

The two basic decisions to be made concern where to canvass and what types of canvassing are to be utilized. The statistical analyses discussed in Chapters 14 and 15 should be used in assigning priorities to areas within the electoral constituency. One should never make the mistake of canvassing at random. At best, this is likely to be a waste of time and effort;

at worst, it might stir up the opponent's supporters. A study of demographic statistics, past election returns, and, if available, polling results should suggest where canvassing can prove to be most valuable.

Canvassing is perhaps most useful in developing and maximizing existent strengths. Rarely will a voter who is committed to the opposition be totally turned around by a canvassing effort. The odds against this happening are such that an area identified as "hostile territory" need not be included in a canvass. The two types of areas most likely to respond well to canvassing are those that might be called "hard-favorable" and "soft-favorable." The former category refers to areas of known strength that can be counted on to produce a favorable vote and thus should be canvassed to maximize turnout. For example, if a black candidate is running for office, he probably will want to canvass thoroughly any area with a high percentage of black voters. Such is likely to be a strong area for him, and he will want to be sure that the voters there are aware of his candidacy and will turn out in large numbers on election day. Likewise, a conservative Republican candidate would consider as "hard-favorable" an upper-income area with a high percentage of registered Republicans. The key is to identify strengths and then maximize them.

The "soft-favorable" area raises different questions since it is one that *could* prove to be an asset in terms of vote margins but, for some reason, cannot be considered "solid." Canvassing as a method of persuasion becomes necessary to give undecided voters (or "weak identifiers") a push in the right direction. Such areas are those where voting turnout is erratic (i.e., people vote only occasionally), where a given issue must be addressed in a certain way to galvanize the voters, or where political allegiances do not already exist and thus must be developed. These areas are said to "lean Democratic" or to "lean Republican," and the idea behind canvassing is to change them from "soft-favorable" to "hard-favorable."

## Types of Canvassing

Canvassing may be conducted over the telephone or on a door-to-door basis. The door-to-door technique lends itself to several variations:

——"Information-gathering": a means of determining a voter's registration and party status, his preferences and views as to issues and candidates, thus providing an important input in overall strategy planning for the campaign.

——"Hit-and-run": i.e., brief contact with the voter, perhaps merely to leave some campaign literature.

——"In-depth-issue": voter education through a presentation on aspects of the issues or candidacy on which the campaign is based.

The most common use of canvassing is for information-gathering purposes. An effective canvass of this type can provide a campaign with essential indicators as to how it might best proceed, answering such questions as which voters are registered; which voters are favorable, unfavorable, or undecided; which issues are most important to the voter; which voters would like to volunteer for campaign work; which voters need further information or assistance on election day. This type of canvass is similar to formal campaign polling, but it lacks a poll's scientific precision and should not, if possible, be considered a substitute for a poll. (See Chapter 15 on Polling.) In some states, where mobile voting registrars are allowed, the canvassing can serve as a voter registration drive. This type of canvassing requires that time be spent talking to someone in each household visited, so a fair number of canvassers will be required to cover any sizable area. Efficiency in gathering the information from the voter cannot be overemphasized; the canvasser must know how to elicit information quickly and politely, and then he must move on. The worker in this type or any other type of canvassing operation is the official representative of the campaign, and the voter's impression of the canvasser most likely will influence his impression of the campaign as a whole. (Some suggestions on canvasser training are included later in this chapter.)

If canvassers are in short supply or information gathering is not necessary, the "hit-and-run" canvass can prove useful. When a candidate is concerned about name recognition or for any other reason wants his campaign to have at least *some* direct contact with as many voters as possible, a less substantive canvass might meet his needs. Usually a "hit-and-run" canvass takes the form of a brief exchange with the voter ("Candidate X wants you to know he is running for Office Y and he would appreciate your support") and the leaving of campaign literature, a bumper sticker, or some other electoral materials. Obviously, there are definite parameters as to the effectiveness of such canvassing, but it does provide visibility when something more substantive is not feasible.

On the other end of the spectrum is "in-depth" issue canvassing, a particularly valuable tool when trying to win the support of "undecided" voters. This amounts to taking the campaign into the voter's home and trying to convince him of a particular point of view. The premise underlying this approach is that the undecided voter is an uninformed voter and that by providing him with information his ultimate voting behavior can be influenced. A good example of the utilization of this type of canvassing was the 1968 Eugene McCarthy campaign, particularly in the New Hampshire primary. In that instance, two-person teams (usually college students) went door to door and asked the voters if they could talk with them about the central issue of the campaign—the war in Vietnam. If invited in, they would present Senator McCarthy's views on the war and discuss the voters' own views with them. This type of canvassing proved fruitful in several ways. Antiwar sentiment that was hidden or only partially formed was uncovered and developed into McCarthy votes. Also, regardless of their views on the war or on politics generally, the voters were impressed with the commitment of the McCarthy workers and were appreciative of the kind of campaign approach that appealed to their intelligence rather than relying on typical campaign gimmickry.

However, not every campaign should utilize in-depth canvassing since so much time is spent at each household that it is virtually impossible to cover much ground unless a great number of canvassers are available. Also, the nature of this type of voter contact requires that the canvassers be highly trained and well informed. It would be disastrous if campaign workers were improperly presenting the candidate's views or in some other way failing to conduct the discussion with the voter. But if the campaign is keyed to one issue that requires explanation, some sort of in-depth canvassing might be in order.

76

Telephone canvassing allows contact with individual voters, but because the canvasser's voice is coming over a machine this approach seems less immediate and is likely to have less impact on a voter than a personal visit. (Obviously, it is not a good idea to try an in-depth issue canvass over the telephone.) The telephone, however, can be an effective tool in an information-gathering canvass, since it is fast, can be more closely supervised, and thus requires fewer workers than door-to-door canvassing. It does require expenditures for telephone installation and use, and it depends on the availability of appropriate lists of telephone numbers and on the number of homes in the area with telephones. Perhaps the best use of telephone canvassing is in locales where the door-to-door method is not logistically feasible. It is also highly effective as a means of following up door-to-door canvassing, either to contact people not at home when their area was canvassed or to answer questions raised during the canvasser's visit. A weighing of these factors will allow the campaign manager to develop a proper balance between the in-person and telephone approaches.

## Planning the Canvass

The value of a canvassing operation is largely dependent on the skill with which it is carried out. This is a two-tiered matter: first, the strategy decision as to where and when to conduct the canvass, and second, the operational question as to how well the individual canvassers will perform.

Where to canvass can be determined primarily through reliance on statistical and demographic data. When to canvass depends on what is to be accomplished and on how many canvassers are available. If a goal of canvassing is to register new voters, this should be done early before other campaign activity reaches its peak. Information-gathering canvassing should begin, at least in part, early in the campaign so planning and general strategy decisions can have the benefit of input from the voters. For instance, early canvassing might indicate a high degree of voter interest in an issue that the candidate had not realized was going to be important. Whatever the type of canvassing undertaken, it must be scheduled according to the availability of canvassers.

As noted above, an in-depth issue canvass is a slow process, so it probably should begin quite early unless there is an almost unlimited supply of canvassers (a situation that rarely occurs). The speed of a "hit-and-run" canvass allows it to operate with fewer canvassers, making it most useful in the latter stages of a campaign. A canvassing calendar probably should include a mix of types and timing. A possible schedule might include:

——Twenty weeks before the election, begin selective voter registration canvassing. This may continue for ten weeks.

——Fifteen weeks before the election, begin in-depth issue canvassing and hold a trial run of the information-gathering canvass.

——Ten weeks before the election, end voter registration canvassing, begin full-scale information-gathering canvass, and continue in-depth issue canvassing in selected areas.

——Four weeks before the election, begin telephone follow-up to information-gathering canvass.

——Three weeks before the election, begin hit-and-run canvass in targeted areas not covered by other canvassing.

Obviously, every campaign has different needs and capabilities with regard to canvassing, but a schedule similar to the above is fairly common. Such a plan has the potential to produce votes and valuable information. The campaign manager must ensure that this potential is fully realized.

While developing the grand scheme of the canvassing operation, it is important not to lose sight of the fact that a great deal depends on the performance of the individual canvasser. Most canvassers are volunteers armed with the best intentions but often with little practical political experience. They will have to learn most of their politics in the field through trial and error, but for the sake of the campaign and the canvassers themselves, they should be given some fundamental training.

A word about paid canvassers should be interjected here. Some campaigns have favored the use of paid canvassers because often an adequate supply of volunteers is not available and because paid employees are generally more reliable. There is a division of opinion as to how voters react to paid as opposed to volunteer canvassers and as to whether the actual performance of a paid worker is as politically effective as that of a volunteer.

For example, even though a paid canvasser might be more reliable, voters might consider him a "mercenary." There is also the omnipresent problem of money: few campaigns can afford to pay canvassers.

The canvasser, whether volunteer or paid, must be able to work quickly and yet efficiently. He must know exactly what he is supposed to do—what information he is to gather from or impart to the voter. This might seem like a rather mechanical function, but there are instances when the canvasser will be asked to make his own value judgments. For example, the canvass might seek to determine voter attitudes toward a candidate, with each canvassed voter being rated on a 1-to-5 (friendly-to-hostile) scale. If the canvasser must assign this rating, there should be standardized criteria on which he bases his judgment. If there is improper uniformity in such grading, the compilation of the canvass results will be meaningless. It is a good general rule to assume that campaign workers need to be told exactly how to do everything. In some cases the instructions might be superfluous, but this is better than risking inaccurate information flowing from the canvass. This emphasis on precision should extend to the canvasser's knowledge of his candidate's position on issues. A campaign is likely to find itself in trouble if its canvassers confuse their *own* views with those of the candidate when responding to voters' questions. If there is *any* doubt in the canvasser's mind as to the campaign's official stance on an issue, he should tell the inquiring voter that he will answer the question with a follow-up telephone call or some campaign literature specifically addressed to that issue. A little sloppiness can do a great deal of damage to an otherwise efficient canvass, so necessary precautions should be taken.

Every canvasser must master to some extent "door-to-door psychology" since he is seen by the voter as an official representative of the campaign, the candidate's surrogate, and, in many cases, is the only direct contact between the voter and the campaign. Therefore, the canvasser who makes a well-informed, pleasant presentation is a great political asset, while a canvasser whose behavior alienates those people he visits is throwing away votes. Some basic rules for canvassers include:

——Avoid lengthy discussions even if with a friendly voter (unless such are part of an in-depth issue canvass). An explanation that a large area needs to be canvassed and a promise to the voter that he will be sent further information should suffice.

——Likewise, avoid arguing with a hostile voter. This is a waste of time and is far more likely to lead to increased hostility than to a conversion.

——Look presentable and dress appropriately for the area to be canvassed (for example, do not overdress in a lower income area); wear some sort of campaign identification. This will increase the chances of receiving something more than a perfunctory reception.

——Address your remarks to the head of the household but, if possible, each potential voter in the household should be contacted. Do not spend time with people who are not eligible to vote (e.g., children, those registered to vote elsewhere).

——Canvass at appropriate times; hours from 9:00 A.M. to 9:00 P.M. are generally best, but avoid meal hours and certain times when the voter is likely to be watching a television program that he prefers to politics. Also, consider when the voter is most likely to be at home.

——Practice asking for the needed information in a way that is businesslike but friendly.

——Record the information as received rather than entrusting it to memory to be recorded later.

Training of canvassers can be accomplished in one session. An adequate briefing on what to do and what to expect, when combined with several days of field experience, can produce an effective canvasser.

## Conducting the Canvass

No matter how inherently skilled and enthusiastic canvassers might be, their utility to a campaign is in large part determined by what they are given to work with, in terms of the means to find the voters and to report the results of the canvass.

There is considerable range in the degree of specificity of information provided to the canvasser as to where he is supposed to work. He might be given a computer print-out (based on voter registration lists, property tax rolls, and so on), or he might simply be told to "cover Avenue A between Streets X and Y." Whenever possible, it is a good idea to avoid this latter course and provide the canvasser with at least some idea as to whom he is looking for. Even if sophisticated computer listings are not available, there might well be, particularly in urban areas, a cross-directory (containing the same information as a telephone book, except arranged by address rather than by persons' names). Availability of a listing of this type is essential to a telephone canvass and is very helpful in a door-to-door canvass since it gives the canvasser the name of the person he is addressing and allows him to verify quickly the accuracy of his information.

There are two basic methods (and infinite variations) for recording canvassing information: use of a single sheet for each block (Figure 5-1) or a separate card for each household (Figure 5-2). Which type to use depends on what is going to be done to follow up the canvass. If all future voter contact is to be on a geographical basis (through the use of block captains), the single-sheet approach is adequate. If voters are to be divided into categories other than geographical ones (by ranking them according to party preference), then the separate card system is preferable.

Figure 5-1 illustrates the single-sheet type of canvassing material. The top section indicates how the sheet will look when given to the canvasser; the bottom section appears as it would after canvassing. Depending on what information the campaign manager wants to obtain, the headings at the top of the sheet will vary. This illustration requests such standard information as:

——Is the person a registered voter (Yes or No)?

——What is the person's political party preference (Democrat, Republican, or Independent)?

——What is the canvasser's subjective evaluation of the voter's attitude toward the campaign? In this area the canvasser assigns a status rating to each voter: (1) highly favorable, (2) leaning favorable, (3) undecided, (4) leaning unfavorable, (5) highly unfavorable.

——Is the voter interested in doing volunteer campaign work (Yes or No)? This is a "specialty question" that may be inserted according to specific campaign needs. In this case it appears that this campaign is interested in recruiting additional volunteer workers.

——Does the voter have any specific questions or requests? Anything noted in this column must receive follow-up action from campaign headquarters.

Figure 5-1

PCT.: 214          STREET: Maple

| House # | Name | Telephone | Reg. | PP | Status | Vol. | Com. |
|---------|------|-----------|------|-----|--------|------|------|
| 1301 | Patch, Anthony | 524-1414 | | | | | |
| 1302 | Gilbert, Gloria | 524-1732 | | | | | |
| 1303 | Buchanan, Tom | 523-2236 | | | | | |
| | Buchanan, Daisy | 523-2236 | | | | | |
| 1312 | Diver, Dick | 523-2449 | Y | D | 1 | Y | — |
| 1313 | Blaine, Amory | 524-2645 | Y | R | 5 | — | — |
| 1314 | Calhoun, Ailie | 523-2828 | Y | I | 3 | N | wants econ. info. |
| 1315 | Stahr, Monroe | 525-3162 | Y | D | 2 | N | — |
| | Stahr, Kathleen | 525-3162 | Y | D | 1 | N | needs E. D. trans. |

The Figure 5-1 illustration is based on a hypothetical Democratic campaign canvass. At 1312 Maple, Mr. Diver is a registered Democrat who evidences strong support for this campaign and is interested in doing volunteer work. His name will be given to the volunteer coordinator at headquarters. Because he appears to be a certain favorable vote, his name will be on a high-priority list for get-out-the-vote work on election day. Mr. Blaine, at 1313 Maple, is a registered Republican whom the canvasser considers to have a highly unfavorable outlook toward the campaign. Once the canvasser ascertains this, there is no need to ask further questions of this voter and there is no need to contact him again during the campaign. Ms. Calhoun, at 1314 Maple, is a registered voter who considers herself an independent and is undecided about how she will vote in this election. She asks for information on the candidate's views on economic issues. Headquarters should see to it that she promptly receives campaign literature on the subject. Later in the campaign she should receive at least a telephone follow-up or, if possible, another in-person visit to determine if she needs any further information and if her status rating should be changed. The campaign that pays the most attention to independents is the campaign that is most likely to win their support. At 1315 Maple, Mr. and Mrs. Stahr are both registered Democrats with slightly different outlooks toward the campaign. Mrs. Stahr seems to have made up her mind, but Mr. Stahr appears to need further reinforcement. He should be given some campaign material and, like Ms. Calhoun, included in a follow-up canvass later in the campaign. Even with a "2" rating, he should be included on the priority get-out-the-vote list for election day. Mrs. Stahr has told the canvasser that she will need transportation to the polls on election day. Her name should be added to the appropriate list at headquarters, and she should be contacted just prior to election day to make arrangements.

Even in a canvass such as illustrated here—and this is relatively simple in format—there are numerous categories that might apply to the individual voters. It takes an efficient headquarters operation to ensure that the respective voters' needs are adequately met.

An alternate method of recording canvassing data is the utilization of a separate file card for each household visited. This allows the sorting of information according to criteria other than address. For example, if, in the above hypothetical canvass, the most important information to the campaign is the status rating of each voter, a separate card system would allow easy grouping of all voters rated "1," "2," and so on, for purposes of campaign follow-up and get-out-the-vote planning. Figure 5-2 illustrates a possible canvassing card.

The information on Ms. Calhoun is basically the same as that on the single-sheet canvass illustration. Assuming that the campaign is most interested in the status rating (SR), this can be indicated in the upper right corner to allow easy sorting. The checkmark after "F-U" indicates that some sort of follow-up is required, while the "Comments" section indicates the particular follow-up. The "Follow-Up" section allows a record to be kept on further contact with the voter. In this case, the requested material was mailed on September 25 and the voter was called on October 7, at which time the telephone canvasser determined that Ms. Calhoun was still "undecided" and thus maintained her status rating of "3." If the telephone caller had found, for example, that Ms. Calhoun was "leaning favorable," her SR number would have been changed to "2" and her card transferred accordingly.

Figure 5-2

---

PCT:   214

                                                              SR: 3
   1314 Maple       Calhoun, Ailie       523-2828       F-U:
   REG.: Y          PP: I          VOL.: N
   COMMENTS:  wants economic information
   FOLLOW-UP:   9-25——information mailed
                        10-7 ———telephone call:  SR: 3

---

On a card such as that shown in Figure 5-3, the small squares are perforated, and as the voter responds to each question, the canvasser uses a stylus or penpoint to push out the appropriate square. Because of the high-speed reading ability of a computer, this type of canvass can gather more information than a manually processed operation. As Figure 5-3 illustrates, in addition to the questions asked in the single-sheet and separate card canvasses (Figures 5-1 and 5-2), this canvass seeks data on selected special interest voting groups (union members, unemployed, students), on the voters' evaluation of the president's performance in office, and on voting behavior in the last election. A simple computer program-operation will feed back the completed cards for any category or combination of categories. For example, the campaign manager might want to know the union members in Precinct 214 who voted Democratic in the last election. After the computer program sorts the cards in the proper way (or, in a more sophisticated process, prints out a list of names, addresses,

**Figure 5-3**

Address: _____ Name: _____ Telephone: _____

| Reg. | Status | Pres. Perf. | Last Election | Pct. |
|---|---|---|---|---|

☐ Reg.
☐ Not Reg.

☐ Vol.

☐ D
☐ R
☐ I

Status
☐ 1
☐ 2
☐ 3
☐ 4
☐ 5

Pres. Perf.
☐ Exc.-Good
☐ Fair-Poor

☐ Follow-Up

Spec. Int.
☐ Union
☐ Unemp.
☐ Student

Last Election
☐ D
☐ R
☐ No-Vote

Comments:

Pct.
0 ☐ ☐ ☐
1 ☐ ☐ ☐
2 ☐ ☐ ☐
3 ☐ ☐ ☐
4 ☐ ☐ ☐
5 ☐ ☐ ☐
6 ☐ ☐ ☐
7 ☐ ☐ ☐
8 ☐ ☐ ☐
9 ☐ ☐ ☐

1 2 3 4 5 6 7 8 9 10 11 12 13 14 15 16 17 18 19 20 21 22 23 24 25 26 27 28 29 30 31 32 33 34 35 36 37 38 39 40 41 42 43 44 45 46 47 48 49 50 51 52 53 54 55 56 57

and telephone numbers) and the desired information is put to use, the cards are fed back into the computer, ready to be re-sorted as desired. Those cards requiring follow-up action can be provided to staff members who will read the canvassers' comments on the bottom and then take appropriate action. Not every campaign can afford computer operations, but depending on the nature of the programing, computer costs often turn out to be surprisingly reasonable.

Variations on the type of canvassing and voter identification discussed here have been utilized with increasing frequency and success since 1970. Every campaign probably will find it worthwhile at least to consider (on a cost-benefit basis) the incorporation of such a program in its election strategy.

The most valuable information provided to a campaign by its canvassing efforts is that concerning voter identification—who among the voters are the sure votes, who can be written off, who needs to be wooed. The different strategies aimed at each of these categories will culminate with get-out-the-vote planning on election day (discussed in detail in Chapter 13). There are important additional uses to which this information lends itself. For instance, all canvassed voters given a "1" or "2" status rating might prove good targets in a fund-raising drive. Voters accorded a "1" rating might be approached about contributing several hours of their time to help the campaign on election day. Trends in voters' responses to canvassers' questions can help shape the theme of campaign literature.

However the information is put to use, it is likely to be one of the most important tools in the campaign. The campaign with the most effective canvassing program very often is the winning campaign.

# 6

# Voter Registration

A candidate often finds that considerable numbers of persons who would be likely to support him cannot do so because they are not registered voters. If it is determined that the addition of these people to the voting rolls might make a significant favorable difference in the outcome of the election, a voter registration drive should be included in plans for the campaign.

## Types of Registration

There are a number of factors that dictate the approach that may be taken toward voter registration. Most important is the type of registration provided for by state law. Currently, numerous reform efforts are under way designed to simplify and make more uniform the procedures for registering to vote. Until these efforts reach full fruition, the following are likely to remain the most common methods of registration:

——*Postal* registration, which allows voters to register merely by sending a short application (usually on a post card) to the appropriate governmental office, with the registration certificate sent by return mail to the voter.

——*Centralized* registration, requiring voters to register in person at one location, such as a county courthouse. This format is sometimes modified by opening several substations for more convenient access for registrants.

——*Mobile* registration, allowing deputy registrars to register voters anywhere, including door-to-door registration.

There are advantages and problems inherent in each of these approaches. Postal registration is a simple method, requiring little effort on the part of the voter and providing a similarly streamlined procedure for the administrator of the registration process. Considering that fewer than 50 percent of those eligible to vote do so even in presidential elections, it would seem desirable to try to stimulate voting by making the whole process, beginning with registration, as easy as possible. Assuming that the postal applications could be made available to every household (perhaps as a function of the Census Bureau), the percentage of eligibles who are actually registered should rise drastically. In turn, it might be expected that voting turnout would increase commensurately. Candidates would be able to concentrate on winning the support of an electorate that would be able to vote, and the campaign would not have to spend its time in registering people.

Postal registration has been criticized on the grounds that it is too susceptible to fraud in that a person using the mail and needing to make no personal appearance before a registrar could register several times under fictitious names. Another criticism is based on the theory that it should not be made too easy for people to register and vote since such ease would foster an electorate of disinterested voters who would be herded to the polls as the easy prey of the most glib politicians. These critics seem to feel that registration is something of a test—that is, a voter who goes to the trouble of actually appearing before a registrar to register is likely to go to the trouble of becoming informed on candidates and issues before voting. Sharp debate on the pros and cons of postal registration has taken place in Congress and elsewhere for many years and probably will continue even if a federal postal registration program is instituted.

In terms of convenience, the antithesis of the postal method is a system of centralized registration. The registrant must appear at the proper place at the proper time to register, no matter how complex or simple the actual process might be. In theory, such a stringent procedure discourages fraud, particularly if the registrant is asked to swear to the information he gives to the registrar, and it does limit registered voters to people who have at least some interest in participating. Critics argue that the effect on the amount of fraudulent registration is negligible and, more importantly, the centralized process is fundamentally unfair in its de facto limitation on who will be able to vote. Some people very interested in participating may have good reasons for being unable to register at a location that might be central to some but seriously inconvenient to others. This travel requirement may have the effect of depriving a citizen of his right to vote.

The approach that falls between these two methods is that of mobile registration. Each registrant has personal contact with a deputy registrar, but access to the registration process is relatively easy. Usually it is quite simple to become a deputy registrar so that a campaign may use those volunteers who have been deputized as part of a registration project. Probably the main disadvantage is that of the administrative complexities that arise when large numbers of people serving as registrars are scattered throughout the community. Eventually all their paper work will have to be gathered and the master voting lists compiled.

Depending on state law, any of these basic methods might be modified or combined with each other to produce a registration system that will incorporate its own peculiarities. Any campaign organization must be fully familiar with the legal aspects of registration. This must include not only the procedure by which individuals are registered, but also the requirements that may exist concerning purging of the rolls (i.e., removing the names of persons who are deceased, have moved away, or for some other reason are not eligible to vote), the need for reregistration after a given number of years, and any other matter that affects voting rights.

The candidate who wants to engage in voter registration must conform his efforts to the type of registration created by statute. Whatever the method of registration in use, a place does exist for the campaign organization desirous of increasing the number of persons who will be able to vote on election day. The determinations of who to register and how to go about doing so are among the most important decisions that a campaign manager will have to make.

## Selective Registration

When a campaign undertakes a voter registration project, the fundamental goal of such an effort will be to allow more people to vote. This altruism is tempered by the fact that registration is not something to be pursued in a haphazard way, trying to cover the entire constituency, but rather must be concentrated among those who are most likely to vote in accord with the candidate's interests after they have been registered. One must not forget that a registration drive is a campaign tactic just like any other and that the sponsoring candidate's interests will be of primary concern.

By analyzing statistics that indicate areas in which there is considerable disparity between population size and the number of people registered, potential registration targets can be determined. These targets should be ranked according to the likelihood of their support of the candidate. There is no foolproof way to assign priorities, but proper utilization of demographic and political data should allow reasonable prediction of voting behavior. Factors to be considered include voting patterns of those registered in the area, socioeconomic indicators (e.g., predominantly student, predominately labor), and political indicators such as polling results. The ideal registration target is the area in which those who are already registered indicate affiliation with the candidate's party, where the socioeconomic profile is such as may be considered of favorable potential (e.g., a lower-income minority group neighborhood is generally considered to be potentially strong Democratic), and where polls indicate that the candidate is recognized and popular. In such an area a registration drive may be tantamount to enlisting sure votes. Registration efforts should first be directed at the most desirable targets. Other areas may then be covered on the basis of their priority ranking and according to how much time and effort the campaign can afford to spend on registration. It may be decided that after the areas of highest priority have been covered, other aspects of the campaign should take precedence. The question that is the basis of such decision making remains constant: What type of campaign activity is going to generate the most votes?

## Timing of Registration

In most states, voter registration may take place at any time except during a short period immediately preceding election day. This allows a candidate who begins his political efforts early to initiate a precampaign registration drive. Such a project has a number of advantages, including:

——Providing a means for keeping political activists involved at times when electoral activity is light. A registration drive allows the candidate to give these people something to do and thus he "holds on" to them while awaiting the beginning of his major campaign effort.

——Serving as a proving ground for campaign organization. By starting early, the candidate will be able to enjoy that most elusive of luxuries—time. A precampaign registration drive can be conducted at a pace that will allow personnel to be shuffled and different tactics to be tried. If, for example, the type of canvassing being utilized is not producing the desired results, it may be replaced by another approach. In the more pressurized environment of the full campaign, such transitions might be too disruptive to be feasible. The results of this test period can prove helpful when planning strategy for the rest of the campaign.

——Enabling the staff to begin building lists of prospective volunteers and voters. Records should be kept detailing the results of any registration drive, at the very least providing a list of new registrants, and, whenever possible, listing those who while being registered express an interest in doing volunteer work or otherwise helping in a campaign. If a precampaign registration drive is not feasible, it will be necessary to integrate registration with other campaign activities. A proper balance must be struck among these activities; registration should not unduly detract from the conducting of other campaign business. The campaign manager must be prepared to make highly selective decisions about what sort of registration program to initiate. As other campaign activities become more urgent and as election day looms ever closer, registration can be undertaken only when a cost-benefit ratio—expressed in terms of effort and votes—appears highly favorable.

### Registration Techniques

The canvassing techniques discussed in Chapter 5 generally lend themselves well to registration work. This is particularly true when canvassers can serve as registrars or, if postal registration is in use, when canvassers can distribute to constituents any information and materials they might require to register.

If mobile registration is allowed, but a door-to-door canvass is not practicable due to insufficient manpower or for any other reason, a bit of ingenuity will be required. The limited number of registrars should be deployed to locations at which it is likely that large numbers of potential registrants will congregate. Registration booths might be opened at shopping centers, at factories during lunch break or shift changes, on college campuses, and anywhere else where a few registrars will be available to many people. Even a small-scale effort of this sort has the potential of benefiting the campaign.

The speed and efficiency of registrars often can be improved through the use of "bird dogs"—campaign workers who in a door-to-door project will operate slightly ahead of the registrars, finding out quickly which households contain potential new registrants and which may be skipped as being fully registered or for some reason not eligible. These "bird dogs" are particularly helpful when only a limited number of canvassers can be deputized as registrars. When using a registration booth at a set location, the "bird dogs" can act as publicity agents, directing people to the registrars. If an adequate number of personnel are avilable and can be properly organized, "bird dogs" can beneficially affect the rate of new registrations.

If the only method of registration is the centralized or fixed-location type, the campaign interested in registering voters is faced with a far more difficult task. Since the registration process cannot be taken to the voters, the voters must be taken or sent to wherever they can register. Because of the added work involved in such a situation, a registration drive of this type is best undertaken at the precampaign stage, before energies must be devoted to other matters.

Many people may need to be convinced that it is worth their while to make the effort to register. Public education, in the form of advertising or handout literature, is useful in explaining the reasons for registering and the procedure for doing so. Once the public has been exposed to this "selling" influence, the campaign must take the initiative in managing the logistics of registration. This often includes scheduling transportation, providing babysitters or other assistance when needed, and generally shepherding constituents along the way to registration. To be most effective, this service should follow a period of canvassing (either in-person or telephone) that has produced a list of persons who need to be registered. If a geographic area of relatively small size (such as one or two city blocks) appears to contain a high percentage of people who need to be registered, a registration "blitz" might prove useful. This may consist of a highly visible mobilization, using sound trucks and buses in an effort to gather everyone who is to be registered at one time and take them (with appropriate fanfare) to the registrar. This tactic is useful in making registration a campaign event—the candidate could make an appearance, news media might attend, and votes as well as registrations might be won.

In deciding what type of registration effort a campaign should incorporate in its planning, careful consideration should be given to the financial aspects of this part of the campaign. A full-scale push to register voters can be extremely expensive, especially when the registration cannot take place as part of a door-to-door canvass. Sometimes it is possible for even a low-budget campaign to stimulate an increased rate of registration by involving nonpartisan organizations—such as the League of Women Voters and various civic groups—in the registration drive. These organizations often have funding sources not available to campaigns, and if they concentrate their political efforts on voter registration they might well do a good job. The campaign organization might not be able to direct the drive, but people will be registered.

The basic political consideration underlying any decision about voter registration concerns *who* is to be registered. A campaign does not want to register great numbers of people who will proceed to vote for the opposition. No registration drive can be conducted with a guarantee of unanimously favorable results, but a small dose of political common sense should indicate, on the basis of demographic and political analyses, where support is likely to be found. Although politicians will proclaim the virtues of registering *everyone*, they will want to register "every one" of their supporters first. This political outlook is not wholly irreconcilable with political altruism, but it should be kept in mind particularly when an opposing candidate begins to talk about "nonpartisan" efforts to register voters.

# 7
# Campaign Issues

Much of the work of a political campaign may be classified as "mechanical"—identifying voters, devising a means to reach them, and mobilizing them so as to generate the desired electoral behavior. Part of this process, however, requires a combination of intellectual and organizational skills: developing campaign issues that will stimulate a positive voter response to the candidate. The following factors are involved in the issue-related aspects of campaigning:

——Identifying issues of political significance. There are some issues in which many voters are intensely interested, others that create little concern. The candidate must determine the issues on which he should concentrate.

——Rendering a given issue "campaignable." After an issue has been selected for its salience among voters or because of the candidate's interest in the subject, it must be reduced to a form that is presentable to voters and which will also lend itself to such techniques of campaigning as use in canvassers' presentations, adaptability to the format of campaign brochures, and so forth.

——Presenting the campaign position. The candidate must be able to communicate his views and persuade voters that he is giving them a reason to vote for him.

The effectiveness of issue campaigning is largely dependent upon how well these basic factors are combined to create a coherent policy presentation for the voters' consideration. Poorly conceived treatment of an issue can prove detrimental to the overall campaign effort, while skillful articulation of a candidate's platform can be immensely helpful as the voters seek to make their choices from among the field of candidates.

## Identifying the Salient Issues

In order to avoid confusing the voters and weakening the thrust of the treatment of issues, only a limited number of issues should be considered "major" for campaign purposes. In other words, although a candidate must be familiar with and have positions on a great number of policy matters, he must choose several from among these that he will adopt as his special areas of concentration during the campaign. For these issues, in-depth position statements and background documentation should be developed. The goal of such efforts is for the candidate and the issue to be linked together in the minds of voters. A candidate who acts upon an issue that has captured the public's interest can build most of his campaign on the foundation of that issue. Good examples of this practice are the 1968 Eugene McCarthy presidential campaign and other candidacies in 1968 and 1970 that were based on the issue of opposition to the war in Vietnam.

Public opinion polling can provide accurate indications of what the public is thinking—what issues they feel are important or unimportant and, more specifically, what positions on those issues are most in line with their own thinking. This polling information can be obtained in a variety of ways: professionally conducted on behalf of the campaign; for an outside entity (e.g., newspaper, market research survey); or as part of the campaign's canvassing program. The format of the polling may vary, utilizing one or several of the following means of questioning the voters:

——Provide a list of five or six issues and ask the voter to rank them in order of importance.

——Select one or two issues and ask the voter to choose from among a list of possible solutions.

——Present the voter with an open-ended question, such as "What do you think is today's most pressing issue and what do you think should be done about it?"

The objective of such polling is to determine what, if any, pronounced trends or preferences exist with regard to the issues. Provided with such information, the candidate can establish priorities as to the issues on which he should concentrate as well as integrate voters' ideas on solutions with his own thoughts on the relevant matters. This process provides no foolproof formula for selecting issues on which to campaign, but it does provide input that will prevent the candidate from making his choice of issues in a manner that is overly insulated from public sentiment. (A detailed discussion of polling techniques is found in Chapter 15.)

As another means of detecting public sentiment or stimulating voter interest, "trial balloons" might be launched. This involves the candidate's trying out a new issue in several speeches and in press briefings to determine if the subject matter has any potential as a political issue. If some public interest is evidenced, the issue may be more fully developed. If there appears to be little interest, the candidate can move on to other subjects.

The campaign committee (discussed in Chapter 4) can serve as another source in identifying salient issues. This advisory body, composed of representatives of the voters in the candidate's constituency, should have sufficient ties to the community to allow appraisals of voters' opinions on given issues. A well-coordinated group of this sort, representing diverse viewpoints, can supplement any information acquired through polling. Depending upon how much time committee members have available for campaign work, it may be possible to create special subcommittees to formulate position statements on various matters. In addition to members of the campaign committee, additional persons possessing expertise in given policy areas might be recruited to lend assistance to the tasks of evaluating the significance of certain issues and polishing the candidate's platform. Members of the academic community often become involved in this aspect of campaign work. For example, a political science professor who is an expert in the field of Soviet studies might be asked for assistance in developing certain foreign policy issue positions for the candidate. Someone on the main campaign staff (perhaps the research director) should be in charge of coordinating this work—assigning ideas about issues for further development and evaluating reports from campaign workers in the field about current voter attitudes and interests. Maintaining up-to-date knowledge about what the voters are thinking is of great importance to a candidate since his campaign is likely to have greater immediate effect if he addresses issues with which the voters already have some familiarity rather than those about which they must be educated. This is not to say that a candidate should avoid developing issues on his own rather than merely responding to current voter interests. There always is a need for candidates to probe policy areas of public importance that have yet to be "discovered" by the electorate. But the candidate who proceeds into new fields should at least have some knowledge of the extent of public understanding of the given subject and thus have an idea of how intensive an effort must be made to educate the public and convince voters of the rectitude of his position.

The observant candidate will be able to find additional indicators of public opinion if he looks beyond the limits of his own campaign organization. Much can be learned from an examination of coverage accorded by the news media to various subjects over a period of time. Newspaper editorials and signed editorial-page columns should be added to the candidate's files on issues and should be watched as a barometer of public opinion. Editorials generally reflect the views of the majority of a newspaper's readership. Examination of the "letters to the editor" column is a further means of ascertaining public opinion about events in the news and may provide indications of the extent to which readers agree or disagree with editorial policy on given issues. Straight news articles also should be examined in terms of what events are receiving how much coverage. This sort of analysis should be applied to broadcast as well as print media. If an issue is subject to extensive background or investigative coverage, the candidate may wish to include his views on that issue in his current speeches and other campaign statements since he may assume that the heavy coverage by the media has increased public awareness of the issue. Furthermore, the news coverage might provide the campaign's research staff with jumping-off points for development of position papers for the candidate. For example, if the news media have uncovered evidence that a local officeholder has accepted illegal campaign contributions and this disclosure receives heavy coverage, featuring in-depth investigative reporting, the candidate may contribute to the furor first by joining in the attack on the official (assuming that the charges are found to be accurate) and then by proceeding to the more substantive task of developing some well-researched proposals for campaign finance reform. If the candidate acts promptly, his proposals will reach a public that, because of exposure to the news coverage, has some knowledge of the subject matter and may be ready for a politician who takes a positive approach to the problem.

The treatment other candidates accord an issue, and the public's response to that treatment, should be watched in order to detect any "sleeper" issues that may have escaped the candidate's notice in his campaign planning. This watchfulness should extend to candidates of the same party who are running for other offices as well as to candidates of the other party, including the direct opposition. If one's opponent finds a popular issue, he must not be allowed to enjoy sole possession simply because he found it first. A politically astute candidate should be able to develop his own position on such an issue and promptly take it to the voters. Merely echoing the opposition will not suffice; the latecomer must provide a new twist in approaching the issue if he is to "take it away" from his opponent or at least neutralize any claim by the opponent that it is "his" issue.

To all these techniques of identifying the most politically potent issues must be added the intangible ingredient of political intuition. The candidate and his staff must be able to detect voter response however it is manifested—the cheers of a crowd on hearing the candidate hammer away at a point in a speech, an upsurge in contributions and offers of volunteer help after a certain issue is addressed, favorable trends in the polls, increased interest encountered by canvassers, or any other indication that the campaign has struck a responsive chord within the electorate.

It is the ability to combine an articulate presentation of issues with the acumen of a solid campaign organization that will find "campaignable" issues that can produce a winning candidate.

## Creating a "Campaignable" Issue

After determining the issues in which the voters are most interested as well as those in which the candidate, for whatever reasons, takes special interest, the task becomes one of finding an approach to each issue that will render it an effective campaign tool.

Particularly if the issue is one that the candidate believes important but it is not widely recognized as such by the public, some basic educational groundwork must be developed before effective campaigning can commence. Part of this work the candidate can do himself through his campaign organization. In speeches and meetings with small groups of voters, he can present the facts relevant to the issue, emphasizing background material and reasons why the subject is important. Similar written material can be distributed by the campaign organization, low-key in the sense that it is directed at increasing awareness of the issue rather than soliciting votes. For example, if the candidate is concerned about potential pollution of drinking water due to the dumping of factory wastes into a river, but the public does not seem to recognize the problem, the gravity of the situation will have to be established before the candidate can expect to affect voting behavior by proposing solutions.

If the candidate has found a truly legitimate issue, he may be able to secure assistance in his efforts from the news media. Again utilizing the example of the environmental issue, it is possible that an enterprising newspaper or broadcast reporter will independently investigate the pollution situation. If there is a problem, as the candidate has charged, news stories on the subject will begin to appear. Even if such stories do not mention that the candidate called the matter to the public's attention, his cause still is served since the news coverage will make more people aware of the issue and thus allow him to proceed with his own substantive proposals.

A candidate must be careful not to assume that the public knows more than it really does. If such an assumption is made and the candidate moves too quickly to present his ideas on an issue, his proposals—no matter how valid—are likely to reach only an uncomprehending audience. This matter points out yet another reason why a campaign should begin with as much lead time before the election as possible. Except for an issue that is of crisis proportions and well established in the public consciousness, recognition of the significance of an issue will take time.

Another caveat for the candidate relates to how the substance of an issue is to be explained to the voters. Many people have neither the time nor the inclination (nor perhaps the ability) to master intricate material relating to various campaign issues. The candidate, without seeming condescending, should strive to reduce issues to their most basic terms when he introduces them. This process will not obviate the necessity for developing extensive background material; it merely places emphasis on ensuring that the voters will find issues material understandable and thus relevant to their decision on how to cast their votes. As the campaign progresses and the voters' familiarity with an issue increases, more sophisticated information might be utilized. The candidate and campaign manager must determine the pace for this educational process. Certain groups of voters may require special treatment depending on their interests. For example, a local chapter of the Sierra Club will not require introductory educational treatment on environmental issues; detailed campaign proposals on such issues should be made available to such an audience immediately. For most effective campaigning, the candidate must neither overestimate nor underestimate the abilities of his constituents to digest the issues materials presented to them.

As a general rule, an issue is most useful when it is presented in positive terms. It is easier to incorporate issues framed in this way into a campaign effort that does not rely solely upon attacking the opposition. The candidate should try to avoid mere criticism or commentary. Voters will be far more impressed by definitive proposals. The ultimate goal for each issue utilized for campaign purposes should be: the candidate's positive policy suggestions supported by an outline of basic facts plus more detailed statements treating various aspects of the issue with

101

specificity. Such an approach is likely to enhance the "campaignability" of any issue.

## Presenting the Issue Position

After an issue has been identified as relevant and of political interest to the electorate, and after consideration has been given to the format of the issue for campaign purposes, the specific content of the candidate's position must be determined. Two basic matters should be considered: the relationship of the issue per se to the constituency and the relationship of the candidate's proposals concerning the issue to the constituency.

Except for issues of obvious importance with which the public is familiar to some degree, the voter's response to a given issue is likely to be, "Why should I care about this?" The candidate cannot expect his views on an issue to have much political effect when he meets with this response. Even a vague public awareness of the ramifications of a policy matter will have to be developed further. For example, with the candidate who wants to campaign on the issue of environmental pollution, the educational process discussed earlier must include not only general explanations of the subject, but also must establish that the voter's self-interest requires cognizance of and action on the matter. In other words, the candidate must move from a mere "pollution is evil" approach to a "pollution is destroying *your* health" argument supported by specific examples. The voter's realization that he is personally involved in a campaign issue is likely to increase his receptivity to a candidate's proposals.

Once this relationship has been established, it becomes necessary to relate the candidate's specific proposals to the voter's interests. The proposed solutions to the problem should logically develop from the general explanation of the issue. In the pollution example, a candidate's proposals might include: "Enact legislation to restrict dumping of wastes into rivers. In our city this would reduce the toxicity of our water supply by 90 percent." The first sentence of this proposal, if standing alone, might seem to the voters to be a good idea on general principles. But the second sentence, with its reference to "our city" and "our water supply," brings home the fact that the voters have a stake in seeing the idea reach fruition. Self-interest often can be a decisive factor in determining voting behavior. The candidate must recognize this fact when he presents his positions on issues to the public.

As the presentation of an issue is being shaped, the campaign committee again should be asked for assistance. Different segments of the candidate's constituency may perceive issues in different ways. To ensure maximum effect, the campaign may desire to stress different aspects of the same issue to diverse groups of voters. For any given issue, members of the campaign committee should be asked what type of approach would be best suited to their respective constituencies. For example, on the pollution issue, a labor union representative might point out the concern of workers that strict environmental controls could force some factories to close and thus increase unemployment. The candidate should consider these fears when developing his detailed statements on the issue and should address himself directly to this problem in any speeches to labor groups and in any material to be distributed to union members.

The candidate must beware of trying to be all things to all people by seeking to please the special interests of every group within the electorate. If he attempts such an approach, he almost inevitably will stumble over his own contradictory statements made to different groups at different times. Should he fall into this trap, he will be highly vulnerable to attacks by the opposition charging him with putting expediency above all else. The politician faces the difficult task of recognizing and representing many divergent interests in a manner that accords equal treatment to all. At times this will not be possible, but the candidate should accept this political fact of life and concern himself with developing positions on issues that conform to the most important demands of conscience and consistency.

## The "Localized" Issue

Related to the concept of presenting a specialized issue position to a given interest group is the practice of conducting an issue identification and presentation process aimed at selected geographical areas within the candidate's constituency.

This approach can be particularly useful in a smaller election, such as for city council or other local office. Through polling or other means of identifying the most salient issues, concerns unique to a certain neighborhood might be detected. For example, in a suburban area recently hit with a large increase in the crime rate, voters might be concerned with virtually no other issue. In such a case, the candidate's basic position on controlling crime should be supplemented with material directed specifically at these voters and made available in a simply printed handout. The text might read:

> I share your concern about the frightening fact that crime has increased 6 percent in this community in the past six months. On Walnut Street alone, three burglaries occurred in June. Neither you, the citizens, nor your elected officials should tolerate this situation. Here is what I propose to do about crime if I am elected:
>
> [*The candidate's standard crime control message would follow here, perhaps including some particular suggestions for the target community.*]

This sort of appeal is likely to be far more effective than reliance on a standard approach designed to be applied uniformly to the entire district.

In all aspects of the treatment of campaign issues—from the identification of salient subjects to the presentation of the candidate's views—the use of innovative techniques (such as localized issues) can move a campaign beyond the realm of "politics as usual" and give the voter a means by which he will remember a candidate and seriously consider supporting the candidacy. On election day such campaign efforts may be found to have paid significant dividends.

# 8

# Media Usage

Modern political campaigns increasingly have incorporated the use of news and advertising media into the planning of campaign strategy. Some candidates have been accused of being "creatures of the media," more concerned with being properly telegenic than with taking substantive stands on the issues. In recent years political scientists and others have expressed fears that extensive media usage is perverting our political system in that voters could be improperly manipulated in their voting behavior by the same media techniques utilized to sell used cars and aspirin. There always exists the danger that voters might be fooled by a clever merchandising campaign with a candidate as the product. But most voters seem sufficiently sophisticated in their attitudes toward politics to be able to resist—and often resent—a candidate who appears to be solely a product of media packaging. Furthermore, an opponent of a "media candidate" may find in this subject area a potent issue, attacking his foe as an exponent of dehumanized, electronic politics. Thus, the task for the candidate and campaign manager is to determine how media usage may best be integrated into their planning and utilized to its greatest benefit without making the campaign dependent upon it.

## Planning the Use of Media

Different campaigns have different media requirements. For example, a candidate for city council from a geographically small district probably would be wasting money if he purchased expensive television advertising time since the televised message would reach far beyond the boundaries of his constituency. By way of example, all or part of 18 different congressional districts are to be found within New York City, as are far greater numbers of state and local offices. As with other facets of campaigning, the secret is to reach those people .who need to be reached and not dissipate strength through too broad an appeal. There is no firm formula for deciding what type of media campaign is best for a given candidate, but the following criteria are among those that are helpful in determining optimal media usage:

——*Nature of the media available.* Although major metropolitan areas usually have a great variety of electronic and print media, many areas are far more limited, there might be one television outlet, two or three local radio stations, and one newspaper. Whatever the lineup might be of media facilities, an analysis of each market should be made—who listens to which radio station, who reads the newspaper, and any other questions that will aid in targeting an audience. On the basis of such information, the campaign manager and the public relations adviser can determine the best feasible media campaign.

——*Size of the media budget.* Difficult decisions must be made as to how much of the total campaign budget is to be allotted to media work. Any campaign interested in extensive television advertising must plan on spending considerable sums. Large amounts also may be spent on radio, billboard, and newspaper advertising, but the same amount of money is likely to buy more time or space in these media than on television. An early evaluation of funding is essential since the possible amount of exposure will determine the type of programing. For example, a large media budget will allow the advertising to develop over a period of time and to coincide with the overall pace of the campaign. A smaller budget might demand a concentration on a "media blitz" in the final days of the campaign, with the early part of the campaign conducted without a concurrent media effort. The amount of funding available also will affect the production of the media material, determining the nature and amount of any professional assistance that can be utilized in developing media presentations. The use of professionals is generally advisable, since a poor media campaign (with inane television and radio spots or ugly billboards) can be worse than no media effort at all.

——*Nature of the constituency.* As with any other aspect of campaign planning, a thorough knowledge of the constituency is essential in determining what type of media is likely to reach the most voters and what type of message is likely to be most effective. For example, if an area's population includes a large number of Spanish-speaking citizens, it might be wise to advertise on any Spanish-language radio stations or in Spanish newspapers. If a district contains a college campus with its own radio station, special advertisements might be devised for the campus audience. If many residents commute to work by automobile, billboards on commuter arteries might achieve high visibility. There is no sense in blindly scheduling political media efforts; to do so may be tantamount to throwing away money.

——*Theme of the campaign.* The nature of a media appeal should be compatible with the general approach the candidate is pursuing in the campaign. If he is stressing economic issues, his media work can illustrate the problems caused by inflation, unemployment, or other such matters. A campaign slogan (e.g., "Let's put America back to work") or general name identification can be embedded in a voter's consciousness through skillful use of media. There should be a general coordination of the media campaign with campaign literature and the candidate's speeches. In other words, it is best not to bombard the electorate with too many different types of appeals for votes; such is likely to result in confusion on the part of the voter.

——*Media usage by other campaigns.* All political media usage should be monitored throughout the campaign for a number of reasons. It might be advantageous, particularly if party identification is favorable, to try joint media work with another candidate of the same party. This might save money and could prove mutually beneficial in terms of gaining votes from each other's supporters. In terms of opposing candidates, it is always useful to know what the opposition is saying to the voters since some of their media work might be susceptible to a response. For example, if the opposing candidate is an incumbent whose approach to economic issues is "We've never had it so good," the challenger might (if the circumstances allow) counterattack using the "We've never had it so good" theme in a sarcastic way, contrasting that claim with current unemployment, inflation, or other economic statistics that favor his position. This example indicates the importance of thoughtful media planning. One must beware of aiding the opposition through the boomerang effect.

As these considerations indicate, it is important that all media work be fully integrated with other parts of the campaign. Even the most lavish media presentations are of little use if they fail to fit into the campaign's overall theme. One of the campaign manager's responsibilities is to control the direction necessary to ensure this conformity.

Unless there is sufficient funding to allow a consistent rate of media usage throughout the entire campaign, it may be best to concentrate the media effort in the last three weeks. This will avoid the dilution of exposure and will reach voters when their interest is likely to be at its highest level. Most voters who consider themselves "undecided" during the campaign do not make final decisions until the last week, and often not until election day. It makes good sense to make a maximum media effort when these voters will be making up their minds and thus perhaps be receptive to a final appeal for their votes. The main value of using media spots earlier in the campaign is to increase the visibility of the candidate, but unless ample funding is at hand, it usually is best to rely on regular news coverage or less expensive forms of advertising at this stage.

Related to the general question of timing is the matter of frequency. Media work is designed to provide visibility for the campaign, and the more consistent the visibility, the more likely it is to be noticed by, and have an effect on, the voter. Constant visibility might also generate something of a "bandwagon" effect: if the voter regularly sees some manifestation of the candidacy (e.g., television spots, billboards), he is likely to think that the campaign is a viable enterprise and worthy of his consideration. Frequency may even be more important than the "reach" of the message—it might be better to purchase time for several spots that will reach a smaller audience than time for only one spot that will reach a larger audience. In the long run, multiple spots are likely to reach different people who are exposed to the spots at different times, whereas a single showing's effect is dependent on the size of the audience the one time it is presented. As a practical matter, it is rare that any single media presentation is so good that its one-shot usage will have much effect on voters. Thus, the general rule is: the more, the better. Once the fact of the existence of the candidacy has found a place in the voter's consciousness, it will be easier to go about winning his vote.

## Broadcast Media

Proper use of broadcast media is a science in itself. It is not easy to predict how well one will communicate on television or radio—the medium may magnify minor flaws (such as a voice of unusual timbre) or provide a shield for candidates who lack true substance but "project" well with the aid of electronic gadgetry. In using television, some basic rules should be kept in mind and applied to the particular campaign situation. Generally, people view television *programs*, not stations (when there are several stations), as opposed to radio, where listeners tend to tune into a favorite station. This theory is useful in determining how to reach a given constituency, since a target voter can be found as part of a target audience. This assumption is prone to be proved wrong at times, as is the case with all stereotyping, but it does have some foundation in logic. For example, if a candidate wants to reach a blue-collar audience, he might buy an advertising spot on a sports program. If women voters are the desired audience, daytime soap operas may present valuable access to these viewers. Since several candidates might have this theory of audience identification in mind, it is necessary to purchase the desired time slots well in advance. It is important that the candidate and his manager understand any statutes or other controls on the purchase of television time for political advertising. For example, "equal access" rules entitle candidates to purchase equal amounts of time if they so desire, but this usually means *available* time. In other words the candidate cannot wait until the week before the election and expect to find prime-time slots available for election eve. The campaign that buys early will be able to secure the best slots. This, in turn, requires that the financial planning for the campaign be such that these early expenditures are possible. (See, for example, the discussion in Chapter 4 about the duties of the finance chairman.)

There is no ideal master plan for scheduling television spots, but if the budget allows, a schedule such as the following might be used for 30-second spots:

Daily——1 spot in prime-time (7:30 P.M.-10:30 P.M.)

2 spots in daytime (8:00 A.M.-4:30 P.M.)

2 spots in evening (4:30 P.M.-7:30 P.M.)

Plus—— 7 spots per week in late-night (10:30 P.M.-12 P.M.), concentrating on Friday and Saturday nights.

If possible, this schedule should be intensified in the days immediately preceding the election. Also, the frequency of the spots may be geared to campaign events, such as a visit by the candidate to a given area, a large campaign rally, or a voter registration drive.

Some debate has occurred in recent years on the subject of the length of television spots. It has been argued that spots of less than 30 seconds should be banned because it is virtually impossible to present a message of any substance in less than a half-minute, and those 10- or 15-second spots that are aired must depend on "Madison Avenue" gimmickry in presenting their quick appeal. Advocates of such a ban contend that the use of television in politics must be restricted to responsible campaigning on the issues and not be allowed to degenerate into a potentially dangerous contest of showmanship. This debate has reached no definitive conclusions, but it is important that every candidate recognize the potential for abuse inherent in the use of a tool as far-reaching as television. A conscientious political leader can use television as a means of providing the public with information; a demagogue could use it as his most powerful weapon.

In recent national campaigns the political power of television has become an increasingly important factor in affecting voting behavior. The 1960 Kennedy-Nixon televised debates were significant not for their discussion of issues, but for the "images" projected by the candidates. Prior to the debates, Kennedy at times had been portrayed as being too young and inexperienced in comparison with Nixon, but Kennedy's television performance in which he seemed both confident and competent proved to be the "great equalizer" in terms of image. He was able to capitalize on the nebulous quality of personal "style" throughout the rest of the campaign (and during his presidency).

In 1964 television advertising was used with devastating effect by the Lyndon Johnson campaign to portray Barry Goldwater as a political extremist. This issue was not created by the advertising spots, but their effect was to amplify Goldwater's alleged faults and exacerbate his problems of political credibility.

In 1968, and to some extent in 1972, the Nixon campaign utilized carefully planned and controlled television exposure. By screening audiences, rehearsing formats, and spending the time and money on the technical aspects of television, the campaign was able to reverse its 1960 experience and use television politics to advantage.

These examples of the use of television in national politics contain valuable lessons even for local candidates. The most basic is the inherent power of television to create a popular image of a candidate or campaign. It is the responsibility of politicians and the general public to demand that this imagery be founded on a basis of fact and that political integrity not become subrogated to the technical aspects of this type of broadcasting.

The purchase of radio time involves many of the same considerations as occur in television work. To determine the nature of the radio audience, one must examine the programing format. Stations with emphasis on country-western, "soul," or classical music will be listened to by different segments of the electorate, a fact that allows more definitive targeting of audience groups than does television. It also encourages a campaign to develop different spots for different stations, matching the style of the spot to the format of the programing, whenever possible.

Market research often can indicate who listens to what station at what time. This sort of information, usually gathered by commercial advertisers, can be put to good use in a political campaign when reaching a certain audience is deemed important. The peak listening times are generally these (they may vary according to locale):

111

——"Morning" time, perhaps the highest audience period; in rural areas this will be from 5:00 A.M. to 7:00 A.M., in urban areas from 7:00 A.M. to 9:00 A.M.

——"Afternoon drive" time, from 3:30 P.M. to 6:30 P.M.

——"Housewife" time, from 10:00 A.M. to 3:00 P.M.

These general rules of audience identification, coupled with a cost factor that is relatively lower than that of television (in terms of both time-buying and production costs), make radio a highly useful campaign tool. Radio is the broadcast medium that a campaign might try to dominate by running spots with great frequency. Since many people turn on a radio at some point in the day, often for only a short time, high frequency of spots is necessary if this maximum audience is to be reached. If the budget allows, radio can provide a good means of increasing the candidate's name identification early in the campaign and a consistent level of exposure throughout the campaign. If it is not feasible to secure radio time of this sort, it is best to concentrate on the two weeks prior to the election. A good high-intensity schedule for this time might be use of sixty 30-second spots per week per selected station. If money is in short supply and the schedule for the radio spots has to be revised, the importance of repetition must be kept in mind. Therefore, the first cutback should be in the length of the overall schedule (e.g., reduction from two weeks to ten days). Then, if further revisions are necessary, the number of stations on which the spots are carried should be reduced. What is to be avoided if at all possible is reducing the number of spots per station, on the theory (sometimes contested) that isolated spots, even if occurring on several stations, have little effect.

In the preparation of television and radio spots, great care should be given to all aspects of production. In technical matters, even when a high degree of polish is not feasible, basic professionalism will turn out a satisfactory spot. Voters are likely to be unimpressed by shoddy workmanship as exemplified by a garbled sound track, nonexistent lighting, or other such failings. On the other hand, a technically well done spot can produce a lasting image in the minds of the audience. To hold the attention of the viewer or listener, any spot (particularly one longer than 30 seconds) must have some "entertainment" value. This does not mean that political advertising should adopt the style of a soap opera or game show, but the technical possibilities for creating good electronic media programing should be used to their fullest. In television work this might mean good graphic design, "candid" (rather than studio) filming, and use of settings that will attract the viewer's attention. For radio spots, a campaign theme song (if not too corny) can stimulate voter recognition of the candidate.

In addition to the technical quality of the spots, the actual content must be properly developed. If the candidate is simply making a direct statement on a subject, it should be in basic, easy-to-understand terms. It must be kept in mind that the audience is being asked to make a mental transition from the entertainment context of the regular program to the political context of the spot. The impact of the text of the spot can be heightened by its presentation. For example, the candidate's views on unemployment problems might be presented as he converses with construction workers, a position on education might be presented as a voice-over with a film of children in a schoolyard. Examples of this sort can be improved upon by the exercise of imagination. An innovative approach to media work is likely to be remembered by the voter and is more likely to affect how votes are cast than is a drab, *pro forma* television or radio spot.

### Outdoor Advertising

A simple, but highly useful type of political medium is outdoor advertising. This consists of billboards, yard signs, cards on the sides of buses, and any other such placards. With the emphasis on *visibility*, outdoor advertising is perhaps the least effective medium for communicating a position, but it is one of the most effective for increasing name identification. The byword in the use of outdoor advertising is *simplicity*. The basic message should consist of the name of the candidate, the office sought, and, if desired, the party affiliation and/or ideology. A billboard or other sign cluttered with a wordy presentation is virtually unreadable. (See Figure 8-1.) With this type of advertising, the viewing public usually will be in motion. This must be kept in mind when preparing the message and when choosing locations for placement. Traffic patterns should also be studied before renting outdoor space. A billboard on a side street probably can be rented for a low price, but few people will see it.

Yard signs are a particularly valuable type of outdoor campaign advertising. They are miniature billboards that are relatively inexpensive to produce and, since they are placed on the lawns of supporters, no rental costs are involved. The name identification of a candidate can be considerably enhanced through a wide distribution of these signs. Their proliferation also can create something of a bandwagon effect—that is, a voter constantly spotting yard signs might think, "If so many people are supporting this candidacy, I probably should consider it too."

## Print Media

Newspaper advertising provides the vehicle for an issue-oriented presentation. People can take time to read material in a newspaper that they might just glance at on a billboard. However, the basic rules of political advertising still must be adhered to—conciseness and good graphic design. If the format of the message is too cluttered, the reader will pass it by. The advertisement must compete for the reader's attention with the rest of the advertising and other printed material in the paper. In many communities anywhere from 50 to 75 percent of the households receive a newspaper, and this percentage is greater among the higher socioeconomic classes. Thus, the potential exposure level is high enough to make some use of newspaper advertising worthwhile. Small ads, accentuating the candidate's name and a consistent theme, can produce an effect similar to that of radio advertising if used repetitively throughout the campaign. In addition, several related advertisements might be scattered through each day's newspapers (when daily papers are available). This will serve one of the basic purposes of campaign advertising—to put the candidate's name frequently before the voters' eyes.

The full-page or half-page newspaper advertisement is a different matter. Even if the cost is not prohibitive, large

114

Figure 8-1 SAMPLE BILLBOARD COPY

# FRANK T. SMITH
## for
## Congress
- - - - - - - - - - - - - - -
# Vote Republican

BILLBOARD A

Simple message; easy to read.

# JOE JONES
## Your Kind of Candidate for U. S. Congress

For: Law and Order    Against: Everything else
No more taxes
Motherhood            Vote The Straight
Apple Pie             Democratic Ticket
The Flag              on November 5th

BILLBOARD B

Too much material; difficult to read quickly.

newspaper ads are most effective when used only occasionally, perhaps even just once, shortly prior to the election. A large amount of copy will fit onto a half or full page, and sometimes a campaign will present a detailed exposition on a matter, particularly if the expected readership is likely to take the time to read the material (e.g., advertising by candidates and causes in the Sunday *New York Times* often includes lengthy sections of straight copy). Generally, the advertisement still must be sufficiently eye-catching to hold the reader's attention.

One type of newspaper advertising often used by campaigns is the endorsement ad, usually composed of a brief message and a list of community leaders who support the candidate. Such endorsements can be quite effective if they reach readers who might know little about the campaign but who are familiar with some of the endorsers. The endorsement might stimulate the interest of the reader to the extent that he starts thinking about supporting the endorsed candidate.

Variations on standard newspaper advertising might be used in publications appearing weekly or less frequently. These periodicals are the sort for which one-time-only advertisements may be advisable. Some campaigns prepare tabloid inserts of various lengths for inclusion in newspapers. Before such a complicated tactic is utilized, evaluations should be made concerning how likely it is that people will read the material. Even the most masterfully produced advertising supplement is of no political value if only a few people take the time to examine it.

Media usage is yet another area that requires careful study of pertinent laws and regulations. Complex formulas are often applied to determine the rates to be charged for political advertising. In addition there might be ways to secure volume discounts and to avoid such costs as advertising commissions. With regard to the broadcast media, the Federal Communications Commission carefully scrutinizes all rates and other matters of access to the media when political activities are involved. The campaign's legal counsel and public relations adviser should jointly examine all such matters.

## Maximizing News Coverage

The news aspects of media should not be neglected in the campaign's search for public exposure. Although news coverage, unlike advertising time, cannot be purchased, the nature of the coverage a campaign receives often can be enhanced by proper planning. News reporting is legitimately stimulated and supplemented by means of press releases. Releases ensure that the news media will know of a campaign event or statement by the candidate and will allow the candidate to present his position on any matter of importance. The use made of a press release varies; rarely will a news story reflect the partisan viewpoint of a release, but a release often will serve as a jumping-off point from which a reporter might begin his research. The following are some matters that need consideration when planning press releases:

——*Timing*: The frequency with which press releases are issued may determine how much attention is paid to them. An unending wave of releases on trivial matters detracts from the notice likely to be given important information. The campaign that issues releases only when there is a truly newsworthy subject is more likely to receive coverage when it is most desired. The compulsion to issue releases about everything should be fought. (A notable spoof of this principle occurred in the following release from the Texas State Comptroller's Office. In its entirety, it read: "Nothing happened Wednesday at the comptroller's office. 'I guess it was just a slow day,' the Comptroller remarked.") When releases are issued, timing is important since the news media operate on deadline schedules that are fairly inflexible. The press secretary must be thoroughly familiar with all deadlines and must allow reporters adequate time to write and file their stories after the issuance of the release.

——*Audience*: The press secretary should compile a mailing list of all broadcast and print news media operating within the candidate's district. This list should include the names of specific contact persons and should indicate any special interest media (e.g., foreign language radio stations, labor union magazines, etc.) for which specially prepared releases might prove helpful. This list should also include notations concerning frequency of publicaticn and deadline times.

——*Format*: The press release is not a position paper. It should state the basic facts of the matter involved, using the form of a newspaper news story, and should be as brief as possible. If the subject matter is lengthy—such as a speech text—the release itself should serve as a brief covering document, noting the main points and perhaps using a few quotations from the longer material. At times, the campaign might wish to supply photographs to accompany the release. Because of the cost involved, this should be done only when a newsworthy photograph is available. The material normally covered by press releases includes speech texts, the candidate's schedule, advance information about campaign events (such as appearances by the candidate), and background or position papers.

An innovative press secretary might introduce some variations in the typical press release. Audio press releases in the form of tapes can be sent to radio stations for incorporation in their news broadcasts. A more sophisticated version of this technique can be utilized by preparing videotape releases for television stations. When using these forms of releases, it is important that the material be objectively presented. If the tapes are merely thinly disguised advertisements, news broadcasts will not use them.

When all the different aspects of media usage are tied together by coordinated planning, the campaign will benefit from one of the most effective tools in winning recognition and support from the voters.

# 9

# Campaign Materials

Almost every voter is all too familiar with the vast amount of campaign paraphernalia that deluges an election district in the course of a campaign. At first glance the funds spent on bumper stickers, buttons, pamphlets, might seem to have been wasted on mere trappings as opposed to substantive necessities. In many cases this is true, because in an effort to enliven a campaign through artificial means, the true political value of properly prepared campaign materials might be overlooked.

## Purpose and Distribution

As with other campaign activities, the purpose behind the preparation of campaign materials must be the winning of electoral support. Campaign literature—such as brochures, broadsides, and more detailed written pieces—can be used to communicate virtually any political message, even if fundamentally complex. Most campaign materials, however, are best utilized in the task of increasing the candidate's name identification. Good campaign material is a form of political advertising since it introduces its subject matter into the minds of its audience and serves as one of the many stimuli that eventually will lead to a decision on how to vote.

If a campaign utilizes election materials, the quality of those materials should be such that they appeal to the voters sufficiently to be read or displayed as they are meant to be. Using materials of poor quality probably is worse than using none at all; equivalent to throwing away money, it leaves the voters with the impression that the campaign is being poorly run. Good quality does not necessarily mean expensive. A multicolored, glow-in-the-dark button is not likely to be any more effective than a simpler (and less expensive) item. There often is a tendency to overemphasize the novelty aspect of campaign materials at the expense of their political value. The materials should be interesting enough to appeal to the voter, but they should not be considered mere toys.

Once the nature of the material has been determined, plans must be made for it to reach the public. Ample time must be allowed for all stages of production, including design and de-livery. A slow-moving manufacturer can disrupt a campaign by failure to perform properly, so any contracts for such work should include stringent time-of-delivery clauses. A proper flow of materials should be maintained throughout the campaign, so that there is never an inadequate supply of needed material nor an overabundance sitting in warehouses. The latter becomes a problem if changes in strategy or extraneous events suddenly render certain materials obsolete and require wholly new efforts (e.g., the sudden obsolescence of McGovern-Eagleton buttons in 1972).

One staff member (perhaps the office manager) should be assigned the task of supervising the flow of campaign material and maintaining inventories at the desired level. This person can keep track of what items are most in demand as well as receive periodic reports from canvassers and others about voter response to given materials. Since it is unlikely that there can be found any consistently successful way to predict the demand for materials, flexibility must be emphasized. This sort of informa-tion can be used by the campaign manager in devising the general campaign plans for use of materials. Decisions on such matters usually should be made by the upper echelon of the campaign staff in order to ensure that no political faux pas is committed through the medium of campaign materials. For example, if the candidate has been endorsed by a controversial figure, the advantages and disadvantages of publicizing that endorsement through the "private media" of campaign materials must be carefully weighed. Likewise, it is important that the distribution of materials be coordinated with other aspects of the campaign; that is, if the candidate chooses to begin emphasizing a certain issue, campaign literature explicating his views on that subject should be readily available. Also, materials such as buttons and bumper stickers should be available in large quantities immediately preceding and following appearances by the candidate.

The method of distribution of campaign materials will vary according to the nature of the constituency. A mass mailing has the potential to reach the greatest number of people, but the effectiveness of the material might be limited. Many people have a negative reaction to anything they might classify as "junk mail" and will not even look at it. Person-to-person distribution is preferable. This may be accomplished by utilizing a form of canvassing, most probably the "hit-and-run" technique (see Chapter 5), in which a campaign worker delivers the material on a door-to-door sweep of a neighborhood, briefly speaking with anyone who answers his door ("Candidate X would appreciate it if you would read this material and consider supporting him") or leaving material with a similarly brief note when there is no answer. This type of distribution is most effective when brochures describing the candidacy and presenting positions on issues are being used—that is, giving the voter something to read. A small packet of material may be prepared—including the brochure, a button, and a bumper sticker—and left with the voter. The basic goal of materials distribution is to get the material into the hands of the voter. Beyond that stage, the voter's own discretion will determine how the material is utilized and, thus, how effective it will be in influencing his outlook on the campaign.

## Preparation of Materials

Campaign literature requires the same careful preparation as that accorded to television spots, the candidate's speeches, or any other representation of the campaign to the voters. The format of the printed piece is crucial; it must catch and hold the reader's attention. There should be enough copy to convey the desired message but not so much as to discourage the average voter from reading the material. Photographs or drawings should be included and two-color printing used whenever feasible. Different sizes of paper folded in different ways will produce varying numbers of panels on which the message may be presented. Rarely should every panel be filled with unbroken copy—chances are too great that it will go unread. If a large portion of one outside panel is left blank, the piece may be utilized as a "self-mailer"—the address of the voter is written in the blank area, a stamp is added, and it is ready for mailing without the need for an envelope. If a self-mailer is not used, it is important that brochures be the size of standard envelopes. Not a few campaigns have found themselves in the embarrassing position of having to chop off a quarter-inch of every brochure before a mass mailing could be undertaken.

Determining the actual content of a piece of campaign literature is a test of both imagination and political acumen. Most campaign brochures are designed to stimulate voter interest and encourage consideration of the campaign. It is unrealistic to expect a piece of campaign literature on its own to win votes; therefore, the content should remain quite simple, presenting an outline of the campaign's goals and discussing in broad terms the issues involved. Campaign literature often is attacked as being so oversimplified as to distort issues. Simplicity does have its price, but most voters will not take the trouble to read a detailed position statement, particularly if they are getting only their first glimpse of the campaign.

To offset this tendency to generalize, specialized materials aimed at specific audiences should be prepared. For example, a special brochure might be written for mailing to labor union members, emphasizing the candidate's stands on labor-oriented issues and including any available endorsements by labor leaders. Similar materials might be prepared in foreign languages for ethnic groups, for students, women, minority groups, farmers— virtually any identifiable section of the constituency. If early campaign planning provides for this type of approach, the identification of targeted voters can be made one of the duties of canvassers (e.g., a question on the canvass form might read,

"Are any members of this household members of a labor union?"). Once this information is obtained, a list of voters requiring distribution of special material may be compiled. A further use of specialized material is in the targeting of small geographic areas. For example, if a six-square-block area has inadequate street lighting and the voters are concerned about this, a candidate (particularly, but not exclusively, one for a post such as city council) might distribute material promising to do something about the problem. This sort of limited distribution does not require the preparation of elaborate material—simple mimeographed flyers will suffice. This will keep costs within reason and should not hamper effectiveness. Many voters are far more concerned about issues that are "close to home" than those of more grandiose dimensions. Any successful candidate will recognize this and make sure that he covers *all* the issues about which the voters are concerned. Polling (see Chapter 15) can be most helpful in determining which issues are considered most important by which voters.

In developing these specialized appeals, it is essential that the positions set forth in any one piece of material be consistent with those of other campaign pronouncements. Although the campaign will determine to whom the materials are to be directed, other people—belonging to other classifications of voters—might well see materials not designed specifically for them. If a candidate's pronouncement sent to farmers advocates boosting farm prices while a brochure distributed to urban consumers vows to lower food prices in any way possible, and copies of both pieces of campaign literature reach the hands of the other group, the candidate might find that rather than winning support through his specialized approaches, he has alienated everyone. The central campaign organization must assume final responsibility for all literature issued supporting the candidate. If, in the course of a large-scale campaign, various organizations endorse the candidate and distribute their own campaign literature, it is quite possible that some inconsistencies in approach will occur that could embarrass the candidate. The member of the central campaign staff who is in charge of "propaganda" distribution should seek to limit the production of extraneous materials. If an endorsing organization wants to assist in this area, campaign headquarters may either provide the organization with standard materials for distribution, the organization might provide the campaign personnel with a mailing list, or the campaign may design prototype brochures or other materials that the endorsing group may adapt for its own use. Maintaining some sort of coordination in this area is essential.

## "Dirty Tricks" Material

Political "dirty tricks" occur with some frequency in the use of campaign materials. The most common problem is that of phony campaign literature, ostensibly issued by one candidate when in fact it is the opposition that has produced the piece. This material usually will contain flaws that will embarrass the supposed originator when brought to the public's attention. Such subterfuge is difficult to combat, so a campaign staff must remain sufficiently alert to detect the circulation of such items. Then a disclaimer must be issued and an attempt should be made to discover the culprit. Sometimes, blatantly slanderous documents (usually anonymous) are found in circulation while a campaign is in progress. These can do some damage, but most voters will not let themselves be swayed by such material.

As with other aspects of campaigning, there is no standard, foolproof formula to be utilized in the production of campaign literature. Because of the need to purchase most commercially prepared materials in quantity and well in advance of when they are needed, the trial-and-error method of finding the best format is a rare luxury. If possible, professional graphics experts should be consulted; the improved quality of the material will make the consulting fee worthwhile. Figure 9-1 indicates what a properly designed standard campaign brochure might look like.

Of less substance, but still valuable, are such campaign materials as buttons and bumper stickers. These are, in effect, miniature billboards that serve as a means of bringing the candidate's name into public view. They also represent endorsements by the persons who display them. In terms of the subliminal generation of political support, these campaign materials serve the important function of increasing voter awareness of the campaign. If a voter's first reaction to a candidate's appeal for support is, "I never heard of that person," this nonrecognition is a factor that somehow must be overcome while the individual's vote is being sought. If, however, the voter has even a vague familiarity with the existence of the candidacy, gained perhaps from seeing the candidate's name on the back bumpers of automobiles, this initial obstacle of recognition might be easily overcome.

Since name recognition is the main goal of utilizing buttons and bumper stickers, there is no need to waste money on lavish forms for these materials. A simple message usually is the most effectively communicated message. Figure 9-2 illustrates basic formats for a campaign button and a bumper sticker. Since most people will only catch a glimpse of these in passing, the message should be brief and uncluttered in form. At the same time, the materials must be sufficiently attractive to encourage their display. In-person materials distribution is important in order to minimize waste. In addition to door-to-door distribution, efforts to reach voters might be made at shopping centers or other places where there are likely to be large numbers of passersby. The campaign workers who undertake this task must do so with considerable tact since campaign literature should not be thrust upon an unprepared person. This is the time for some efficient politicking—a brief conversation and an offer of literature can be an effective way to win support.

## Miscellaneous Materials

Few other campaign materials are necessary. Some need may exist for various banners, balloons, and insignia for use at rallies or other campaign events, but expenditures in this area should be kept to a minimum. Novelty items can be sold as a fund-raising technique, but a campaign must resist the temptation to purchase unnecessary gadgetry. Rarely does the political value match the cost of ball-point pens, nail files, matchbooks, or other such items.

The main legal consideration with respect to campaign materials is simple but important and usually strictly enforced. Most states require that all forms of political advertising—including the use of campaign materials—contain a statement of

125

**Figure 9-1** (SELF-MAILER)

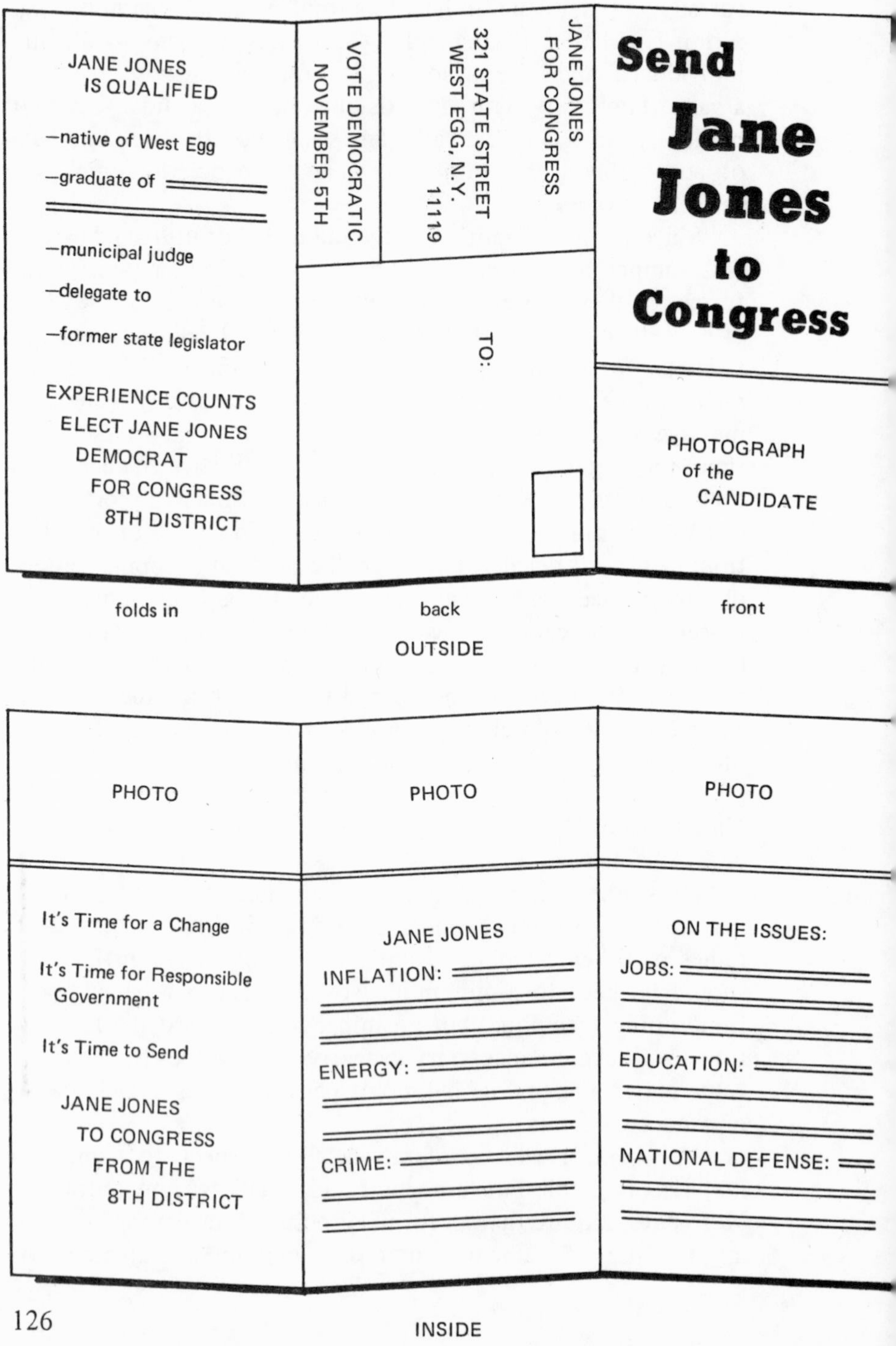

---

**OUTSIDE**

**folds in:**

JANE JONES
IS QUALIFIED

—native of West Egg

—graduate of ════════

—municipal judge

—delegate to

—former state legislator

EXPERIENCE COUNTS
ELECT JANE JONES
DEMOCRAT
FOR CONGRESS
8TH DISTRICT

**back:**

VOTE DEMOCRATIC
NOVEMBER 5TH

321 STATE STREET
WEST EGG, N.Y.
11119

JANE JONES
FOR CONGRESS

TO:

**front:**

**Send Jane Jones to Congress**

PHOTOGRAPH
of the
CANDIDATE

---

**INSIDE**

PHOTO

PHOTO

PHOTO

It's Time for a Change

It's Time for Responsible
Government

It's Time to Send

JANE JONES
TO CONGRESS
FROM THE
8TH DISTRICT

JANE JONES

INFLATION: ════════

ENERGY: ════════

CRIME: ════════

ON THE ISSUES:

JOBS: ════════

EDUCATION: ════════

NATIONAL DEFENSE: ════

126

attribution naming the person and organization responsible for the issuance of such material. This usually takes the form of, "Paid for by Jones for Congress Committee; John Smith, Campaign Manager," inscribed in fine print somewhere on the material. The purpose of this type of regulation is to prevent anonymous (and perhaps scurrilous) material from circulating during a campaign. Failure to include this information can result in legal problems as well as claims by the opposition that the offending campaign is ashamed to assume responsibility for its own materials. This may or may not prove to be a serious issue in a given campaign, but as a general rule there can be no sense in handing the opposition potential ammunition, particularly when the problem can be easily avoided.

**Figure 9-2**  BASIC FORMATS FOR CAMPAIGN BUTTON AND BUMPER STICKER

# 10

# Fund-raising

Fund-raising is an aspect of politics that has received increasing public attention in recent years. The high costs involved in campaigning have grown at such a rate that either personal wealth or access to the resources of wealthy people have often been a *sine qua non* to a candidacy. Such reliance on financial support from others has the effect of undermining the democratic nature of government—politicians who win elections with the support of rich backers take office with a built-in obligation to extend preferential treatment to these supporters. In turn, elected officials have used the power of their respective offices to apply political strong-arm tactics to potential contributors. All in all, the situation has reached intolerable proportions, with the Watergate scandal merely indicating that no level of politics is safe from financial or other types of corruption.

While statutory controls and public scrutiny have begun to curb some of the more flagrant abuses of political fund raising, virtually every campaign remains faced with the problem of building a campaign treasury that will meet the unavoidable costs of politics. This chapter will examine some of the fund-raising techniques utilized by campaigns of various offices. Chapter 16 presents an overview of the nationwide status of political fund raising, discussing some specific reforms that have been developed in an effort to control the intricate practices of campaign finance.

### Direct-Mail Fund-Raising

One type of fund raising that has proven highly effective in reaching a large number of contributors (particularly small contributors) and in securing an adequate rate of return is direct-mail solicitation. National candidates such as George McGovern and George Wallace have raised millions of dollars, mostly in contributions of less than twenty dollars, from a broad cross-section of voters by using this method.

This direct-mail technique is by no means limited to national politicians. Any candidate for any office can develop a direct-mail operation that meets his needs. Although the primary use of this technique is fund raising, it also is valuable in that it provides general exposure to the voters through the material used in the solicitation. Some campaigns utilize direct mail solely as a means to communicate positions rather than to raise money. The basic method of operation remains the same, however, and it would seem somewhat wasteful to pass up any such opportunity to seek financial assistance for the campaign.

Basically, direct-mail fund raising consists of a letter discussing the purpose of a given campaign and asking for financial assistance. Usually, the mailing will contain some sort of reply card or envelope. The material is mailed to individuals who have been identified through mailing lists acquired by the campaign.

Usually, it takes considerable time for a direct-mail campaign to produce its maximal return. The underlying methodology of direct-mail work is the development of mailing lists. The compilation of a list of donors requires a trial-and-error process by means of which virtually any mailing list, obtained from any possible source, is culled for contributors. Initial returns will be small, increasing only as the "quality" of the list is improved through the inclusion of persons who have demonstrated support and the exclusion of those who apparently are unresponsive. Only rarely will a campaign begin with a good list that will generate an immediate favorable return rate. An example of this sort of success was found in the early days of the 1972 McGovern presidential candidacy. The McGovern fund-raising solicitation was sent to a list of persons who previously had responded to a televised appeal for funds to aid the antiwar movement. These people were deemed likely to be responsive to a McGovern candidacy based on an ideology close to that of the antiwar movement. The assumptions proved to be correct and the fund-raising effort was successfully launched.

When the valuable resource of a list of proven merit is not available, and it is necessary to "start from scratch," the degree of success can be predicted based on the following determinative factors:

——The nature and quality of the lists to be utilized;

——The amount of time and money available for test mailings; that is, the thoroughness with which lists and types of approaches may be tested before initiating mass mailings;

——The degree to which the campaign is relying on direct mail, that is, how extensive the direct-mail effort is going to be.

The most valuable lists are those of previous contributors or other people who have in some way evidenced support for the candidacy. Even a candidate who has never before run for office should be able to compile a list of friends and associates who are likely to have a favorable attitude toward his candidacy. The bulk of the mailing list, however, for a direct-mail effort—particularly that of a first-time candidate—must be made up of strangers, people whose degree of support (if any) remains to be discovered. Among the sources for building a mailing list are the following:

——Contributors to other campaigns or political causes;

——Voter registration records;

——City cross-directory (to target specific demographic areas);

——Property tax rolls;

——Driver's license lists;

——Membership lists of professional organizations;

——University or other specialized directories;

——Publications subscription lists.

Often these mailing lists must be purchased or rented. Sometimes they are available on computer tapes. Depending on the size and potential value of the list, these costs can be substantial, so list acquisition should not be undertaken blindly. Past experience and perhaps the advice of a professional fund-raising consultant should give some indication of what lists are likely to be most valuable.

Specialized lists can allow for specialized appeals; for example, if a list of members of a medical association can be obtained, a special letter discussing issues of concern to doctors can be the basis of an appeal for funds. Similarly, a campus directory allows incorporation into the fund-raising process of a student population that may be responsive to a well-designed, specialized solicitation. Of course, a single standardized appeal may be sent to everyone, but the success of the project (in terms of money received) is likely to be directly proportional to the imagination with which the drive is conducted.

Even if a promising mailing list can be compiled, *testing* is necessary to ascertain the type of appeal that is most effective. Among the matters to be tested are:

——Is a short or long letter requesting support more effective?

——Should the tone of the letter be positive or should it primarily attack the opposition?

——Should a form letter be utilized?

——Should the campaign prepay return postage?

By coding the reply materials included in the mailings, it is possible to ascertain with considerable accuracy the reactions to the various approaches. For example, if the test involves short versus long letters, the reply envelopes in the short mailing may be printed in blue, those in the long mailing in green. If the total of blue envelopes actually returned greatly outnumbers the green returns, this indicates that the shorter appeal was better received. Thus, when the major (nontest) mailing is prepared, a shorter message might best be utilized. Other testing might be conducted to determine quality of a given list. For instance, if a Democratic candidate has acquired a list of 10,000 subscribers to a magazine of liberal editorial orientation, a test mailing to 500 randomly selected persons from the list can indicate how worthwhile it might be to contact the entire list.

Testing of this type requires much advance planning plus appropriate allocations from the campaign budget. Due to time or financial constraints, it may be necessary to proceed with a direct-mail program without testing. However, if at all possible some preliminary work should be done. It is far better to lose a relatively small amount of money in a test yielding negative results than to gamble with a larger sum of money in an untested major mailing.

The procedure involved in conducting a direct-mail project can become quite complex. There is a constant stream of material being mailed and an erratic flow of replies. The following hypothetical situation has been greatly simplified—the numbers involved in the mailings and for costs have been kept low and rounded off so that the core concepts of the cyclical process of direct mail can be understood in basic terms. Any given campaign situation will impose numerous complicating exigencies on the situation.

## PROSPECT MAILING:

|  |  | *Cost* | *Income* |
|---|---|---|---|
| *Mail to*: | 50,000 prospects @ $100/M | $5,000 | |
| *Response*: | 1% (500) @ $10 | | $5,000 |
| *Yield*: | 500 identified contributors | | |

A mere 1 percent return on a prospect mailing is not unusually low; 5 percent or higher return from an untried list is considered extraordinarily high. Although there is no monetary profit realized from this first mailing, there has been a valuable return in that 500 new contributors have been identified. Someone who has contributed once is likely to do so again.

## SECOND MAILING:

|  |  | *Cost* | *Income* |
|---|---|---|---|
| *Mail to*: | 500 identified donors @ $100/M | $50 | |
| *Response*: | 20% (100) @ $10 | | $1,000 |
| *Yield*: | $950 | | |

The second mailing, conducted after a decent interval following the first solicitation, is likely to be a high-yield effort. The nature of the appeal is very important in this case—these people have indicated that they will contribute, but since they already have given money, the campaign's letter must express thanks for the first contribution and explain why more funds are needed. A contributor never can be taken for granted if his continuing assistance is desired. It is this type of mailing that is likely to be the most worthwhile direct-mail effort—the rate of return (as in this example) can be quite high.

---

THIRD MAILING:

|  |  | Cost | Income |
|---|---|---|---|
| *Mail to*: | 400 identified donors who failed to respond to SECOND MAILING @ $100/M | $40 | |
| *Response*: | 10% (40) @ $10 | | $ 400 |
| *Yield*: | Net income from SECOND and THIRD MAILINGS | | $1,310 |

---

The third mailing is aimed at previous contributors who did not respond to a second mailing. Although the return rate is less than that of the second mailing, it still is far higher than the response percentage from an untried list.

In this hypothetical case, a $5,000 investment produced a $1,310 financial gain plus exposure (via the first mailing) to 50,000 voters. For a direct-mail program to reach its true potential as a political tool, the largest possible audience should be contacted. For example, while the second mailing in this case was being sent, another first-run mailing should have been in preparation for another large, untried list. The coordination of this activity is likely to require a full-time staff assignment. For, in addition to generating the mailings on a tight schedule, careful record keeping is essential. Since names of persons will be moved from list to list depending on their response, each reply must be noted so that any appropriate follow-up mailing can be made. If adequate finances are available, computers may be used to maintain the mailing lists. This facilitates keeping lists up to date and allows retrieving of separate lists of special interest groups or other categories of contributors. For example, a labor union list might be given a particular computer code and contributors to a past campaign another code. With the aid of the computer, a list of labor union members who have contributed in past campaigns can be compiled quite easily. Even if test mailings have been utilized earlier, all response patterns should be analyzed to determine if there are any particular aspects of the mailings that are encouraging or deterring contributions. Also, many campaign financing statutes require that information on every contribution be filed with a government office, thus requiring complete records.

An effective direct-mail campaign cannot be created on the spur of the moment. The development of lists, preparing the text of the material, printing, and actual mailing all take time. Since several test mailings are desirable, they should be started three or four months prior to the election. For any single mailing, two or three weeks should be allowed for the full mailing process (from initial planning of the letter to actual posting). It will be another two weeks before 50 percent of the total returns will have arrived for evaluation. This entire process can be squeezed into a shorter period of time (primarily by limiting testing), but a minimum of approximately four weeks is necessary for direct mail to have any value greater than that of a "one-time-only" effort. If bulk mail rates can be used (a helpful way to cut down on costs), some additional "in-the-mail" time should be allowed.

Conducting a direct-mail project obviously requires a certain degree of expertise. A campaign that does not have a staff member fully capable of undertaking the direction of such a project should consider hiring a professional fund-raising consultant who has direct-mail experience. A consulting fee is an additional burden on the campaign budget, but the costs of running a direct-mail solicitation, as well as the potential for valuable financial return, are good reasons why it is unwise to risk conducting the project in a way that is not highly efficient.

## Other Fund Raising Methods

Direct-mail is increasingly favored as a fund-raising tool by politicians because of its proven success at many levels of campaigning. However, it rarely is a simple (or, initially, inexpensive) process. Nor is it guaranteed to reach all potential contributors. Therefore, a campaign might undertake additional or alternative fund-raising endeavors; these include:

——*Receptions and dinners.* The $1,000-per-plate political dinner is a well-known fund-raising device used primarily by the national political parties to tap their wealthiest supporters. New campaign financing regulations have made the selling of such expensive meals something of an anachronism, but on a smaller scale this still can be an effective means of raising money. Almost any campaign can organize a cocktail party or dinner with tickets priced in the range of $25 to $100. Attendance probably will not be great, but this is a simple way to give the campaign treasury a quick transfusion. If a political celebrity (in addition to the candidate) can be found who is willing to be the "star" of such a gathering, such an appearance might boost attendance. To reach a larger number of people, a low-cost ($3 to $5 per person) "spaghetti dinner" type of gathering might be held. The finance chairman should make the determination of the function that is likely to be best suited to the given constituency. This is an important decision, since any such event requires a capital outlay by the campaign, particularly if a high-priced, somewhat lavish dinner is being planned. An overestimation of ticket sales or improper planning can easily turn such a fund-raising event into a financial disaster since overhead costs can run extremely high.

——*Concerts*. Since many people are tired of the mediocre food that usually is a feature of political dinners, they may desire an alternative type of political-social event as a basis for a contribution. If entertainers who support a candidate are willing to donate some of their time and talent, an activity such as a concert can prove highly lucrative for the campaign. If, for instance, the election district contains a college campus, a concert might well be the best way to raise money from the student members of the electorate. (The 1972 McGovern campaign raised several hundred thousand dollars in a series of concerts.) This same basic technique is just as useful on a smaller scale at the local level.

——*Campaign paraphernalia sales*. Some novelty items, such as fancy campaign buttons, tieclips, ball-point pens, etc., can be sold. Such sales are unlikely to raise much money, and it might not be worth the trouble to engage in such a project. However, one advantage of this type of selling is the fact that people who buy such items, then, will be advertising for the campaign whenever they use the material.

136

——*Solicitation through advertising.* Many political professionals argue that no piece of campaign advertising is complete without a request for contributions. Campaign brochures might include a tear-off coupon to be returned to the campaign with a contribution. Advertising directed specifically at fund raising also might be utilized. Newspaper ads, radio or television spots, and handbills of various sorts might generate income for the campaign. Reply coupons should be provided in any printed fund-raising advertisement. This will aid the campaign's record keeping and may be necessary in meeting statutory guidelines pertaining to the reporting of contributions.

——*Pledges.* Contributions made on an installment plan can provide the campaign with a regular flow of income. Pledges should be solicited early in the campaign. The general format of the payment system is that the contributor will pay a set amount (for example, $10) on the first of each month during the campaign. The main problem with such a system is the bookkeeping involved for both the contributor and the campaign. If a payment is missed, the contributor must be sent a reminder. If the contributor decides to renege on his pledge, there is little that can be done. To be on the safe side, a campaign's financial planning should take into account the likelihood that at least a few of the pledges made are likely to go unfulfilled. Failure to recognize this possibility can lead to overestimating campaign income, thus creating an out-of-balance budget.

——*In-kind donations.* Sometimes in-kind contributions are easier to secure and more valuable than cash. Such contributions might take the form of office space to be used as a campaign headquarters, use of a mimeograph machine, free food for campaign workers, or anything else that is helpful to the campaign effort. It should be noted that most campaign laws treat in-kind contributions just as if they were cash contributions for the market value of the donation; that is, limitations and reporting procedures will apply.

For any given constituency, there are likely to be particular fund-raising techniques that have good chances of generating campaign funds. Careful planning by the finance chairman and others involved in raising funds is necessary to maximize response from the electorate. A mere *pro forma* effort at fund raising probably will produce only a minimal rate of contributions. As with other aspects of campaigning, imagination and energy are crucial factors.

Many candidates intensely dislike having to ask for money, whether from friends or strangers. As understandable as such sentiments might be, it is necessary for anyone who becomes involved in a campaign to recognize that fund raising is an absolutely essential task, no matter how unpleasant it might seem. Many campaigns have met electoral failure largely because of an inability to keep pace financially with the opposition. For example, while one campaign is mounting an advertising blitz in the last days of the campaign, the opposing campaign might find its financial resources exhausted. As a result, the voters go to the polls having taken a good last look at one candidate, but not at the other. Until the system of financing campaigns is changed drastically, fund raising must continue to be one of the most important campaign activities.

# 11

# Scheduling and
# Advance Work

Efficiency is often an illusory quality in a campaign. A candidate is to be commended for trying to avoid turning his campaign into a dehumanized, assembly-line process, but at the same time politics requires the conducting of so many concurrent activities that a campaign lacking the highest degree of organization is unlikely to reach its electoral potential. The great variety of campaign activities necessitates an organization that must be diffuse even while efficiency remains a paramount concern. The center of the campaign's organizational universe must be the candidate and his activity.

All campaign activities basically exist as support functions for the candidate. Fund raising, advertising, canvassing—all are designed to facilitate the candidate's presentation of his case to the voters for their electoral support. The day-to-day personal activities of the candidate are but a part of this effort to convey the basic concept of "the candidacy" to the public. The scheduling and advance operations must provide the efficiency necessarily underlying the candidate-to-voter communication.

## Planning the Schedule

The scheduler is responsible for planning the movements of the candidate to ensure most effective coverage of areas and events that have been determined by the campaign manager to offer good opportunities for exposure. Scheduling requires solid familiarity with basic demographic information—a knowledge of who the voters are and where they are. The candidate must know with whom from among his constituents he will be meeting and how best to find those he wants to meet, that is, those people who might support him. The scheduler must see to it that this information is available and that the candidate's political interests and campaign activities coincide. The scheduler must also be completely familiar with the personal working habits of the candidate. Some seem never to require food or rest and can be scheduled at a consistently arduous pace. Others will insist on a free hour for lunch and several half-hour breaks to unwind in the course of a day's campaigning. The schedule must be made with cognizance of such requirements.

Early in the campaign, the scheduler should contact local party officials for information on all forthcoming political events. When this information is assembled as a complete calendar, plans can be made for the candidate to attend what appear to be the most valuable events. When deciding on which rallies, receptions, or other such activities to attend, it is wise to coordinate planning with candidates for other offices from the same party. There may be events at which the entire slate of a party's candidates should appear, and yet there may be other times when the number of attendees can reach a point of diminishing returns in terms of effectiveness. A voter who sees ten candidates at a single gathering is likely to remember none of them. If there are desirable events on the calendar to which the candidate has not been invited, it might be necessary to "fish" for an invitation through local contacts. This usually is not too difficult; a scheduler should not hesitate to utilize this tactic if the event is deemed worthy of the candidate's participation. The scheduler may best pursue this course if the campaign manager has reviewed the calendar of potential events and has assigned priorities to the various activities for each day or week.

The handling of invitations often requires considerable delicacy. The candidate should defer to his scheduler on virtually all invitations, whether they are to be accepted or rejected. If accepted, the scheduler can secure basic information on arrangements (preferably utilizing a standardized recording form) and will then remain in contact with the host until the time of the event. If a refusal is in order, it will be the scheduler, not the candidate, who should be the target of any ill-feeling caused by the rejection. It is important for the scheduler to beware of offhand verbal invitations; all invitations should be supported by specific written confirmation before they are added to the schedule. In all matters relating to invitiations, the scheduler must work closely with the campaign manager.

Sometimes—because of scheduling conflicts or other matters —it will be necessary to turn down an invitation to an event at which the candidate should be represented. When such a situation arises, it might be worthwhile for the candidate to send a taped or written message or to send a surrogate to read a message, to deliver a speech on his own, or just generally to be present to represent the candidate's interests. Two basic conditions must be met if a surrogate is to be utilized. First, the inviting group or individual must agree to accept a stand-in. Second, the candidate must be able to call on someone who can fulfill the task as necessary. Attendees at the function will look upon the stand-in in much the same way they would examine the candidate. A surrogate who is unprepared or for some reason creates a bad impression can do considerable harm. If no one is available who commands the full confidence of the candidate to play such a role, it is better not to send anyone. In such a case it still might be feasible to send a telegram or other message to the gathering as evidence that the candidate is aware of his missed opportunity.

In campaigns that must reach large constituencies, it is necessary to coordinate the schedule planning with local party leaders who might be asked to submit suggestions for the candidate's itinerary—where he should go, what audiences he should seek. Depending on the campaign manager's appraisal of the political abilities of these local leaders, the suggestions may or may not be incorporated into the schedule. Local contacts can provide valuable insight into the political situation in their areas (often through merely reporting the current political gossip), and any reports they make should be passed on to the campaign manager for inclusion in the campaign's information files. Even though this sort of information flow can prove valuable, a campaign should not allow itself to become too entangled in the machinations of local party affairs. Direction of the candidate's schedule never should be fully delegated to anyone that is not a member of the central campaign staff. All local suggestions should be considered, but they should always be treated simply as suggestions, not orders.

Whatever method of treating suggestions from local contacts is utilized, the central campaign organization should make a concerted effort to keep all local representatives fully informed of campaign activities in their areas. A person seeking to aid a candidate "loses face" politically if he finds out about campaign activities from outside sources. It is impossible to keep everybody associated with a campaign happy all the time (particularly since political egos bruise easily), but in the interest of efficiency some attempt should be made to maintain harmony. The scheduler can play an important role in this effort through his treatment of suggestions from local contacts and by working to keep these contacts apprised of when and where the candidate will appear and when other campaign activities will occur.

Some politicians of the candidate's party are likely to prove uncooperative or even hostile for political or personal reasons. They might disagree with the candidate's position on certain issues, or they might be rivals of the candidate for power within the party. Whatever the reasons for such problems, the candidate and his manager must be able to spot such situations and deal with them objectively. Picking a fight rarely is a good idea. It is better simply to avoid contact with a troublesome politician and assign one of the candidate's supporters to undertake any necessary functions in that politician's place. The most important task is to be able to recognize such problems when they exist.

By compiling information gleaned from local contacts and from general campaign files, an "in-house" annotated schedule should be prepared for the candidate's personal use. This would provide the candidate with background material concerning each event on the schedule—who issued the invitation, what the event consists of, and what the reason is for attending. Also included might be some suggestions for the general political approach to the occasion—what issues should be discussed and what items most need to be emphasized. A candidate who is following a crowded schedule often needs this sort of concise briefing in order to perform most effectively. After some time is spent campaigning, all rallies or luncheons begin to look the same, and to some extent, a candidate is likely to lapse into performing mechanically if he is unable to differentiate among the array of people and places that pass before him. The campaign staff has the responsibility of helping to keep the candidate as sharp as possible. In addition to general information on the event, it might be helpful to include a list of the persons the candidate is likely to encounter and should know. Even the slightest bit of familiarity with a mass of names can be helpful. Following is an example of what such an annotated schedule might include for one event:

12:00 NOON: Tarleton Civic Association luncheon. Thirty-minute speech; twenty minutes for questions and answers. This organization includes most of Tarleton's leading professionals and businessmen. They pride themselves on their interest in political matters, particularly those relating to economic issues. Be prepared for some tough questions (often with a conservative bias) from the audience after your speech. Robert Jordan is the current president and will introduce you; he supports us vocally and is a contributor ($100). Many of the other attendees are supporting the opposition, but any open hostility is unlikely. According to Jordan, if you take a stand against governmental deficit spending, such a position is likely to be well received. Other people whom you will meet will include: Tarleton Mayor Richard Bailey and Tarleton bank president John S. Mill.

A candidate primed with this sort of information is likely to appear knowledgeable, confident, and generally will seem more impressive than one who is relatively unprepared. The scheduler should coordinate the preparation of this material, drawing on the resources of the political research staff, who may have prepared an even more detailed background report (e.g., including data on the city of Tarleton) for the candidate's briefing book. (See Chapter 4 for a description of the duties of the research director.)

On most days during a campaign, it will not be possible (or perhaps desirable) to schedule major events in a solid, back-to-back array. There are likely to be gaps in the schedule, but even these time periods should be planned so that they are not wasted. An occasional fifteen-minute period should be set aside for the candidate to have some time to himself so that he may rest, read over his briefing material, or just generally regroup his mental faculties. Just as it is obvious when a candidate is poorly prepared for an appearance, so also it is clear when he is "burned out" and stumbles through a campaign event. Few voters are fully appreciative of the physical demands imposed by a campaign schedule, and therefore they are unlikely to be sympathetic to a candidate who appears to lack stamina. There is no escaping the fact that some voters at least partially base their choice of a candidate on the nebulous concept of "image." The candidate shapes his own image, largely through his general demeanor in the course of campaigning. Certain important events should always be scheduled to include a short preparatory period. For example, if a candidate is going to debate his opponent on television—an event in which the style as well as substance of the performance can be decisive—the schedule for the day should not call for a last-minute dash to the television studio from a handshaking appearance at a factory gate. The nature and extent of preparation for an event such as a television appearance *can* make a difference in voter response. The scheduler of any campaign must keep this in mind as he plans the candidate's daily pace.

Breaks in the schedule of appearances also allow the candidate time to meet with his campaign manager, press secretary, or other key staff members in order to discuss any matters of campaign business that require his personal attention. Most of the day-to-day management of the campaign will be conducted entirely as a staff function, but the candidate must be kept fully aware of all activities taking place on his behalf. Short briefing sessions normally are adequate as an updating procedure, with longer sessions scheduled periodically for full reviews of the campaign situation.

Some "invisible" campaigning can take place during open periods in a day's schedule. A candidate should contact all local leaders of his party when campaigning in their bailiwicks. These contacts, quite brief, can be made in person or by telephone. (Many candidates prefer using the telephone in such cases because it does not require as much time or effort as "granting an audience" to the local politician.) These contacts are primarily a function of political courtesy; even if there are no substantive matters to discuss, the local leader will appreciate the fact that he has been recognized by the candidate as someone worth consulting. For the candidate this is an almost effortless and yet often valuable task—still another activity that the scheduler should keep in mind when plotting the schedule and planning how much time to leave between formal events.

An additional consideration in planning the sequence of campaign activities is the need for the news media to have time not only to cover an event, but also to prepare and file their reports. Copies of the daily schedule distributed to the press should indicate an occasional fifteen-minute interval set aside for "press filing." These times should be keyed to the deadlines faced by reporters. Similarly, the timing of a campaign event may be determinative of the nature of the press coverage. For example, a late-afternoon appearance by the candidate is unlikely to receive extensive coverage on the evening television news if only because there is inadequate time to develop the newsfilm of the event. Since press coverage is such an important part of the campaign, these considerations must always be a part of planning the schedule.

Attention also should be paid to the geography of the candidate's schedule. At some times it might be impossible to avoid moving the candidate from one end of the district to the other to make his appearances. Whenever possible, however, there should be a geographical coherence to the day's schedule so an inordinate amount of time need not be spent in traveling. Travel time usually is lost time in terms of voter contact (except for the rare occasions when a motorcade is utilized), so it should be kept to a minimum. The best schedule is that which moves the candidate in a steady progression across a given area, keeping distances between points short and avoiding the necessity to retrace steps.

The scheduler will allot a certain amount of time for each day's events. The precision with which this is done is important.

Too little time might impair the candidate's effectiveness, while too much time is wasteful. The schedule should be such that the candidate can give his speech, talk to some voters, shake a few hands or do whatever else is required, and then promptly move on to the next event. For the sake of general efficiency, the schedule should rarely be changed once it has been set and the candidate has developed an idea of what sort of performance will be expected of him on a given day. If some miscalculation causes the candidate to fall behind schedule, he still should try to cover all the planned events, catching up as best he can. If there is some clear time in the schedule, it can be sacrificed to allow lost time to be made up. (See Figure 11-1: sample campaign schedule.)

### Advancing the Candidate

In the face of all the various contingencies of scheduling, it is no easy task for the candidate's many appearances to be run with the precision that a heavy schedule necessitates and that is essential to maximizing the effectiveness of contact with the voters. The task of bringing this precision to the campaign falls to the staff members who do the "advance work" for the candidate. Advance people not only are charged with making the schedule an operational reality, thus ensuring optimal use of the candidate's time, but their efforts can also do much to create the aura of a successful campaign. A campaign is constantly scrutinized by the press and public. The appearance of political professionalism can impress these observers and will reflect favorably upon the candidate's competence. This blending of reality and illusion is part of any successful campaign. If the two forces are kept in proper balance, they can help generate a sense of confidence and momentum within the campaign organization itself as well as with regard to the opinions of the campaign held by the voting public. All who work on the campaign *can* contribute to this sense of cohesion; advance people *must* work with professional smoothness if their job is to be done properly.

The extent of the work done in advance of the candidate's appearance depends on the importance of the event and on the

146

time available for advance work. Physical arrangements are a standard concern of the advance person. Whether the candidate is going to take a walking tour of a neighborhood or make a speech at a fixed location, all his movements should be planned (whenever possible) and any necessary equipment made ready. For example, if a walking tour is planned, an advance person should devise a route that will cover the desired area, allow contact with some voters, and provide the news media with opportunities for coverage. If the candidate is to deliver a speech, a podium, public-address sytem, and any other necessary equipment must be on hand. The location at which the speech is to be given should be examined for planning the entrance and exit of the candidate, accommodations for the press, security, and so on. Particular attention should be paid to crowd capacity. A standard rule is to try to find a location that will hold fewer people than are expected. News reports tend to stress attendance in terms of "sparsely attended" or "standing room only" based on the density of the crowd, regardless of the actual number of people in attendance. For example, if a reasonable attendance prediction is 400 persons, the advance people normally will seek a meeting area designed for 300, rather than one designed for 500.

Within the limits imposed by the main schedule, the advance person must devise mini-schedules for each event—how much time for the candidate to move from point A to point B, when and where to talk with the press, when to move on to the next event. This attention to detail is not to imply that the candidate is a mindless robot who must have his every step programed. It is necessary to remember that any given event is but one of many in a typical day of campaigning. The candidate will welcome, and often will demand, his job being made as simple as possible. He will want to concentrate on winning votes, not on searching for the rostrum from which he is to speak. Here again, efficiency on the part of the advance people should allow ease and effectiveness on the part of the candidate.

In conjunction with the press secretary, the advance person might have the responsibility of stimulating press coverage of an event. Press representatives should be contacted and given any available advance information (schedule, speech text, candidate's biography, etc.) concerning the appearance. Particularly if the candidate is appearing at a place where he is not well known, it is helpful to have an on-scene advance person available to talk with local press about the campaign. Similarly, local political leaders may require briefings on the campaign prior to being asked for assistance. A politically astute advance person can establish valuable contacts on behalf of the candidate and increase the amount of local cooperation that the campaign might receive.

Depending on the personality of the candidate, the advance people might be faced with an additional, time-consuming task—that of taking care of personal arrangements for the candidate and whatever entourage might be accompanying him. Some of the most sensible, down-to-earth politicians have been known to be virtual prima donnas about the quality of their hotel rooms, the availability of good food (and drink), and the general avoidance of all the minor annoyances common to traveling. The advance person who has to take care of such matters must try not to let his political tasks suffer as a result, but should treat the personal requirements of the candidate with the same efficiency accorded political needs. For his part, a candidate should realize that it might be necessary to forego certain amenities while campaigning, thus allowing his staff to devote their full efforts to the vote-getting process.

One of the more challenging tasks for the advance person is that of building a crowd for a campaign event. Poor attendance at appearances can be disheartening to the candidate and staff and, when reported by the press, can cast the pall of impending defeat over the campaign. For an event such as a major public address by the candidate for which a large turnout has been deemed important, the following potential sources should be contacted:

——*Local political workers.* Any mailing lists made available by a party or candidate organization should be utilized. "Hard core" campaign workers are likely to be an interested and reliable audience.

*——Labor unions, business organizations, and civic groups.* Members of such organizations often have common interests related to the issues of the campaign. If so, a large delegation might attend the event.

*——Students.* Government and political science teachers at nearby high schools and colleges should be notified of the candidate's appearance and asked to encourage students to attend to catch a glimpse of actual campaigning.

*——Senior citizens.* If there are identifiable senior citizen organizations or housing areas nearby, numerous spectators might be found, particularly if the campaign will furnish transportation.

*——Bands.* If the event is to be held outdoors or involves a motorcade, high school or other bands can enliven the occasion and help attract a crowd.

Once these disparate sources have been contacted, the advance person must prod them (with varying degrees of gentleness) to ensure a reasonable turnout. An aggravating aspect of advance work is the fact that no matter how many assurances are given as to the number of people who will certainly attend, there is no sure way to know what the attendance will be until the event takes place. This uncertainty is part of a larger, persistent problem of advance work: the advance person must rely on no one but himself. Advance work presents an important exception to the general rule that it is best to delegate authority whenever possible. The advance person will be working primarily with people with whom he is unfamiliar and therefore must check and recheck *every*thing himself. If anything goes wrong, the responsibility will be his, and it is he who will feel the candidate's wrath. At the time of the event, an advance person must shepherd the candidate through his duties as well as serve as "commander-in-chief" of all the logistical and other aspects of the event that he has arranged.

At the conclusion of any particular event, the advance person should file a report with the main campaign headquarters covering two major areas:

*——Thank-you's and fence mending.* Local officials, representatives of the campaign, and anyone else who was helpful should receive a letter of thanks from the candidate. If any

feelings have been ruffled by the staging of the event, some effort at reconciliation should be made. These efforts can pay noticeable dividends if some of the same people must be asked for assistance later in the campaign.

——*General political intelligence.* Any information on local political situations, persons who expressed an interest in aiding the campaign, general voter opinions about the candidate, and any other bits of information that might somehow prove useful should be filed by the campaign manager or other senior staff members.

The scheduling and advancing of the candidate are among the campaign activities of which the voters see only the results, not the constant efforts required of the members of the campaign staff. There is always "one more trip" to schedule and advance and one more set of political factors that must be mastered as part of the process of presenting the candidate and winning votes. As "invisible" as this arduous part of campaigning might be, no evaluation of a given campaign can be complete without an appreciation of the value of efficiency in this area of political work.

Figure 11-1
(SAMPLE MORNING CAMPAIGN SCHEDULE)

A.M.  5:45  United Motors factory gate. Handshaking at shift change.

6:15  depart United Motors; proceed to WXYZ radio station.

6:35  arrive WXYZ.

6:45  10-minute interview on WXYZ "Morning Show."

7:00  depart WXYZ for Plaza Hotel.

7:15  arrive Plaza Hotel; proceed to Meeting Room A breakfast meeting with representatives of Trade Union Council.

8:30  depart Plaza Hotel; proceed to campaign headquarters.

8:45  arrive campaign headquarters; schedule is clear until 9:30.

9:30  depart campaign headquarters; proceed to Central State College campus.

9:55    arrive Central State College; proceed to Room 311, Main Building, for question-and-answer session with political science students.

10:45   depart Room 311; proceed to Room 220 (same building) for meeting with Professor H. S. Thompson concerning preparation of issues papers for the campaign.

11:15   depart Central State College; proceed by car to Tarleton (25 miles).

11:55   arrive Martin's Restaurant, Tarleton, for luncheon speech to Tarleton Civic Association.

*(The pace of the afternoon schedule will be similar and will usually continue until late into the night.)*

# 12

# Campaign Headquarters

In every campaign there is a central "nerve center" into which flows a constant stream of information concerning the progress of the campaign and from which issue the decisions that shape ongoing political strategy. In a small campaign the headquarters might be a room in the candidate's home. In a national campaign entire office buildings are often needed. Whatever the degree of complexity of the headquarters operation, the candidate and campaign manager should realize that a well-organized headquarters can greatly benefit the campaign effort, while an inefficient command center can prove to be a serious detriment.

## Organizing the Headquarters

Just as political tasks are divided among campaign personnel, so should areas of responsibility be physically separated at headquarters. The goal involved is the avoidance of isolation of staff members conducting campaign business, while still allowing the proper degree of operational autonomy. The integration of information is not always easily accomplished, but the campaign manager—who must orchestrate all the diverse functions of the campaign—needs a headquarters operation that facilitates his acquisition of knowledge of all the factors that will influence his and the candidate's planning of strategy.

153

An additional function of campaign headquarters is that of maintaining contact with the public. Interested voters may call or visit the headquarters, seeking information or volunteering their services. The headquarters thus is a representation of the campaign as a whole and should be designed and operated in a fashion that will serve the candidate's interests in this respect. A voter who visits a headquarters that appears to be in a shambles is unlikely to be favorably impressed. If adequate space is available, part of the headquarters might be designated a "public area" for the use of visitors. Campaign literature, bumper stickers, buttons, and other giveaway items should be available as would any campaign novelties that are being sold to raise funds. (Even with free items, a contribution box should always be visible.) A staff member should be available to greet any visitors and answer questions, particularly those in reference to working for the campaign. This area might also be used as a gathering place for volunteers prior to embarking on a canvassing sweep or other field activities.

By establishing such an area separate from the main business portion of the headquarters, the comings and goings of visitors are less likely to disturb staff members at work. Assuming that the campaign staff structure is similar to that discussed in Chapter 4, the physical layout of the headquarters can be quite simple. If the luxury of private offices is not available, clearly designated areas or desks should be assigned to specific staff members and campaign functions. For example, the scheduler should be given a location where he can post his oversized calendars on which he charts campaign events. Whoever is engaged in political research should be granted a fixed location where he may assemble the maps, statistical records, and other information that he utilizes. An area should be set aside for the use of office volunteers who may need substantial space for collating, envelope stuffing, or other such functions.

Security of the headquarters should not be overlooked. Certain materials—such as lists of contributors, results of canvassing, and research information—may be irreplaceable and could be useful to the opposition if somehow acquired. Access to this material should be limited. A campaign headquarters need not be turned into a bank vault, but cognizance of the possibility of theft or vandalism can reduce the dangers that might arise through simple carelessness.

In searching for a location for the headquarters, several factors in addition to the floor plan and overall size should be considered. These include the adequacy of the lighting, plumbing, heating and/or air conditioning. Staff members will be laboring long and hard at the headquarters and the physical conditions should be such as to facilitate their work as much as possible. Special attention should be paid to the electrical power available. A campaign that plans to use electric typewriters, mimeograph, copying, and postage machines will face serious problems if the number or capacity of electrical outlets is inadequate. Similarly, ample storage space is a necessity, particularly if mailing operations are being conducted directly from the headquarters, thus requiring stockpiling of envelopes and materials to be mailed. The office manager should see to it that the physical environment of the headquarters is well maintained and should keep track of all equipment and supplies, anticipating all demands on these operational resources. In addition to the supplies needed in the operation of any office, equipment specifically necessary to the campaign (such as duplicating machines) should be available. It is worth the expenditures involved in leasing or buying supplies and equipment to ensure that campaign operations will not be hampered by their absence. Special consideration must be given to the installation of telephones. Most campaigns will require the availability of a large number of telephones, mainly for use in polling and canvassing. There is a considerable cost factor involved, but the necessity of telephones should not be underestimated. Sometimes a friendly business or labor union will allow campaign workers to use their telephones after regular working hours. All such potential sources should be investigated.

Some care should be exercised in the selection of a location for the headquarters. Normally, it should be near the center of the district's most populated area and preferably in a neighborhood of friendly voters. To encourage the enlistment of volunteer workers, it should be easily accessible, close to public transportation and parking. The headquarters should be visible and so decorated with signs or banners that it serves as a campaign advertisement. In some campaigns a supporter might wish to lend the use of a vacant storefront or suite of offices. This can be a great aid to the campaign's financial situation, but the legal counsel and finance chairman should be aware that such a loan, or any similar in-kind donation or loan, might be classified as a campaign contribution and thus need to be reported as pertinent statutes may require.

In addition to a central headquarters, many campaigns will need to establish auxiliary headquarters in outlying parts of the district. These need not be as large or as completely equipped as the main headquarters since their chief functions are to serve as a visible manifestation of the existence of the campaign and as a substation for distribution of materials to campaign workers in the area. A local headquarters can allow campaign activities to become more fully integrated with the life of the community and can serve to establish a permanent campaign presence as a stimulus to the political interests of local voters. Indigenous personnel should staff the local headquarters, making community acceptance more likely. The nature of a headquarters and its staff should match the nature of the community; for example, a headquarters located in a constituency that includes a large number of Spanish-speaking residents should be staffed by at least some Spanish-speaking campaign workers. This concept of local auxiliary headquarters is a facet of the basic theory that the more a voter sees of a campaign (up to the point of over-saturation), the more likely he is to cast a vote in favor of that campaign as opposed to one with which he is less familiar.

The local campaign headquarters can be more than simply a staging ground for campaign activity; it can serve as an important political tool in itself. An effective means of undertaking this expanded role is through the utilization of campaign headquarters as "neighborhood centers" from which both political and nonpolitical activities are conducted. For example, in an inner-city constituency a headquarters might be established that included the following functions: sponsorship of recreational activities, coordination of a job referral pool, provision of information on government services (the ombudsman role of helping citizens cope with governmental bureaucracy), as well as direction of the more standard political activities such as canvassing and voter registration. By becoming a part of the community through increased involvement in various aspects of neighborhood life, the campaign will increase its political effectiveness. This approach is reminiscent of the local political clubs that served as the bases of power for many of the big-city political machines.

To some politicians, anything even slightly resembling "machine politics" is anathema, but before rejecting the neighborhood center idea on that basis, it might be wise to consider what the role of a political headquarters in a community should be. If one feels that the headquarters should serve only as a warehouse and business office, then there is no need to expand the scope of headquarters activities. But if one believes that a candidate seeking people's votes incurs an obligation to respond to their political wants and needs, then the headquarters can and should be more than merely functional for logistical purposes. If this outlook seems somewhat idealistic, it also makes pragmatic political sense. A well-run neighborhood headquarters that is an integral part of the community is likely to have a head start over other political enterprises when it comes to winning votes. If staff and funding are available, it might be possible to make the neighborhood center a permanent operation, giving a politician the means by which he may remain attuned to the political life of the community. The specific activities of such centers will vary according to the nature of the constituency, but any sort of innovative political endeavor such as this is likely to benefit both the candidate and the public at large.

## Orchestrating the Campaign Effort

The operation of the central headquarters will be reflective of the overall pace of the campaign. It is important that a consistent rate of activitiy be maintained throughout by the candidate and workers. The primary responsibility for sustaining smooth performance rests with the campaign manager. His role is not unlike that of an orchestra conductor—he must solicit the highest level of performance from each member of the staff and integrate individual efforts into the larger scope of campaign activity.

On any given day in the course of the campaign, a diverse assortment of political projects must be in progress simultaneously. Most of this work is clerical in nature. The campaign manager will try to amass as much political information as is available, including data on voter attitudes, status of plans for future campaign events, news of any quarrels among political factions, names of new potential supporters, and any other items of information that might be relevant to the campaign effort. Acquisition of such material usually is no easy task—it requires a network of attentive political field operatives plus staff members who can sift through the material reaching headquarters and put it into usable shape. An example of this process is to be found in considering a hypothetical election district that includes 100 precincts. An information card, maintained for each precinct, should include: recent election returns, voter registration figures, name of the precinct chairman, and any basic demographic information on the nature of the precinct. This information should constantly be updated with reports on how the campaign is progressing in that precinct—is the precinct chairman contacting voters, has the area been covered in a canvass, have supporters erected yard signs, has the opposition campaigned in the area, what is the general attitude of the precinct's voters toward the candidate? The campaign manager should be able at any time to pick up the file card for a given precinct and find information that can help him decide on the best strategy to reach the voters in that area. This sort of information usually is available. The staff's function is to find it and put it into a form in which it is most useful.

There is a considerable amount of campaign material for public dissemination that must be prepared on a continuing basis. Press releases, position papers, speech texts, brochures, and other materials for distribution all require concerted efforts by staff members who must research and prepare these pieces. Unforeseen issues may arise in the course of a campaign, and the candidate's organization must be able to respond swiftly and sensibly. The successful candidate is one who takes command of an issue rather than allowing himself to be buffeted by events that he does not control. Voters are quick to perceive the presence or absence of the ability to exercise leadership. For example, if, in the midst of a race for the state legislature, the governor unexpectedly announces an increase in taxes, every candidate will be expected to respond with comments or counter-proposals. Some candidates will issue only the most vacuous statements in praise or condemnation; others will present researched, thoughtful suggestions. If the voters take time to reflect on the situation, they are likely to pay more attention to politicians falling within the latter category. Any number of crises or sudden changes in the political situation can occur during a campaign. The day-to-day operation of the campaign organization should be such that virtually any political event may be taken in stride and an appropriate response fashioned for the candidate. Staff members should not merely await the advent of a crisis situation. Ideally, the staff will constantly be generating new ideas and suggestions on how to improve the campaign effort. In management terms what is needed is a free flow of ideas and creation of adequate channels to allow new concepts to reach fruition. Facilitating this process is yet another task for the campaign manager, who must be the focal point for the internal communications system, directing assignments and suggestions within the staff structure.

During the campaign, regularly scheduled staff meetings are useful to ensure that everyone has at least some awareness of what is going on at the various levels of campaign activity. A daily, early morning meeting of key staff members provides the campaign manager with a useful forum for briefing the staff on any matters he or the candidate may wish to raise. The best staff meeting usually is a short staff meeting. Not much time is required for status reports and answering questions.

In addition to these and similar elements of coordination of the campaign organization, there is a less tangible aspect of day-to-day campaign management: the development and maintenance of the kind of motivation that will elicit the best work efforts from the entire staff. The pressures involved in campaign work cannot be overstated. In addition to the high volume of work, there is an unceasing intensity that pervades political activity. Crises arise frequently, and staff members know that the quality of their responses to any given situation can decisively affect voting behavior. Since long working hours are a necessity and pay is usually minimal (or nonexistent), campaign workers must be sustained primarily by their faith in a cause or a candidate. The campaign manager should be sensitive to these factors and do what he can to foster an esprit de corps within the organization. When staff members start demanding overtime pay or protesting about stuffing envelopes, a campaign is in trouble. Although neither the candidate nor the campaign manager can "baby-sit" with individual staff members, an occasional appearance and a few words of encouragement from the candidate can let staff members know that their efforts are appreciated and, in turn, can spur them on to continued achievement.

All the many campaign activities discussed in previous chapters will proceed at varied paces unified solely by their common purpose—to secure support for the candidate. The campaign manager cannot personally supervise every aspect of every project, but he can maintain a broad overview of the campaign as a whole and can see to it that certain efforts are emphasized at given times. To some extent, the campaign must run itself. As long as full communication is maintained within the organization, a certain amount of autonomy should be encouraged. For example, an advance person preparing for an appearance by the candidate should not be expected to consult with headquarters on every detail of the event, but must be encouraged to exercise his own judgment when proper. There should be a mutuality of faith; everyone is working toward a common election day goal.

Thus, day-to-day campaign management is not so much a function of a "grand scheme" of political organization as it is a manifestation of segmented efforts loosely, but efficiently, unified. The whole may turn out to be greater than the sum of its individual parts.

# 13
# Election Day Activities

The many months of planning and campaigning culminate in the events of a single day—election day. No matter what the public opinion polls may have indicated or what the politician's intuition tells him of the public's mood, the only accurate measure of the people's political desires will be found in the counting of this day's ballots. Even though the electorate determines the final outcome in response to the politician's exhortations, the candidate must not assume that the events of election day are beyond the scope of his campaign planning. Election day is very much a time of final competition between candidates, with the results of many an election turning on the relative preparedness of the electoral contestants.

## Getting Out the Vote

One of the campaign's major efforts must be that of seeing to it that all the voters whose support has been won actually make their support felt at the polls. Politicians' nightmares are composed of counting the friendly voters who stay at home on election day. At some point in the campaign, well in advance of the day, the campaign manager should appoint a staff member to begin planning election day activities. The most important of these events will be a concerted get-out-the-vote drive. The success of the drive will depend on how well organized and well executed it is, attributes requiring careful advance preparations.

The first step in developing a get-out-the-vote program is targeting. Unless the given race covers only a small constituency, it may not be feasible to contact all voters on election day. The drive must concentrate on areas of strength where supporters have been identified throughout the campaign. Results of voter registration and canvassing efforts should be compiled so as to allow development of a list of high-priority precincts in which there is evidence of substantial support for the candidate. These are the areas where a heavy election day turnout is virtually certain to prove beneficial. Depending on the nature of the canvassing utilized during the campaign, it may be possible to build a list of priority individuals as well as priority areas. If a rating system such as that discussed in Chapter 5 is used, persons rated "1" or "2" should be contacted as part of the get-out-the-vote effort even if they do not live in a priority area.

The premise underlying this sort of activity is that the candidate wants to exercise some control over who votes, just as in a voter registration drive, when attention is directed at persons who are likely to vote for the given candidate. There is nothing necessarily improper in this concept of "control." No effort is made to prevent anyone from voting; an attempt is merely made to increase favorable turnout through organizational efficiency. It is a matter of simple common sense that efforts to increase voter participation in an election should first be aimed at one's own supporters. Generally, there is an automatic "ripple effect" in that the effort to increase turnout in one area is likely to stimulate turnout in other areas as well. As with most other aspects of campaigning, the question here is one of deciding how priorities are to be assigned.

When decisions are made as to the areas and individuals to be targeted, plans must be devised concerning how these people are going to be encouraged to vote and what sort of assistance is to be provided them. Get-out-the-vote is one part of campaigning that requires direct voter contact; that is, media usage alone will not suffice. Individual voters must be provided with information on the basic mechanics of voting—where to vote, when the polls are open, and what the ballot will look like, particularly with regard to where the candidate's name will appear. Once the voters have been informed how to vote, get-out-the-vote coordinators must ensure that they do so on election day by offering constant reminders and providing transportation to the polls when needed. Depending on the volume of activity, these tasks may require highly complex scheduling, since voters can be expected to go to the polls only at their own convenience. Cars or buses driven by campaign volunteers need to be in constant use, transporting voters whenever and wherever the ongoing canvass indicates that the need exists. In addition to drivers, the get-out-the-vote project will require a sizable number of election day volunteers to conduct telephone and door-to-door canvassing. The telephoning should be conducted from a central "telephone bank"—a large number of telephones installed at headquarters for use in telephone canvassing. This centralization allows easy supervision and facilitates any changes in the canvassing plan that might be dictated by the day's events. The day's schedule should include the following:

5:30 A.M.—headquarters opens, personnel report.

6:00 A.M.—leaflet distribution at factory gates and any other early-morning openings involving large numbers of people.

7:00 A.M.—polls open.

9:30 A.M.—telephone canvass begins, continues until 6:30 P.M.

10:00 A.M.—check made on target precincts to determine turnout. These checks are to be made every two hours with results called in to headquarters to allow increased activity in precincts where turnout is too low.

11:00 A.M.—sound trucks move through target areas, continuing until 1:00 P.M.

1:00 P.M.—door-to-door canvass begins in order to stimulate turnout in target areas.

3:00 P.M.—intensified telephoning begins, directed at precincts in which turnout has been low.

4:00 P.M.—"human billboards" holding signs about voting take up stations along heavy traffic routes.

4:30 P.M.—sound trucks make one-hour sweep of target areas.

5:30 P.M.—final telephone and door-to-door canvassing blitz begins, aimed at target areas with low turnout and at targeted individuals who have not yet voted. Voter transportation should be made available at this time.

7:00 P.M.—polls close.

All this activity will not work miracles, but a successful get-out-the-vote drive might increase turnout by roughly 5 percent, an amount that in a close election could be very important. As in most other areas of campaigning, a comprehensive knowledge of election laws is essential. In some states a candidate's poll watchers may be allowed access to the voting lists at each polling place so that the names of persons who have voted may be checked off the campaign's registration lists or priority voter lists. Campaign workers then can direct their efforts at persons known not to have voted. If the law does not allow this approach, the canvass will unavoidably be reaching some people who have already voted. Their names should be crossed off the lists as soon as possible so that the final canvassing efforts reach those who most need to be contacted.

Another aspect of get-out-the-vote planning that some campaigns might consider is absentee balloting. If, in the course of the campaign, it becomes evident that there is support to be found among people who will be unable to go to the polls due to illness, old age, or some other factor, these persons should be supplied with absentee ballots. State laws vary as to procedures for absentee voting, but when a genuine need exists ballots will be made available. Usually the absentee vote is a very small percentage of the total vote, so the campaign manager may decide that it is not worth the effort to pursue this matter. However, in a very close election, these votes can make a difference.

One of the keys to success for a get-out-the-vote drive is that it be the logical culmination of activities that have been conducted throughout the campaign. With some adjustments of responsibilities, the entire machinery of the campaign organization should be geared for the final push to turn out the vote. The election day coordinator should move into a preeminent position with the campaign manager in taking command of the campaign's final activities. Since efficient communication is essential on election day, two types of telephone "hot lines" might be put to use. The first would be for the use of the public to direct inquiries and requests concerning voting, such as questions about voting locations and transportation to the polls. Such a telephone service, if publicized properly, could uncover

164

some "hidden" voters who might have been missed by the canvassing or who find themselves needing some last-minute assistance before voting. The second type of hot line is for internal purposes, serving to aid general dispatch and coordination of activities and to receive news of any problems that might develop. As unfortunate as it might seem, "incidents" that might be unethical or illegal do occur on election day. It is wise to have the campaign's legal counsel standing by throughout the day until the final ballots are counted. He must be ready to act promptly if the need arises, such as by obtaining a court order to seal ballot boxes if irregularities are reported. Again, it must be stressed that speed is of the essence on election day. Everything must move smoothly and any problems must be solved promptly; in terms of the campaign, there is no tomorrow.

## Working the Polls

Election day efforts will require the mobilization of a large number of campaign workers. In addition to those engaged in the get-out-the-vote activities discussed above, workers must be stationed at every polling location. These poll workers perform several functions. Since they constitute the campaign's final effort at electioneering by being a very visible representation of the candidacy, they should wear large campaign buttons or other appropriate insignia and should distribute a short piece of campaign literature that urges support for the candidate. (NB: Many election codes require that poll workers remain a certain distance—such as 100 yards—from the polling place if they will be actively proselytizing for their candidate.) Voters may resent anything they interpret as being an attempt to apply pressure to their vote casting, so poll workers should concentrate on visibility rather than verbal campaigning. Just as the mere presence of a candidate's workers serves as a final reminder to voters, so also may it serve to inhibit any improper behavior related to voting. It is at polling places unwatched by candidates that "irregularities" tend to be found.

Poll watchers also will act as reporters to headquarters concerning the voter turnout. An effective poll-watching operation will leave the voting public with a good final impression of the campaign. It is proof of a thorough campaign organization and

165

thus evidence of a highly competent candidate. This impression is one of those political intangibles that might be hard to explain and yet still seems to influence voting behavior. Because of the important role of poll watchers and other election day workers, and because of the high degree of tension surrounding all election day activities, it is important that adequate support and supervision be provided by campaign headquarters. The long day should be divided to allow several shifts of workers, food should be provided even for those watching polls in the most distant precincts, and whenever a "crisis" of any magnitude is reported, a staff member should respond promptly. Again, this sort of efficiency is bound to pay political dividends.

If election laws permit, the election day organization should include *challengers*—representatives of the candidate stationed in the voting area (as opposed to the area designated for other poll workers) to oversee voting procedures and guard against any fraudulent practices. In many instances, when challengers are allowed, each party, rather than each candidate, is permitted to station a challenger at the polling place. Challengers observe activity at the polls from the time the voting equipment is readied for use until the ballots have all been counted or voting machine totals have been ascertained and reported. The mere presence of challengers tends to encourage proper conduct at the polling places, but any apparent impropriety must be questioned immediately. The challengers must receive training in the basic provisions of the election code, have some knowledge of what types of election frauds most commonly occur, and be fully informed as to the procedure for reporting any violations of law. Challengers are the watchmen of the election process, protectors of their party's most vital political interests; and their election day work must be given high priority within the campaign organization. The legal counsel should monitor all challengers' reports throughout the day, responding immediately to requests for assistance or to situations in which improper conduct is evident. As with other election day activities, immediacy is the byword. Protests by a candidate usually must be filed before the election is certified, but it is most important that whenever possible the challenge be raised as soon as the questionable procedure is discovered so that it may be determined exactly what part of the balloting is affected. For example, if it appears that a voting machine has been tampered with, a prompt protest might result in no further use of that machine, thus limiting the potential damage, particularly if for some reason the challenge is later disallowed.

An additional task for the challenger might be the maintaining of a list of persons who vote. Depending on the procedure at the polling place, the challenger might be the only campaign worker who will have access to the voting lists. The challenger's list should be picked up at regular intervals by a messenger from campaign headquarters and the information put to use in the get-out-the-vote effort. After the polls close and the challenger has observed all vote-counting and reporting procedures, he should report the totals from his polling place to campaign headquarters so a current tabulation of returns may be maintained.

Fraudulent practices of various types always have plagued the election process. The challenger must be familiar with some of the more common election frauds in order to spot them when they occur. Increased public scrutiny of the administration of voting has perhaps led to a decrease in massive election fraud schemes, but smaller precinct-level improprieties continue to exist and their cumulative effect can severely change the outcome of an election. Following are some not uncommon frauds to which challengers and other poll workers should be alerted so they can spot them (but not perpetrate them):

——Last-minute substitution of the voting judge or clerk. In the event of an unforeseen vacancy at a polling place, a non-partisan or bipartisan substitute should be found, rather than a volunteer from a campaign staff.

——"Chain" balloting, in which the compliant voter is given a premarked ballot (when paper ballots are in use).

——Jammed or rigged voting machine. Sometimes a voting machine, because of accident or tampering, will not properly register votes. The challenger should check the counter on the machine to make sure that the number of votes registered coincides with the number of votes cast. If a voting lever is broken or if the machine is working in any way other than perfectly, its use should be discontinued immediately and the campaign headquarters notified so that a protest may be filed. A related problem that has been know to arise is that of improperly printed ballots or improperly labeled voting machines that alto-gether omit a candidate's name. On arrival at the polling place, the challenger should check to make certain that this catastrophe has not occurred. If it has, a new election might be necessary.

——Vote buying. If this occurs, it usually does not take place near the polling area, but the challenger should watch for any suspicious appearance of cash.

——"Assistance" for voters. State laws vary, but many do not even allow the voter to take printed material (such as sample ballot or campaign literature) into the voting booth. Usually only handicapped persons are allowed to have other persons (representatives of both parties) in the voting booth with them. Some voters are too susceptible to being told how to vote. The challenger must be sure that the autonomy of these and other voters is preserved.

——Multiple voters. As a result of fraud committed at an earlier time, perhaps during registration, an individual might try to vote several times using different names. One example of this is "graveyard voting," which is voting by assuming the identify of a deceased person whose name still appears on the voting roles. The challenger should try to keep watch for faces that appear several times during the day and make sure that any person whose identity is questionable presents adequate identi-fication before being allowed to vote.

——Harassment of voters. Basically, if a person is registered and can properly identify himself, he should be allowed to vote. Extraneous questions, demands for excessive proof of registra-tion, or any other tactics utilized to discourage voting can literally drive potential voters away from the polls. In the past such procedures have been directed against minority group members, among others. Any such attempts to curtail voting rights must be challenged. Any time an election official disqual-ifies a voter, good cause must be shown. Standards as to qualifi-cations for voting must be applied identically to all voters.

——Ballot-counting fraud. Particularly when paper ballots are used rather than voting machines, the vote-counting process can be a source of numerous improprieties. Election codes usually require that to be valid a ballot must be properly marked and may be disqualified if it is not. Someone desiring to disqualify ballots could do so by surreptitiously spoiling them—marking votes for more than one candidate, tearing the ballot, or defacing it in any way that would allow disqualification. Similarly, a ballot might be wrongly disqualified by stretching the meaning of the election law beyond its actual limits, claiming that even a small ink smear "spoils" and thus disqualifies an otherwise valid ballot. The challenger should keep close watch on the handling of the ballots and examine any that are to be disqualified. The counting of the ballots often is highly susceptible both to honest error and fraud. If the challenger thinks the procedure being used in counting the votes is flawed, he should protest. When the votes have been counted, he should be sure that the final tally is a sum equal to the number of people who appeared to cast ballots. These matters are so crucial that if the challenger even *senses* something that might be improper, he should contact his campaign's legal counsel. It is better to get a court order to suspend vote counting until an election supervisor is available than to take a chance on fraudulent vote totals. Another related voting fraud is the sudden "discovery" of additional ballots. Any late-arriving ballots should be questioned stringently, since they may have been created to try to offset early voting trends. In this, as in other vote-counting matters, the challenger must not be afraid to assert any demands he may be allowed.

To ensure that challengers and other poll workers are thoroughly familiar with all their assigned responsibilities, an intensive training session should be held shortly before election day. At this time all duties and potential problems can be discussed. By election day it will be too late to explain what needs to be done. The feasibility of these election day projects will depend in large part on the number of campaign workers who are available. Recruiting for the various tasks should be initiated well in advance.

In the course of the day, as the voting continues, staff members at campaign headquarters must be kept up to date on all events occurring in the field. If turnout is unexpectedly low in a certain area of potential strength, there must be enough flexibility in the election day organization to shift personnel to increase the canvassing effort. At the same time the need for flexibility must not be met at the cost of an organization that is too loose to respond promptly to any problem. Nothing can be put off until tomorrow; all decisions are, by definition, final and, by circumstance, crucial.

## After the Polls Close

Even after the polls close, the election day campaign effort continues since the most important activity is that of keeping close track of the tabulation of returns. It might seem that this serves little purpose since "what is done, is done." That may be true—the voters have completed their electoral activity—but elections have been "stolen" after the polls have closed. Just as challengers at individual polling places must keep watch for frauds such as those mentioned above, so too must the campaign manager and the legal counsel maintain an overview of the entire election returns system. If the election is close, there are bound to be demands for recounts by one side or the other, and the candidate's organization must be able to amass any information that will be of use in making or withstanding a challenge to election day activities or results.

Some of the most emotionally charged hours of a campaign are those spent in watching the vote totals mount—the impersonal numbers representing the fruit of months of exhaustive efforts by everyone from the candidate to the part-time volunteer. Whether election night ends in the ecstasy of victory or the agony of defeat, the candidate must recognize his obligation to all those who have made up his political "family." However inadequate words of thanks might seem, they must be said and are best presented in the same terms with which the candidacy was launched. Although election day marks the end of a campaign, it should not mark the end of the political involvement of the candidates or their supporters. Win or lose, the commitment to politics as the highest form of public service must be kept alive.

# 14

# Uses of
# Aggregate Data

Aggregate data is the most widely used form of data with which to analyze and plan the strategy for a political campaign.[1] This data is usually a matter of public record, and it only requires the locating of either the public official, library, or archive that keeps such records to obtain such data. Aggregate data differs from individual data, discussed in Chapter 15, in that it consists of the distribution of whole populations among various categories of classifications; for example, votes cast for Democratic or Republican candidates in a particular race at the precinct, county, or state level, or census-type information such as the percentage of nonwhite population in a city block. It is readily available data and therefore utilized extensively for the planning of election campaigns and for study of electoral behavior. Some of the most important information required for a campaign can be derived from aggregate data: partisan vote, candidate strength, voter turnout, and swing vote. It is a reservoir of information on the characteristics and behavior of *groups of people*, and with some imaginative interpretation it can add much useful information about political behavior.

Aggregate data has several advantages as raw material which invites utilization. To begin with, it is, as already stated, easy and relatively inexpensive to obtain. At one time or another, most nations have published election returns or conducted censuses and published reports of social and economic information about their populations. On the other hand, to secure reliable *survey* data requires not only skilled personnel but a fairly elaborate research organization such as the Gallup Poll or the Survey Research Center at the University of Michigan.

Because it is easily obtained and inexpensive, aggregate data lends itself to replicated and comparative studies of electoral behavior. Another virtue of aggregate data is its "hardness," that is, it is almost completely bias-free. The individual interpreting the aggregate data does not directly interact with the basic sources of information—for example, the voter—whereas in polling there is always the problem of "interviewer bias." Therefore, this kind of data is not suspect, as is survey data, because with survey data the researcher must infer behavior from a small sample which may be subject to sampling error in a larger universe.

Anyone who uses aggregate data must be aware of some potential hazards in the collection and analyzation of it, one important limitation being the "ecological fallacy," which is the erroneous practice of making inferences concerning the actions of individuals on the basis of correlations observed in groups of people. For example, consider the election results of a precinct with a total of 2,206 persons voting. Both the Democratic congressional candidate and the Democratic state treasurer candidate received 816 votes. Were these votes cast by the same voters? In other words, aggregate data cannot be relied upon to produce reliable descriptions or explanations of the behavior of individuals? The sole object of inquiry when using aggregate data should be the behavior of electorates.

Another example concerns the "coattail effect" in presidential elections. This is the degree to which the presidential candidate is able to pull into office with him other members of his party. Examination of this phenomenon in the press is usually done in terms of the president's total vote compared with the votes of those running with him. If the president ran ahead, this would indicate the president's pulling power; if he ran behind, his coattails were useless to those running with him. This has been challenged by Warren Miller with the argument that, to the extent the president runs ahead, he has not been able to attract votes to others of his own party; thus, the greater the president's margin over his teammates, the *less* his coattails' effect.[3] Even if the president and his running mates received an identical percentage of the vote, one should be wary about inferring straight-ticket voting without actually seeing the ballots or talking to the voters individually.

Another somewhat similar problem calls for caution to be exercised with respect to high correlations among characteristics of electorates. For example, does a Jew vote for the Democratic party strictly because of the party or because of other reasons? A multitude of reasons may affect how and why an individual votes for a given candidate: party label, ethnic name, various issue stands of the candidate, place on the ballot, or personal appeal as a friend. Therefore, caution should again be exercised in making inferences based on correlation characteristics of electorates regarding the causes of their voting behavior.

Any analysis that uses electoral data or census data over a span of years is bound to encounter another problem: changing boundaries. Many times boundary changes go unnoticed or unrecorded in public records. There are several ways this comes about:

——Voting precincts are usually created for the convenience of the voter or because of the availability of a public building, (school, fire station, etc.) in order to forego the paying of rent.

——The change from paper ballots to voting machines usually is accompanied by an increase in the size of the precinct (i.e., from 600 to 1,200 voters) thus requiring boundary changes to maximize the utilization of the voting machine.

——In many states there are limits placed on the size of a voting precinct. If there is an area increase in voting-age adults, a precinct may be split into two new precincts with different geographic characterisitcs. This usually occurs following the taking of the census. Precincts may also be renumbered or renamed for administrative reasons. Regardless of the changes, this creates problems in attempting to make comparative studies over a span of time and simultaneously retain a precinct as a unit of analysis. If, for instance, conversion is possible for the past two years but impossible for the past four years, the study would have to be done with two-year statistics only. This is not preferable, but in many cases it would have to suffice.

There are a couple of other problems concerned with time and the fact that things change. Precincts and census tracts are only geographical areas, while the American populace is not composed of serfs tied to a particular location. In fact, census statistics indicate that an average of 25 percent of the population moves every year. In the case of census tracts, where the statistics are based on a survey taken once in every ten years, this simply means that with the passing of every year thereafter, the census data becomes less trustworthy. However, precincts have new elections at least every two years, thus lessening problems of mobility. It does, though, create another problem that requires care in interpreting aggregate data. What effect does the change of population have on votes cast for candidates? For example, if a candidate receives 10 percent fewer votes in 1974 than he received in 1972, it cannot be said that 10 percent of the people changed their minds, since there is no way of knowing if the same people voted in both elections.

A related problem is that census tracts and voting precincts rarely coincide exactly in boundaries. This requires interpretative analysis that may not easily resolve the problem at hand. A researcher who wishes to use these election units as his basic units cannot rely solely on census reports for determining the various social and economic characteristics of the population.

One way of making these and other judgments as they relate to boundary or name changes is to secure maps, current and old, and compare their boundary structures.

The limitations discussed are inherent in the use of aggregate data, but this does not detract from their political value. Identifying them actually makes them more valuable in that this kind of data can then be used correctly. All of these problems can be overcome, but it is first necessary to be aware of them.

## Massaging the Data

It is an oversimplification to say that after the basic data has been chosen, gathered, and checked, the next step is to consider analyzing it. The data to be used for electoral considerations usually lends itself to elementary analysis not requiring complicated statistical procedures. Some of the calculations are time-consuming, but not difficult. As indicated earlier, in order for aggregate data to be meaningfully utilized, comparative analysis of several elections over time must be considered. With the advent of the electronic computer, the level of the analysis problem is not severe. Computers make it possible to enter, store, and calculate large amounts of data from a larger number of units. With such facilities, the computer allows the aggregate data researcher to go down to the lowest unit, the precinct. The ease of data handling brought about by the computer does not, however, reduce the increase in management burden involved in acquiring, entering, verifying, and storing large amounts of data. Simple problems can be devised to perform the repetitive computations of precinct-by-precinct analysis. Among the measures and formulas utilized are the following:

——The total raw vote and percentage of total vote (two-party or multiparty) for each office by each candidate over several elections.

——Number and percentage of eligible voters:

*Formula*: $\dfrac{\text{Total voting-age population}}{\text{Total population}} \times 100$

——Number and percentage of registered voters who voted:

*Formula*: $\dfrac{\text{Number of votes cast}}{\text{Number of registered voters}} \times 100$

——Percentage of voters turning out who actually voted for one or the other candidate for each office (the voter-fatigue factor):

*Formula*:

$$\dfrac{\text{Total Democratic and Republican vote of selected race}}{\text{Total voter turnout}} \times 100$$

——The ticket-splitters vote—the percentage of the actual vote received by one candidate over another candidate of the party (in calculating the ticket-splitter vote, a high-visibility race should be considered, for example, U.S. Senate race, as opposed to the state treasurer's race that might be a "bedrock" of partisan vote for one of the parties):

*Formula*: Percentage difference between the highest and lowest vote-getters on a party ticket = ticket-splitters

——Percentage differences among the votes received by candidates from several different races in the same election year, or by candidates for a single office over a number of elections. This will measure the precinct performance of a selected party candidate (the performance quotient). For example, to measure the performance quotient for a Democratic candidate, the following formula would be utilized:

*Formula*:

$$\frac{\text{Total precinct vote of (D+R) selected race No. I}}{\text{Democratic vote of selected race}} \times 100$$

This will give the Democratic precinct performance quotient for one race. To calculate this for three races, the formula above should be repeated utilizing the appropriate precinct data. After these calculations have been completed for three races, to calculate the performance quotient for each precinct the formula is as follows:

*Formula*: $\dfrac{\text{Race 1 + Race 2 + Race 3}}{3}$ = performance quotient for each precinct

——Percentage differences among the votes received by candidates from several different races in the same election year, or by candidates for a single office over a number of elections.

——Gross vote totals of one candidate over his opponent for each office.

——Vote concentration analysis augmenting the percentage analysis by identifying the areas in which a candidate is receiving most of his support or lack of it. These calculations are made by dividing the number of votes received in an area by the number of votes cast in a race:

*Formula*: $\dfrac{\text{Total votes in an area (precinct)}}{\text{Total votes cast in a race}}$

This calculation is used when analysis is needed in several subareas (cities) of a congressional district.

In addition to the above, the following census data needs to be surveyed and, where necessary, utilized to provide a more comprehensive picture of the constituency.

——*Income* (median, below poverty line, over $15,000): This will provide a general economic view of the constituency, as well as providing insights into the constituency's issue orientation.

——*Social background* (race and ethnic origin): This is important not only in considering the issues and policy orientation of the candidate, but also in helping assess the overall thrust of a campaign.

——*Age* (eighteen years or over and sixty-two years or over).

——*Occupations*: This will provide an indicator as to which economic issues might be important.

——*Education* (median educational attainment; secondary school, high school, college): This is an important variable in considering the type of media campaign to be utilized and also how education relates to policies and issues.

——*Residential patterns* (percent owner occupied, median property values, percent rental, median rentals): This variable is important in considering issues of property taxes and housing policies. For campaign analysis purposes, it will dictate the kind of approach that will be utilized in canvassing, telephoning, surveying, and judging voter turnout.

The series of techniques as outlined above are not by any means a definitive catalogue of the methods one can utilize to analyze voter information. But just as other procedures should be employed to utilize election data, so should the campaign researcher or strategist look to other kinds of aggregate data manipulations for information. For example, more complex statistical analyses (simple and multiple correlations) may provide additional insights into voter behavior.

How can these measures be utilized? In any campaign it is important to identify geographic and political areas of a constituency so as to make campaigning more manageable; this is known as targeting. It is also important to remember that the candidate cannot deal equally with every voter—he should not. If he did, it would mean that he had no campaign strategy. The resources of the candidate are not infinite. Time, money, and other assets are valuable commodities, and the campaign that maximizes their utilization will probably be victorious in the end.

A candidate's constituency will consist of three levels:

——The entire constituency area (e.g., congressional district, entire state for a U.S. senatorial race);

——The intermediate level consisting of major subdivisions (e.g., counties, cities, wards, districts);

——The third level consisting of the precincts, the smallest electoral units.

It is the intermediate and third levels that most interest the campaign strategist because both of these provide the best data sources for electoral analysis. More specifically, intermediate-level targeting provides information concerning the amount of campaign effort that should be expended in the various sub-divisions of a constituency. For example, if a congressional district consists of five cities and a very sparsely populated rural or county area, how much campaign effort should each of these areas receive? Perhaps the rural population may not warrant more than 5 percent of the total effort, while the cities, depending upon their previous electoral performance, may require varying percentages of the campaign effort. The basis of how much effort is allocated to specific areas will depend on analyzing the raw electoral data of at least three to four general elections (e.g., 1974, 1972,* 1970, 1968). Certain types of races provide insights into electoral performance. Examine races that feature a "top vote-getter" of the party (president, U.S. senator, governor) that could furnish some indication of maximum voter turnout. In addition, another race should be selected that reflects "bedrock" partisan voting—that is, an election in which no candidate or issue was particularly important, and people voted their party preference only. When this electoral data is combined with census figures, a campaign strategist is able to reconstruct past electoral performance and make educated guesses regarding issue orientation, voter strength, potential voter turnout, and party organizational strength for a pending electoral contest. In Texas, for example, an office that reflects "bedrock" support on a statewide basis is the state treasurer's office. Intermediate level analysis provides a broad overview of a specific constituency.

Ultimately an analysis of each precinct in a constituency will provide a campaign with a ranking of precincts—in order of importance—so that grass-roots (person-to-person) activities can be directed toward the areas of greatest potential for the campaign. There are three campaign purposes for utilizing precinct targeting: (1) voter registration drives, for door-to-door work and telephoning; (2) persuasion techniques; and (3) getting out the voter on election day. Each of these purposes also requires a different kind of ordering of the precincts. For example, some precincts may have large concentrations of unregistered voters, while others have high concentrations of ticket-splitters, and still others may have law-turnout voters. Each is a unique problem requiring a unique approach.

Targeting relies on past election statistics. It is important to keep in mind that the representative selected from the past for analysis should be analogous to the present situation. There are no hard-and-fast rules that apply here—only good judgment. The best way to approach the selection process is to look at all past data in terms of an entire constituency. Analogous races are those with similar (or the same) candidates and similar issues and races in which normal party performance is best reflected. It is important to remember that targeting will not predict the outcome of an election. What targeting does is to direct the campaign toward those targets that will have the biggest "payoff" in votes for the candidate. In primary elections the key measurements for targeting are usually the size of the precincts and the voter turnout. These elections are intraparty conflicts and very seldom is this conflict cohesive and consistent enough to all the identification of united factions, to judge performances of past candidates, or to identify the group of candidates who did best or worst in previous primary elections. Whereas in the general elections, the label of Democrat, Republican, and so on, greatly assists the researcher in identifying strengths and weaknesses of candidates and parties throughout the electoral process.

Along with the presentation of the various techniques one can use to analyze aggregate data, it is also important to avoid some rather elementary traps. One such trap is the exclusive use of percentages without considering actual votes. Percentages are the most useful device in analyzing election figures since they allow the researcher to make direct comparisons of areas of different size. This is important because it indicates the ratio of support to opposition and gives a quick and accurate count of how close victory might be, but it also creates the "percentage pitfall." An election is not won on percentages but on the plurality vote. A campaign strategist could very easily be trapped into setting a precinct for high-priority consideration when in actuality it had very few votes.

Another trap to be avoided is that of using large units of analysis so that significant differences within the unit are meshed. For example, if all the people of a congressional district were measured according to the percentage that voted Republican, the figure would reflect a percentage between the least and the most Republican subareas. It is conceivable that some of the intermediate areas of the congressional district varied from 80 percent voting Republican to as few as 20 percent voting Republican. These differences, therefore, would be meshed and not actually reflect where true Republican strength was concentrated. This problem also results when intermediate areas are used as units of analysis, thus masking differences found among the various precincts of that constituency.

A further caution in analyzing county-by-county results: one must not consider all counties of equal importance. Each county is unique and unequal in electoral participation; therefore, a political strategist must examine not only the aggregate data of total vote but also the percentages and the pluralities in order to get a realistic picture of where the potential voter is located. For example, in Texas the Dallas-Ft. Worth (population 2,378,353) and the Houston (population 1,999,316) metropolitan areas had a total of 2,376,400 registered voters in 1974 who make up about 30 to 35 percent of the total votes cast in a general election. Here again, care should be exercised since out of the seventeen counties that make up these two metroplexes, three counties alone—Dallas, Harris, and Tarrant—cast a total of 80 percent of the total vote from within these metroplex areas.

There is no doubt but that in utilizing aggregate data analysis the strategy of a campaign may be developed. This data will assist in the planning of radio, television, and newspaper advertising, targeting of direct-mail and person-to-person appeals, literature distribution, and the development of specialized appeals to specific voters. By coupling aggregate data analysis with the polling of a constituency, an even better basis from which to make political judgments is produced.

### Data Records

A large amount of quantitative information is collected by government, quasi-public, and private agencies. Unfortunately this data is not found in any single location; it must be ferreted out from a variety of publications. The following annotated bibliography covers some of the major sources defined within four areas:

——*U.S. Census Materials*: The major data collection in the United States is the Bureau of the Census. Its primary effort is devoted to the decennial census, but the bureau also conducts censuses of agriculture, manufacturers, minerals, transportation, construction, foreign aid, and government. There are three publications issued by the Bureau of the Census that will prove extremely valuable for election studies. If focusing on regions, states, counties, or cities with a population of over 25,000, then the *County and City Data Book*, issued every five years, is useful. The *Congressional District Data Book* has been published since 1962 and provides data by congressional districts. For each metropolitan area, a separate report is prepared called *Census Tract Statistics*, giving the data by census tract.

——*American Electoral Returns*: There is no systematic collection of election data in the United States. For presidential contests, one must combine the resources of several works to yield a record of the presidential vote, by county, from 1836 to the present. These publications are as follows:

Burnham, W. Dean. *Presidential Ballots, 1836–1892*, Baltimore: Johns Hopkins University Press, 1955.

Robinson, Edgar E. *The Presidential Vote, 1896–1932*, Stanford: Stanford University Press, 1934.

*America at the Polls: A Handbook of American Presidential Election Statistics, 1920–1924*, Pittsburgh: University of Pittsburgh Press, 1965.

The county-by-county results for all elections for U.S. senators, U.S. representatives, and U.S. governors since 1952 are found in Richard M. Scammon, *America Votes*, vols. 1–2 (New York: Macmillan and Co.); vols. 3–5 (Pittsburgh: University of Pittsburgh Press, 1958–62); vols. 6–10 (Washington, D.C.: Congressional Quarterly, 1964–72). Also see *Guide to U.S. Elections* (Washington, D.C.: Congressional Quarterly, 1975). Election results for other offices or for smaller subdivisions of the state are more difficult to locate. For such data, inquire at the County Clerk's office or the Election Commission of the Secretary of States's office. State manuals (e.g., *Blue Book*), local election boards, or newspapers are excellent sources for such electoral statistics.

——*State and Local Data*: The primary sources of information on American states and cities are Bureau of the Census publications. Other sources include *The Book of States*, published biennially by the Council of State Governments, which provides data pertaining to each state; the *Municipal Yearbook*, issued annually by the International City Managers Association, reports data on governmental matters for all cities of 10,000 or above in population. For individual states and cities, state manuals and city and planning commission studies can prove valuable. For specific electoral information, the secretaries of state of most states publish voting statistics on a biennial basis. Such data for the local level may be obtained at the County Election Board, County Clerk, or City Secretary's office.

——*Data Archives*: The last two decades have witnessed the development of social science archives for the collecting and storing of quantitative information. The archives obtain, organize, maintain, and disseminate data collected by survey research organizations and individual scholars. There are three prominent data archives: Inter-University Consortium for Political Research (ICPR) at the University of Michigan, the Roper Public Opinion Research Center, and the International Data Library and Reference Service. The Consortium for Political Research—a partnership of more than 100 universities and colleges—has many major surveys on both American and international political behavior. They are also adding to their archives election returns, legislative roll calls, and socioeconomic census data of the United States. The Roper Center is the major repository for the Gallup surveys conducted both in the United States and in other countries of the world. The International Data Library concentrates primarily on surveys from outside the United States, particularly those of developing nations.

In all instances, these archives store the data in machine-readable form (magnetic tapes and computer disk packs) in order to facilitate easy transfer and orderly analysis.

## NOTES

1. For other in-depth treatments of this topic, the following are recommended: Robert Agranoff, *The New Style in Election Campaigns* (Boston Holbrook Press, 1972), Chapters 3-6; Austin Ranney, "The Utility and Limitations of Aggregate Data in the Study of Electoral Behavior," in *Essays on the Behavioral Study of Politics*, ed. Austin Ranney (Urbana: University of Illinois Press, 1962).

2. W. S. Robinson, "Ecological Correlations and the Behavior of Individuals," *American Sociological Review* 15 (1950): 351-57.

3. Warren E. Miller, "Presidential Coattails: A Study of Political Myth and Methodology," *Public Opinion Quarterly* 19 (1955-56): 353-68.

*Data prior to 1972 does not include the enfranchisement of eighteen-year-olds in most states.

# 15

# Polls in Political Life

Polling is now an integral and essential tool of political campaigns. This method provides an important means of gathering information for the candidate for public office, be it mayor, legislator, governor, or U.S. president. When one needs information about people, the most obvious tactic is to ask them.

## Purpose and Use of Polls

Polls serve at least two major functions for those thinking of running for public office. First, they investigate individual social characteristics, opinions, attitudes, knowledge of political affairs or behavior; surveys perform this intelligence-gathering process and in most instances are the only means of effectively tapping such information. This information is also helpful in assisting a candidate to learn which segments of the population most need to be reached. Second, polls serve as a means of counseling those who are running for public office.

A major problem that any candidate must overcome is how to handle the vast amounts of information and advice received from advisers and other well-intentioned individuals. Political advisers are noted for being either overly optimistic or pessimistic, so realistic appraisals of whether a candidate is ahead or behind are not readily available. A scientifically conducted poll provides a candidate with information for a realistic appraisal of his candidacy. In their *Plunging into Politics*, Marshall Loeb and William Safire note that surveys accomplish five important objectives: (1) They can evaluate one candidate's prospects compared to another's. (2) They can regularly measure a party's and a candidate's strength. (3) They can portray a party's image and suggest desirable changes. (4) They can advise about the effect of campaign issues and tactics on the public. (5) Lastly, they are particularly useful in narrowing issues. Most importantly, polls allow the candidate to put into proper perspective the counsel he receives from advisers, thereby providing objective checks on the hunches of loyal supporters. A candidate who prevails is one who effectively responds to the concerns of the people, and there is no better way to learn of these concerns than through a scientifically conducted poll.

In today's world of "razzle-dazzle new politics," there is concern that politicians may cynically assume that the public is impressionable enough to be influenced on any issue by political communications technology. This, in our view, is a naïve assumption. Most political issues affecting the electorate are found among the basic concerns of the people. In the last two decades the telling political issues have come *up* from the people, not *down* from the politicians—racial equality, the economy, law and order, Vietnam, and so on. There is probably no other kind of data more important to a candidate than that indicating the concern of the people; and the candidate who effectively addresses these concerns is the most likely winner. Polling for secondary kinds of data, such as recognition factors of candidates and trial heats, will usually show an upward trend if the candidate has managed to tie in effectively to the public's view of the salient issues. Clearly, the candidate must articulate the issues and in the end must find a way to come to grips with what is on the minds of the people. Governor George Wallace's treatment of the issues of busing and big government in the 1972 Florida presidential primary proved to be the principal concerns of the voters. At the end of the 1972 presidential primary road, Governor Wallace had addressed the voters about the pertinent issues, thereby garnering more votes than any other Democratic presidential hopeful. He was surely touching a sensitive nerve with his rhetoric, although he pointed to nothing on the positive side that might help to solve these problems.

Because resources and time are limited in any campaign it is imperative that a candidate decide how and where he will expend his energy. It may make the difference between victory and defeat. Beyond that are a multitude of decisions regarding promotional activities, media usage, research on the campaign issues, and others similar in nature.

The polls are looked to for answers to many of these questions, but in particular, two problems arise repeatedly in a campaign. The first has to do with the extent to which a candidate is known to the electorate; the second lies in defining the message the candidate should communicate to the voters—in other words, to narrow the issues to a manageable number. Let us examine further each of these problems.

In political circles much is made of the so-called "political recognition" factor of a candidate. Is the candidate known by the voters? Have they heard or read about particular candidates? For example, what initially was the recognition factor of Morris Udall of Arizona, who announced his candidacy for the 1976 presidential race? Research indicates that with rare exceptions most members of the House of Representatives have little, if any, national visibility score. This was a major problem for Udall to overcome if he was to be considered a serious candidate for the presidency.

Politicians tend to stress the importance of these recognition scores, apparently feeling they represent some reliable measure of their popularity, thereby urging their inclusion on most polls. If a candidate ties into the basic concerns of the electorate and addresses himself to the issues of most interest, a little-known person can gain visibility among the voters. In other words, recognition of a candidate is not, in and of itself, all-important. Other factors, such as issues, timing, and the opponent, will affect positively or negatively the candidate's visibility. However, such recognition of a candidate may serve as an indicator of progress being made, even though very little insight can be gained regarding future strategy.

Hints about an opposing candidate's image constitute important intelligence information needed in formulating an effective strategy for a campaign. Polls are useful for "tapping" what an electorate thinks of a candidate as a public figure—name familiarity, deficiencies in performance, past record.

This kind of information is very pertinent since it is negative and it usually never reaches the candidate. It may come as some surprise to a three-term U.S. congressman to find that he is relatively unknown among his constituents and that he may have a negative image or no image at all among the voters.

Another important avenue for minimizing an opponent's strength is to focus on those areas that offer the best chance for picking up votes. Three considerations are in order. First is the need to determine which subgroups in the population are favorable to or oppose the candidate. Second, a campaign will want to pinpoint those voters who currently favor the opposition but are most likely to switch over—appropriately referred to as "switchers." Third, it will be necessary to investigate the attitudinal make-up of present supporters and potential "switchers." Particularly important is the need to know how these voters perceive the priority of problems and how the division of opinion breaks on specific issues. Such polling will also allow a candidate to uncover the weaknesses of his opponent, weaknesses that may be vital in the short or long haul of the campaign. With such information, a campaign can begin to target its efforts. A crucial decision must then follow: Should a candidate campaign on his or her strengths and galvanize them, or admit his own areas of weakness in order to minimize a possible attack by his opponent?

One example of how these considerations are utilized by a candidate is the 1966 senatorial race in Texas. Republican incumbent John Tower employed the services of the John F. Kraft polling organization. The first poll was conducted in the summer of 1965, sixteen months prior to the election, when the Democrats as yet had no announced candidate. This poll estimated Tower's chances against three possible challengers: Governor John Connally, a then-formidable opponent ("not a very hopeful situation"), Congressman James Wright ("unknown to the voters of Texas"), and Attorney General Waggoner Carr ("shows enough strength to make his assessment realistic"). Tower's opponent in 1966 was Carr. This precampaign poll revealed that Tower was well known, but controversial because of his conservative ideology, his pro-Goldwater position in 1964, and various other issue stands. On ideological matters, the poll revealed that Texans classified themselves as one-third conservative, one-third moderate, one-tenth liberal, and the remainder "not sure." Tower's strategy, therefore, was to take over the middle-of-the-road position and force his opponent to the left. The poll further revealed that the race should not be made on issues, for any stand would disaffect more voters than it would please. As a result of this poll, Tower was advised to be moderate and to project a more understanding image. In the course of the campaign, he emerged as the "moderate" candidate to the extent that the Republican voters supported him, but he also won votes from a sizable number of Democrats, ultimately winning by a margin of 198,646 votes, or 56.68 percent, in a predominantly Democratic state.

The above is an example of how a candidate's most effective course was to maximize his strengths. This successful course was decided upon as a result of correctly utilizing the information obtained from a poll.

Utilizing scientific polling in a campaign is not a one-time undertaking. It is important that polling be continuous for the duration of a campaign (at least one poll every four to six weeks). This will provide the candidate with trends—gains and losses—that are occurring within segments of the population and also provide direction as to the salient issues affecting the voters.

These then are some practical applications of polls in politics. With this as a background, it is necessary for us to briefly discuss some of the unfortunate uses of polls.

**Pitfalls of Polling**

Increasingly, for a candidate to be "with it," he must hire a pollster. Is this really necessary, and what are the problems associated therewith?

As we have indicated, polls generate political intelligence. The results derived from a poll are dependent on a multitude of procedural problems that must be overcome. Basically, the procedure used for gathering the information and the degree of sophistication employed in interpreting the results are the keys to the effective utilization of polling. It is relatively easy for the figures and the percentages to become realities in themselves;

yet, they are nothing more or less than responses to specific questions asked of a portion of the population for a declared purpose and at a particular point in time.

It is not enough to simply go out and "take a poll." It must be tailored to the constituency, to the candidate, and to the political situation. The results will be reflected in a trade-off of monies spent, information sought, sample size, and so on. In other words, as the informational base desired and the accuracy of the data sought are increased, the cost of conducting the survey increases substantially.

Specific instances where polls can be used in an unfortunate manner are:

——Trial runs that reportedly pit candidates against each other are usually those most readily reported by the press. This is also the kind of poll to which a political client will turn after receiving the results of his commissioned survey.

The results of these trial heats are not realistic. Challengers ordinarily have less political visibility or political strength, with incumbents naturally better known, especially if they have taken a stand on a controversial issue. Awareness of a candidate comes about once the campaign is in full swing. Trial heats for primary elections are even more transitory and superficial, thereby less reliable. In primaries, there are usually fewer clear-cut alternatives, and party loyalty is not yet effectively perceived or garnered. On occasion, primary elections may even serve a vehicle for protest votes. Finally the personality of the candidate becomes a factor, and there is no way yet discovered to measure the potential strength of an unknown.

A more basic problem—a philosophical one—is that a poll should not be the final determiner of whether or not one should run for public office. Lack of popularity or visibility should not be the major criterion for candidacy. How many potentially excellent candidates have decided not to run for office because of this?

——It is very difficult to properly evaluate the significance of private polls. In most cases the reader is not provided with the basic information of sample size, questions asked, population surveyed, and so forth, thereby limiting the completeness of the reported findings.

The leaking or releasing of a poll may be good political strategy. The one who is ahead will most likely attract contributors because it allows such contributors to know where that candidate stands as compared to other candidates. There is, however, a risk in that contributions may slow down if a candidate is too far ahead of the field. Usually "smart money" is on the leading candidate. In 1972 Muskie contributions slowed down considerably when initial polls from October 1971 through January 1972 showed him far ahead of the other Democratic presidential contenders.

On the other hand, a poor showing in a poll can demoralize a campaign staff, traumatize the candidate, and prematurely terminate a campaign. In short, the loser's staff virtually gives up. Volunteers thrive better on hope than on desperation. Such negative poll reports not only dry up money and kill morale, but as far as the media is concerned, they become self-fulfilling prophecies. If polls are purposefully released, superficially evaluated, and minimally understood by potential contributors, contributions will tend to go to the front runners of polls rather than to the "underdog."

Releasing of poll information may assist a candidate's media coverage since newsmen want to cover the most likely winner. National correspondents for the mass media in 1972 felt that their organizations were not fully utilizing their talents by assigning them to George McGovern's campaign during the initial stages of the presidential primaries.

Polls are also often leaked with the hope of swaying a sufficient portion of the electorate to guarantee victory. The implication here is that the electorate is unsophisticated to be so swayed. Many politicians and their campaign strategists still believe that poll results will induce voters to cast their ballots for the leading candidate. But George Gallup's *Guide to Public Opinion Polls* states:

> The bandwagon theory is one of the oldest delusions of politics. It is a time-honored custom for candidates in an election to announce that they are going to win. The misconception under which these politicians labor is that a good many people will vote for a man regardless of their convictions just to be able to say that they voted for the winner.

191

There may have been a time in American political life when people cared so little about political issues or about candidates that the mere pleasure of telling their friends that they supported the winner was enough to make them vote for him. But in recent years no objective evidence has been found to support the contention that poll predictions influence voters. And there is a mountain of evidence to the contrary. (p. 81)

A comparison criticism involves the underdog psychology— that voters seeing a particular candidate behind in the polls will vote for him merely out of sympathy. Most authorities are in agreement that the bandwagon-underdog syndromes have been vastly exaggerated. According to Professor Joseph Klapper, formerly of Stanford University: "In most elections there is generally about a one percent underdog effect, and they cancel each other out."[1]

A multitude of factors affect the outcome of elections in terms of the individual voter's mentality. People tend to make their voting decisions based not on poll indications, but on voting behavior of family, friends, and close associates or because of social background, party affiliation, issues, and the personality of candidates. In fact a large proportion of the public *does not* follow the polls closely enough to create any sort of bandwagon-underdog affect. Those who are alert to polls and follow them are the most politically active. Research also indicates that these individuals are the ones who identify strongly with their party and are the least likely to be swayed. In the end polls may peripherally affect the voters; but other factors intervene in actual election day vote decision.

——The candidate may wish to reevaluate his campaign strategy when the Harris or Gallup polls are released; if so, he has three alternatives. First, if the poll indicates voter concern on substantive issues to which he is not addressing himself, he may wish to attempt to persuade the public to his views. On the other hand, he may seek to follow the public's concerns on the issues. Lastly, he may just side-step the issues altogether. Whatever strategy is arrived at, there are no absolutes; each is correct depending on the circumstances.

But it is also conceivable that a candidate or one of his strategists may seek to exploit the procedures of such polls.

It is important to know the procedures (methodology) used in a survey for its correct evaluation. *But* there are other procedural concerns of polling which, if known or uncovered, could jeopardize the poll's integrity and results, particularly if it was known that the Harris or Gallup polls are to interview respondents in an area on a particular day of the month. The candidate in question could spend extra funds for television, radio, and newspaper coverage so as to enhance the results of his standing and hopefully affect the direction of issues. It is ultimately the voter whose free choice is affected. There is a need to emphasize here that pollsters cannot be held accountable in a literal sense for the uses made of the information by candidates, their strategists, or political consultants. However, pollsters must be alert to the ends for which their services have been solicited. In the section that follows we address ourselves to the more technical and procedural problems that may affect survey results and also consider the problems of interpretation.

### Techniques of Polling

Much mystery and misunderstanding surround the process of administering a poll.[2] *The quality of the product is most critical.* For example, how can interviews of 1,500 people possibly provide an accurate portrait of the nation as a whole? Why would these 1,500 interviewees grant a pollster the same precision as if he interviewed the entire population? Why would interviews obtained in one state as part of a national sample not be representative of a good sample for that state alone? How can one tell how valid a sample is?

It may seem very inappropriate to analyze the electorate or the population of the United States in a survey of only 1,500 individuals. It would, of course be prohibitively expensive to interview the entire population, so the only way to study the people's response to a candidate or an issue is by interviewing relatively few individuals who accurately represent the entire population. Probability sampling is now relied upon by most opinion researchers in drawing their samples. The essence of this method is to assure that the individuals selected for interviewing are representative of the whole population. If the procedure is carried out fully and accurately, every individual in the population has an equal or known chance of fitting into the sample. If the interviewees are selected in this way, the analyst can be reasonably confident that the characteristics of the sample are approximately the same as for the whole population.

It is, however, very difficult, if not impossible, to make a list of every adult American or every adult eligible to vote and then draw names from the list at random. Therefore, the most common procedure is to divide the overall adult population into separate categories or "strata" according to regions and within communities of differing size in order to guarantee that all sections are represented. In order to further reduce costs and inconvenience for the interviewers, the analyst could concentrate the interviews in a given geographic area selected for sampling. This is known as clustering. One can also sample households rather than individuals, which means that within a sampling area households are enumerated and selected at random. (*A note of caution*: utilization of this procedure means that no interviews will be conducted in dormatories, military bases, hotels, hospitals, or in other places where people do not live in households.)

Another procedure in selecting respondents is quota sampling, used commonly by commercial polling organizations such as Gallup. Although the areas where the interviews are to be conducted may be randomly selected, at the last stage of selection the interviewer is permitted discretion in choosing respondents according to quotas. In this type of sampling, census data is analyzed to identify the distribution of the population by characteristics such as sex, age, education, and income. The interviewers are given assignments in those areas in which the respondents are located according to preselected social characteristics, with the intention of creating a collection of respondents with proportions of quota-controlled characteristics identical to those within the population. For example, the quota might call for half of the respondents to be men, half to be women, one-third to be under 30 years of age, one-third to be between the ages of 31 and 45 years, and one-third to be 46 years or older, and so forth. The idea is that if all the subgroups are given the appropriate amount of representation, the overall sample should then correctly represent the greater population group or universe.

The prime advantage of quota sampling is that it is much faster and less expensive than probability sampling. The disadvantages are critical. With quota sampling, the analyst does not have the assurance that the respondents are representative of the total population because the interviewer introduces biases (conscious and unconscious) when selecting the individuals to be interviewed. He may inadvertently over- or underrepresent individuals of a particular type.

Both methods of sampling depend heavily on the ability and integrity of the interviewer, but probability sampling does not permit interviewers to introduce biases. In recent times quota sampling fell into disrepute when Dewey was chosen to beat Truman in 1948; at that time the main flaw lay in the fact that the pollsters stopped polling more than two weeks prior to the election. Another serious error occurred in 1970 when polls in Great Britain were calling for the defeat of Edward Heath's Conservative party by the Labor party of Harold Wilson, which did not come about. On the other hand, in 1960 Gallup and Roper predicted the Kennedy-Nixon totals within one percentage point of the actual vote. Gallup and Harris were within two percentage points in their final preelection poll of the actual vote in the Johnson landslide in 1964. In 1968 Gallup predicted the actual vote in the presidential election: Nixon 43 percent, Humphrey 42 percent, and Wallace 15 percent. Most of the major polls predicted the precise dimensions of the Nixon landslide of 1972.

Returning now to the original question: How can interviews of 1,500 persons possibly provide an accurate portrait of the nation as a whole? The simplest explanation is found in the following: Suppose a "population" is represented by 4,000 solid plastic balls in a bowl consisting of 2,000 white and 2,000 blue, and we want to draw a probability sample of 200 plastic balls. We must keep in mind that each of the plastic balls must have an equal chance of being drawn. Blindfolded, one would draw the first ball and then, before each subsequent drawing, give the container a thorough shaking. This procedure would be followed until 200 plastic balls had been drawn.

What would be the distribution of white plastic balls to blue ones? It is conceivable, but highly unlikely, that we could draw

1 blue and 199 white plastic balls. It is more likely that, since we had a 50–50 division actually existing in the container, we would draw 100 blue plastic balls and 100 white.

If we continue to repeat this procedure 10, 100, 1,000, or an infinite number of times, the laws of probability forecast that the most frequently drawn combination in the sample of 200 is 100 blue and 100 white plastic balls. The next most frequently drawn combination would be either 99 blue and 101 white or 99 white and 101 blue, and then 98 blue and 102 white or vice versa. A further probability is that ultimately, and in a very extreme and rare drawing, one could draw 200 of one color alone.

This same principle applies to an opinion survey. An infinite number of samples can be drawn from a given population. If each individual in a given population has an equal or known chance of being part of that sample, the laws of probability are such that the sample will be sufficiently representative of the population so as to provide accurate data, as was the case of the blue and white plastic balls—that a representative number of each would be drawn from the bowl.

Another way to illustrate probability is to suppose that one tosses a new coin the weight of which is evenly distributed on both sides 100 times. There are 100 possible outcomes, with a 50–50 chance that heads will appear each time the coin is tossed. Each outcome—the first, second, third, and so forth—is independent of every other, as is the case when selecting respondents for a public opinion poll based on the theory of probability. We can illustrate the coin-tossing technique's anticipated results as follows:

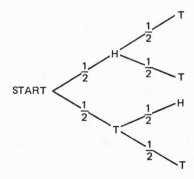

How representative is a sample drawn of the population? If this were the best of all possible research worlds, there would be no random error. It should be emphasized that the dependability (accuracy) of a survey is affected not only by the sampling plan and the faithfulness with which it is carried out, but also by the measurement procedures used. There is *always* chance error, and this can be calculated through the use of statistics. "Sampling error" is the term used to describe the degree to which the results obtained in a single sampling can be expected to vary from the results that would be obtained if an infinite number of sample people were interviewed. Another way of explaining sampling error is the degree to which the results of a random sample would differ from the results if the *entire* population universe were interviewed. Conversely, the pollster using probability sampling can specify the size of the sample (or the sizes of various parts of a complex sample) that he will need if he wants a given degree of certainty that his sample findings do not differ by more than a specified amount from those that a study of the total population would yield. The amount of sampling error for which we allow affects the precision (reliability) of the sample estimate.

No doubt some mechanical and clerical errors occur in sampling. But sampling error in a survey is not error that is caused by inexact answers to poorly worded questions, sloppy sampling procedures, or other types of human error. It is, rather, the result of the fact 'hat an element of chance enters when one is dealing with random samples. How precise (reliable) one demands the sample results to be depends on how much risk one is willing to take in using the data, and this will depend on the intended *use* of the data.

The size of the margin of error to be considered in a given survey depends on the level of confidence desired in the survey. The standard is the 95-percent confidence level. So, in any survey where 5 percent error is permitted or a 95-percent confidence level is set, the assumption is made that 95 samples out of 100 will contain the population value within 5 percent, plus or minus, of the estimate. One might also reason that for any given tolerated error, the sample size needed in order to be 99 percent confident of getting a reliable estimate is necessarily greater than the sample size needed for a 95-percent confidence level.

Below is a table of the maximum simple random sample size to produce sampling estimates within various limits of tolerated error (1 percent to 7 percent) at two levels of confidence (95 percent and 99 percent).

Figure 15-1
Simple Random Size for
Several Degrees of Precision

| | Confidence Levels | |
| Tolerated Error | 95 samples in 100 | 99 samples in 100 |
| --- | --- | --- |
| ±1% | 9,604 | 16,587 |
| ±2% | 2,401 | 4,147 |
| ±3% | 1,067 | 1,843 |
| ±4% | 600 | 1,037 |
| ±5% | 384 | 663 |
| ±6% | 267 | 461 |
| ±7% | 196 | 339 |

SOURCE: Mildred Parten, *Surveys, Polls, and Samples: Practical Procedures* (New York: Harper & Row, 1950), chapter 4.

The table indicates clearly the great price that must be paid for enhanced precision and confidence. Higher precision is an ideal toward which a pollster aims. Because of cost, it is easy to see why most pollsters learn to live with risk estimates. The question might be put: Would it be worth nearly doubling the cost of a survey by increasing the sample size from 600 respondents to 1,067 in order to reduce the expected sampling error from ±4 percentage points to ±3 percentage points? (Perhaps it will be worth the cost of increasing the sample size in an election eve poll.) On the other hand, the size of the population (universe) polled does not dictate the size of the sample to be drawn. Referring to Figure 15-1, to achieve an error of ±2 percentage points requires a sample of 2,401 interviews regardless of whether one is surveying the nation, a state, a county, or a congressional district. This justification is founded in probability theory.

If this be the case, then polls, and especially election eve polls, represent the reading of public opinion and cannot be offered to the community as outright predictions. Polls are time-bound and can also be place-bound. It is for this reason that a poll should not be judged merely on the basis of whether or not it picked the winner. The only valid measure is whether the election results fall within the sampling error. *The key to sampling lies not in having a large or massive sample, but in how that sample is drawn.*

Up to this point, the discussion has stressed that the sample size must be adequate to yield the desired precision; however, having a large sample does not guarantee representation. Once the pollster has fixed the size, a rigorous procedure is demanded for selecting the persons to be interviewed in order to be reasonably sure that they reflect the characteristics under study, within the limits that are assumed by the sampling error.

Thus far the discussion has focused in a general way on the kinds of samples, but to ensure the overall selection of a representative sample of respondents, the pollster should, based on probability statistics, give each interviewee in the population an equal chance of being selected. Since there is no list of all the adult population within a state or the nation as a whole, an alternative method is to use individual households. People, therefore, become part of the sample because of where they live and not because of who they are. The use of households instead of individuals as a basis for selecting the sample does not bias the data. As long as only one person per household is interviewed and as long as the person interviewed has a known chance of getting into the sample, conclusions can then be drawn from the data as though drawn on individuals from the outset. The housing unit in this usage serves only as a means of locating respondents.

But again, it would take an inordinate amount of time and money to list all the households in the United States. Since all households can be linked with a specific area in the country, and since the country is divided into states and states into counties that in turn are divided into smaller units, a lot of time, effort, and money can be saved by using a sampling process which would concentrate on a "cluster" of households in a limited number of small areas. The absence of an adequate list means that no direct sample can be selected; instead, one must go through multiple stages of sampling in order to select the sample. This process of multistage cluster sampling requires that random procedure be followed. What considerations must be made when cluster interviews are conducted? First, a determination must be made as to the number of sampling areas required. At one extreme one interview could be obtained in each interviewing area. Thus, for a 600-case sample, there would be 600 interviewing areas. This approach would be very prohibitive from the standpoint of selecting the household, considering the time and expense involved in dispatching the interviewer. On the other hand, the 600-case sample could be obtained from one interviewing area. The danger of this approach is that the one area selected for representation may not prove representative. Even if the 600 respondents in the sample include various characteristics (age, sex, education, income, religion, etc.) the sample still might not reflect the proper mix of people with regard to institutional and cultural influences of other regions or communities. A balance must be struck between an adequate number of sampling areas and the costs involved. The number of interviews usually conducted in each sampling area ranges from four to ten. The greater the dispersion of interviewing areas and the fewer the interviews per area, the more accurate the representation of the sample to the total population.

### Drawing a Sample

The steps taken in drawing a multistage cluster sample of all adults for the state of Texas will serve as our illustration. Suppose a sample size of 1,000 respondents is decided upon in 500 sampling areas. Since there is no list of adults, a means must be devised of conducting successive samples until a point is reached where a list is compiled. Moreover, because of the shortage of funds and the sheer size of Texas, in the end the sample must be clustered.

For the first stage of the sample, the population of each of the 254 counties of Texas will be classified by city size. These statistics are easily secured from United States Bureau of the Census lists.

The first step is to classify the population of each county by city size. That is, the population of each county is divided into eight categories or strata as follows:

A—500,000 and over    E—10,000 to 49,999
B—250,000 to 499,999 F— 2,500 to 9,999
C—100,000 to 249,999 G—cities of less than 2,499
D— 50,000 to 99,999 H—unincorporated areas of less than 2,499

This procedure requires a very close examination of the population and how it is distributed throughout the state. Certain judgments must be made regarding the number of categories created.

The next step is an examination of each county as to the number of cities that fall within the eight categories we have created. For example, observe Dallas County, Texas (see Figure 15-2). The city of Dallas—population 844,401—is alone in Category A. Dallas County has no cities falling in Categories B and C. In Category D there are three cities with a total of 233,828 in population; in Category E (cities of 10,000 to 49,999 range) there are nine cities with a total of 203,987. Category F contains four cities and Category G, nine cities, where combined populations total 18,379 and 8,164 respectively. Category H totals 13,311.

The identical procedure is followed for all 254 counties in Texas and the results listed in alphabetical order by county on a master table (see Figure 15-3).

The next step in this process is to arrive at a *skip interval*. The skip interval is a systematic skipping device to ensure that the 500 sampling areas are dispersed geographically in order to offer each cluster a known chance to be in the sample. The skip interval is calculated by dividing the total population of Texas (11,196,730) by 500, thereby arriving at a skip interval of 22,393. The first sampling point is determined by a table of random numbers (found in the back of most statistics texts) and it falls somewhere between zero and the interval number of 22,393. In this case it happens to be 13,417.

## Figure 15–2
## Population Categories for Dallas County, Texas–1970

|  | POPULATION CATEGORIES | | | | | | | |
| CITIES | A | B | C | D | E | F | G | H |
| --- | --- | --- | --- | --- | --- | --- | --- | --- |
| Addison | | | | | | | 593 | |
| Balch Springs | | | | | 10,464 | | | |
| Buckingham | | | | | | | 41 | |
| Carrolton | | | | | 13,853 | | | |
| Cedar Hill | | | | | | 2,601 | | |
| Dallas | 844,401 | | | | | | | |
| DeSoto | | | | | | 6,616 | | |
| Duncanville | | | | | 14,105 | | | |
| Farmers Branch | | | | | 27,492 | | | |
| Ferris | | | | | | | 25 | |
| Garland | | | | 81,437 | | | | |
| Grand Prairie | | | | | 47,731 | | | |
| Highland Park | | | | | 10,133 | | | |
| Hutchins | | | | | | | 1,755 | |
| Irving | | | | 97,260 | | | | |
| Kleberg | | | | | | 4,768 | | |
| Lancaster | | | | | 10,522 | | | |
| Mesquite | | | | 55,131 | | | | |
| Richardson | | | | | 46,189 | | | |
| Rowlet | | | | | | | 1,696 | |
| Sachse | | | | | | | 771 | |
| Seagonville | | | | | | 4,390 | | |
| Sunnyvale | | | | | | | 995 | |
| University Park | | | | | 23,498 | | | |
| Wilmer | | | | | | | 1,922 | |
| Woodland Hills | | | | | | | 366 | |
| Unincorporated Areas* | | | | | | | | 13,311 |
| TOTALS | 844,401 | –0– | –0– | 233,828 | 203,987 | 18,379 | 8,164 | 13,311 |

*For purposes of illustration, the 44 tracts that are unincorporated areas in Dallas County with a total population of 13,311 have not been listed. None of these exceeds our eighth category of unincorporated areas of 2,499 or less in population.
SOURCE: *1970 Census Fact Book* (North Central Texas Council of Governments, 1971).

Figure 15-3 ALPHABETIC SAMPLE OF
COUNTY POPULATION BY CATEGORIES

CATEGORIES

| COUNTY | A | B | C | D | E | F | G | H |
|--------|---|---|---|---|---|---|---|---|
| COLLIN | -0- | -0- | -0- | 33,065 | -0- | 2,675 | 14,872 | 16,306 |
| DALLAS | 844,401 | -0- | -0- | 233,828 | 203,987 | 18,379 | 8,164 | 13,311 |
| ERATH | -0- | -0- | -0- | -0- | -0- | 12,087 | -0- | 6,054 |
| WISE | -0- | -0- | -0- | -0- | -0- | 6,854 | 3,004 | 9,824 |

Referring to Figure 15-2, in the Population Category A, the city of Dallas is alone with a population of 844,401. To locate the first starting point of 13,417, refer to the census material, which lists the population of each block in the city of Dallas (see Figure 15-4). Begin with the first block listed and add the population of that block and continue to add the population of each subsequent block until the total reaches 13,417; this will then be the block at which to start. Utilizing this process, the first starting point is Census Tract 52.207, having a population of 91.

To the random starting number, add the interval number 13,417 plus 22,393, which totals 35,810. This will then be the next, or second, sampling point. This procedure is followed until the entire population of the city of Dallas has been exhausted. Using this lengthy and somewhat complicated process, 38 sampling points have been obtained (out of the intended 500 for Texas) in the city of Dallas.

Rather than using population, one can also use the number of housing units in the city of Dallas. The same procedure would be used for finding the first starting point and ultimately arriving at the location of each of the several starting points. The total of these would be the total number of sampling points required in a survey of the city of Dallas.

## Figure 15-4

### Characteristics of Housing Units and Population, by Blocks: 1970—Con.

[Data exclude vacant seasonal and vacant migratory housing units. For minimum base for derived figures (percent, average, etc.) and meaning of symbols, see text]

| Blocks Within Census Tracts | Percent of total population — Total population | In group quarters Negro | Under 18 years | 62 years and over | Year-round housing units Total | Locking some or all plumbing facilities | Units in — One unit structures | Structures of 10 or more units | Owner Total | Owner Locking some or all plumbing facilities | Owner Average number of rooms | Owner Average value (dollars) | Owner Percent Negro | Renter Total | Renter Locking some or all plumbing facilities | Renter Average number of rooms | Renter Average contract rent (dollars) | Renter Present Negro | 1.01 or more persons per room Total | With all plumbing facilities | One person households | With female head of family | With roomers, boarders, or lodgers |
|---|---|---|---|---|---|---|---|---|---|---|---|---|---|---|---|---|---|---|---|---|---|---|---|
| 416 | 52 | — | 25 | 21 | 22 | — | 20 | — | 17 | — | 5.2 | 11400 | ... | 5 | — | 4.0 | 114 | — | 2 | 2 | 6 | 3 | 1 |
| 417 | 93 | — | 18 | 34 | 36 | — | 36 | — | 34 | — | 5.4 | 10000 | — | 5 | — | 4.8 | 72 | — | — | — | 7 | 6 | 1 |
| 51 | 3632 | — | 27 | 25 | 1460 | 19 | 1129 | — | 918 | 7 | 5.4 | 12100 | — | 473 | 11 | 4.1 | 78 | — | 101 | 100 | 352 | 144 | 31 |
| 101 | 22 | — | 14 | 23 | 14 | — | 6 | — | 3 | — | ... | ... | — | 10 | — | 3.5 | 70 | — | — | — | 7 | — | — |
| 102 | 53 | — | 15 | 45 | 32 | 2 | 8 | — | 12 | 1 | 5.8 | 12100 | — | 18 | 5 | 3.7 | 58 | — | 1 | 1 | 15 | 4 | 1 |
| 103 | 42 | — | 26 | 41 | 20 | 5 | 9 | — | 7 | — | 5.9 | 12300 | — | 12 | 5 | 3.6 | 66 | — | 2 | 1 | 10 | 1 | 1 |
| 104 | 69 | — | 31 | 41 | 30 | 1 | 9 | — | 12 | — | 5.3 | 10800 | — | 16 | 1 | 3.9 | 67 | — | 3 | 3 | 9 | 3 | 1 |
| 105 | 33 | — | 32 | 29 | 27 | — | 17 | — | 12 | — | 5.3 | 14400 | — | 11 | — | 3.9 | 82 | — | 3 | 3 | 12 | 4 | 6 |
| 106 | 33 | — | 9 | 24 | 20 | 1 | 8 | — | 14 | — | ... | ... | — | 9 | 1 | 3.1 | 79 | — | 2 | 2 | 9 | 2 | — |
| 107 | 76 | — | 36 | 20 | 27 | 1 | 17 | — | 17 | — | 6.4 | 12000 | — | 9 | — | 3.1 | 69 | — | — | — | 12 | 5 | 1 |
| 108 | 83 | — | 22 | 36 | 37 | 1 | 24 | — | 20 | 1 | 6.4 | 11600 | — | 17 | 1 | 3.8 | 68 | — | 1 | 1 | 6 | 1 | 1 |
| 109 | 107 | — | 41 | 17 | 34 | — | 22 | — | 17 | — | 6.1 | 10500 | — | 15 | — | 4.1 | 84 | — | 5 | 5 | 6 | 7 | 1 |

| Blocks Within Census Tracts | Total population | In group quarters Negro | Under 18 years | 62 years and over |
|---|---|---|---|---|
| 52 | 3820 | — | 27 | 24 |
| 101 | 97 | — | 25 | 10 |
| 102 | 93 | — | 28 | 15 |
| 103 | 113 | — | 37 | 23 |
| 104 | 82 | — | 34 | 20 |
| 105 | 80 | — | 37 | 6 |
| 106 | 59 | — | 43 | 34 |
| 107 | 80 | — | 24 | 6 |
| 108 | 6 | — | — | 100 |
| 109 | 72 | — | 17 | 31 |
| 110 | | | | |
| 111 | 85 | — | 24 | 20 |
| 112 | 90 | — | 20 | 23 |
| 113 | 9 | — | 22 | 24 |
| 114 | 69 | — | 16 | 29 |
| 115 | 49 | — | 31 | 33 |
| 201 | 54 | — | 28 | 27 |
| 202 | 63 | — | 18 | 32 |
| 203 | 66 | — | 24 | 44 |
| 204 | 62 | — | 13 | 46 |
| 205 | 56 | — | 16 | 24 |
| 206 | 91 | — | 33 | 24 |
| → 207 | | | | |

The same procedure would then be followed for all of the other categories until the 500 sampling points that make up the poll are secured.

The next step is to choose the interviewer's starting point. Again, refer to a table of random numbers and in a random fashion choose the first four different single-digit numbers encountered, that is, 1, 5, 3, and 8. Then make a code to represent the block numbers: 1 represents the northwest corner of any block, 5 is the southeast corner, 3 is southwest, and 8 is northeast.

Entering the table of random numbers at any point, again find the first 38 of these four numbers (the number of sampling points for the city of Dallas). In the order that 38 numbers appear in the table, record one of them beside each of the sampling points. The number (1, 5, 3, and 8) next to a sampling point will indicate the corner of the block from which the interviewer is to start. Because the starting corners were chosen randomly, no further randomness would be gained by indicating to the interviewer if he is to move in a clockwise or counterclockwise direction. This decision must be made by the project director.

To ensure a purely random selection of the individuals, a list can be secured of all inhabitants of voting age within a block and the interviewers randomly selected from the list. One can also randomly select households in a given block and, again, in some systematic manner select the person to be interviewed. Having selected the person to be interviewed, no substitutions are permitted. If the interviewer does not find the interviewee at home, every attempt must be made, either by return visits or telephone, to contact the respondent and complete the interview. This process is termed "callback." It is a very costly and time-consuming process, but a necessary one, if the poll is to be a true probability sampling of individuals.

In summary, the cardinal rule to be followed in drawing a random sample is: *leave as much as possible to chance*. As illustrated in this chapter, the flipping-of-the-coin philosophy should dictate every move in order to completely remove personal biases. In random sampling it is well to admit that almost anything one might decide to do, rather than permitting chance to do the "deciding," is a contamination of the survey.

The preceding explanation is only one of the many designs available to those interested in random surveys. It should be emphasized that the respondents or sampling areas are not selected because of their typicality or their representativeness. Rather, each sampling area and each individual falls into the sample by chance and thus contributes a certain uniqueness to the whole. When these unrepresentative elements are added together, the sample should then become representative.

At times, however, it is necessary to improve the composition of the sample so that it more clearly mirrors the characteristics of the population sampled. For example, a given city may have a suburban area containing one-third of its total population. The pollster may be especially interested in a detailed analysis of the households in that area and might feel that one-third of this total sample size would be an insufficient sample. As a result, he may decide to select the same number of households from the suburban area as from the remainder of the city. Households in the suburban area, then, are given a disproportionately better chance of selection than those located elsewhere in the city.

As long as the pollster analyzes the two areas' samples separately or comparatively, he need not worry about the differential sampling. If, on the other hand, he wishes to combine the two samples to create a composite picture of the entire city, he must take the disproportionate sampling into account. How is this done? If $n$ is the number of households selected in each area, then the households in the suburban area have a chance of selection equal to $n$ divided by 2/3 of the total city population. Since the total population of the city and the sample size are the same for both areas, the suburban-area households should be given a $1/3n$, while the remaining households should be given a weight of $2/3n$. This could be simplified by merely giving a weight of 2 to each of the households selected outside of the suburban area. This procedure could give a proportionate representation to each sample element. The population figure would also have to be included in the weighting if population estimates are desired. Following these steps helps produce an unbiased sample.

## Collecting the Data

Once the subjects have been selected, the next step is to gather the required information concerning these subjects. Ultimately, the accuracy of the results will depend on how well the interviewers are trained and how well they follow their instructions.[3]

Survey analysts and pollsters have developed a wide array of questions. Basically there are two types of questions: open and closed. Open-ended questions are those in which no structured alternatives are given. For example: "What do you personally feel are the most important problems to be taken care of by the government in Washington?" The interviewer records the verbatim response. There are advantages to this type of question; they do not force the respondent to fit his responses into pre-conceived categories, and they also make for "richer" responses because once the respondent begins to answer, it is easier to draw him out. This type of question is useful when the dimensions of public views are not readily apparent. On the other hand, these questions take longer to ask, thus limiting the time that can be spent on a topic; it often creates inconvenience for the interviewee. Ultimately, open-ended responses must be crystallized into some intelligible pattern, a process that may introduce particular biases in how this is accomplished.

Closed-ended questions form response alternatives in order to reduce, as far as possible, the introduction of bias. This means that all the positions or alternatives stated should adhere to one dimension of an issue. For instance, if the respondents were presented with only the following two options concerning the policy of the United States in Western Europe, they might be legitimately confused: "The United States should withdraw all its forces because Western Europeans can now defend themselves; *or* the United States should keep some forces in Western Europe until the Western Europeans are able to defend themselves with nuclear weapons." Nowhere is a place provided for the respondent who might, for example, favor the withdrawal of all U.S. forces but does not care if Western Europe can defend herself or not. Other types of closed-ended questions are those that give the respondent a simple yes-no, agree-disagree, true-false choice. The principal weakness here is that they limit the respondent to only two possible answers. There are also multiple-choice questions, those with three or more structured alternatives; these can be used when specific answers are desired, but enough leeway is allowed to give the respondent a wider variety of choices. Most commonly, respondents are given from three to five alternatives: strongly agree, agree, undecided, disagree, and strongly disagree. Last is the ranking-list question, useful when one wishes to determine the respondent's priorities among several objects or reasons. The respondent is then given a printed list of all alternatives and asked to rank them according to some criterion.

Regardless of the type of question asked, care should always be taken to minimize the introduction of bias, which might appear in the wording of the questions or in the sequence in which they appear on the questionnaire. To eliminate such bias, a questionnaire is tested on a limited number of trial respondents—or "pretested." The pretest is run under actual field conditions. Trained interviewers can usually determine the extent to which questions are workable and their sequence influences patterns of responses. Even then, one cannot always be totally confident that a certain amount of bias has not been unknowingly imparted. Only with care and experience can bias be minimized. Because of this threat of bias, the report of survey results should always include the *exact* questions so that the reader can judge the fairness and adequacy of the questions asked.

There are three avenues for posing questions, by mail, by telephone, or in person. Each of these methods has its strengths and weaknesses.

By far, the least expensive way to obtain information is through the mail questionnaire,[4] but in political research, mail polls are not very useful because of the low response rate. Even when gimmicks are used, such as cash incentives, "advance" letters, specifically written cover letters, and mailing the questionnaire by certified mail, the response rate is usually not more than about 45 percent in a general population survey. No matter how intellectually entertaining or intriguing a mail questionnaire may be, it is an imposition. Occasionally the response rate will increase, as when special groups are interviewed (i.e., American Medical Association, American Rifle Association). An interesting problem for further examination might be: Do the people who return questionnaires differ substantially from those who refuse to respond? Lastly, mail surveys have little control over when or how the questionnaire is completed. Some respondents might answer the questions alone, others with help; some might complete their answers while listening to the radio or watching television, others in a quiet room.

Personal interviews and telephones lend themselves better to opinion research on public issues or political matters. Telephone interviews can be a remarkably efficient survey method. In fact, telephone interviewing has become very popular in political polling, especially in privately commissioned surveys. George Wallace, Edmund Muskie, and Presidents Johnson and Nixon, among others, have included widespread telephone surveys in their campaigns. The advantage of telephone polling is that it is quick and cheap, and allows for a greater dispersion of respondents in the sample; in other words, it permits access to the best *and* worst neighborhoods. There are, on the other hand, several disadvantages to telephone interviewing. One, the interview must usually be short—no more than ten to fifteen minutes in length—unless arrangements have been made beforehand. As such, it seldom is practical to ask extended, controversial, or detailed questions. Another drawback is that respondents cannot peruse exhibits during the interview. Third, the interviewer cannot visually observe the respondent, a situation which can be most helpful, since it permits the interviewer to determine a respondent's race or income level, either of which might affect his answers. Further, in rural or outlying areas, some people may not have phones; in the case of ethnic minorities, the interviewers must be bilingual in order to communicate with such persons. Also, new listings and unlisted numbers are problems that must be solved. One solution is to add one digit to each number selected so as to provide a chance to catch unlisted numbers. These, then, are some of the shortcomings of telephone sampling that may introduce bias and, if compounded with sampling error, may cause preelection polls to be "off-the-mark."

Personal interviews suffer only from the disadvantage of high costs in money and time. It has been estimated that personal interviews of a sample of people selected randomly throughout the United States in 1975 may cost $30 or more per interview, even when carried out by organizations that already have staff facilities set up for interviewing. This is opposed to $12 per interview for telephone polling and $5 per interview for a mail questionnaire.

But personal interviews have some very important advantages over the other two forms of polling, which is why they are widely used in spite of the high costs. The interview can be long, sometimes several hours; people often enjoy being interviewed. The interviewer is also in a position to visually check information which may reduce exaggeration; for example, not many persons who live in a shack would dare to report a high income with the interviewer sitting in the shack with them. Another major advantage of the personal interview is that interviewers can probe for further and more detailed information by asking "What do you mean by that?" and so on. Also the interviewer can explain questions that the subject may not understand. It is face-to-face interviews that alone have the flexibility to ferret out the hard information and cases, which in turn leads to a high response rate.

How do we know that personal interviews are not fabricated by the interviewer in his reports? There is little future for a dishonest interviewer, and they will sooner or later be found out. Most professional research organizations will utilize devices to prevent such dishonesty: postal cards may be sent to selected interviewees, asking when and how they were interviewed; "cheater" questions may be asked in such a manner that the dishonest interviewer betrays himself. If an interviewer is suspected of falsifing his reports, then all dubious interviews are discarded.

The choice among mail, telephone, and personal interviews is a delicate one and calls for good judgment on the part of the researcher. All the advantages and disadvantages of the various techniques must be weighed as they apply to a particular project. The trick is to balance the advantages against the disadvantages in order to arrive at the best possible technique for the expenditure of time and money available.

Regardless of the method selected, after the initial data has been collected, it must be rearranged and manipulated to yield the information needed. This is the process of analysis. It begins with standardizing the data and separating it into convenient and interesting categories, and ends with summarizing the statistics and/or the various graphs and tables. A good analysis will show the pertinent data in such a form that it will be clearly understood and the meaning grasped by the reader. For example, there should be a separate table (one enormous master compilation) in which nothing appears obvious. Report only what is discovered and not what the interviewer may wish the data to show.

How are the "don't know," "undecided," and "no opinion" responses interpreted and reported? These percentage responses on a candidate or issue should be reported, because this data may serve as an indicator of the changing loyalties of the populace. The causes of such responses are threefold. First, in some cases it must be assumed that the respondent truly *does not* know or is undecided or has no opinion. Second, the questions asked may be poorly phrased, resulting in such a response. If the pretest has been correctly carried out, it should eliminate such ambiguity in questions, thereby eliciting true "don't know," "undecided," or "no opinion" responses. Lastly, the respondent may not want to commit himself for one reason or another, such as lack of the knowledge or confidence required for a reply. The pollster has the obligation to report these responses, and the reader has the right to know the process by which these responses were analyzed. It is, therefore, imperative to describe findings carefully for what they are, so that unwarranted conclusions are not extrapolated from the data. In other words, do not go beyond the data when the poll results hint at the direction a campaign might take. Good judgment is all that can be relied upon when generalizing from data.

Report methods along with conclusions. Report also what was not learned and the findings that were not significant, along with those that were. Only through practice and experience can one grasp the dynamics of polling and how to interpret the data. There is no simple test (statistical or otherwise) that can be applied to the data to determine what, if any, "significant" conclusions can be drawn therefrom.

How the pollster interprets a poll, and the interpretation placed upon it by a politician, the public, or the press may be completely different. Sweeping inferences are frequently drawn from polls which, in turn, lead to fundamental misunderstandings of what the survey results were and what public opinion actually is. As earlier indicated, a poll is time-bound, and many are place-bound. In other words, it provides us with information at one point in time and on only the questions asked in the poll. Volatility in candidate preference or issue spontaneity occurs frequently, and the problem becomes one of how to interpret the data. Therefore, interpretations and decisions based on polls must be very carefully made. For example, in May of 1975, the Harris Survey conducted a presidential trial heat asking a sample of 1,314 voters: "Now in the presidential race in 1976, suppose it were between President Gerald Ford (Ronald Reagan in the second question) for the Republicans and Senator Edward Kennedy for the Democratic party. If you had to choose right now, would you vote for Ford (Reagan) the Republican or Kennedy the Democrat?"

|          | *Latest* | *April* |
|----------|----------|---------|
| Ford     | 48%      | 43%     |
| Kennedy  | 46%      | 50%     |
| Not sure | 6%       | 7%      |
|          |          |         |
| Kennedy  | 53%      | 52%     |
| Reagan   | 40%      | 38%     |
| Not sure | 7%       | 10%     |

What interpretations can be placed on this data? Specifically, what were the domestic and international events that might have affected this survey, and how will such future events affect subsequent polls? What other candidates offer possible viable challenges to these individuals? Is a Chappaquiddick-type event likely to affect current or future candidates? How should other potential candidates interpret the poll? Will such a poll deter other prospective persons from seeking the presidency?

Polls such as this have relatively little merit. These early poll findings of a trial-heat nature are entertaining to watch, but

they are certainly no basis upon which to make political commitments or form decisions on any campaign strategy. These
surveys may be barometers, but barometers of what? In April
1948, seven months before Harry Truman's surprising victory
over Thomas Dewey, Truman's popularity stood at a low of
36 percent, which suggests that polls can produce tenuous
results. A sequence of polls allows one to decide more authori-
tatively what public opinion is regarding a candidate or an issue.
This, again, is predicated upon the continued positive perceptions of the candidate or the issue by the public and on the fact
that no major catastrophic event has occurred to disturb this
positive correlation.

This discussion has been an overview of perhaps the most
important tool in political research. The many problems associated with polling have evolved through trial and error. Although a costly process, surveys have become powerful vehicles
for the candidate as instruments for intelligence and counsel.
This discussion has attempted to demonstrate the diversity of
this approach, and to make the point that polling is a very
versatile apparatus of inquiry with applicability to not only the
political world but also to the broader functions of the polit-
cal system.

## NOTES

1. Joseph T. Klapper, *The Effect of Mass Communications* (New York: The Free Press, 1960), p.45.

2. The terms "poll," "survey," and "public opinion poll" will be used interchangeably throughout this chapter. For more in-depth treatment of this topic and the methodological problems associated with these techniques, the following are recommended: Earl R. Babbic, *Survey Research Methods* (Belmont, Ca.: Wadsworth Publishing Co., 1973); Charles Backstram and Gerald Hursh, *Survey Research* (Evanston, Ill.: Northwestern University Press, 1963); *Interviewers Manual* (Ann Arbor, Mich.: Institute for Social Research, University of Michigan, 1969); David Leege and Wayne Francis, *Political Research* (New York: Basic Books, 1974); Charles W. Roll and Albert Cantril, *Polls* (New York: Basic Books, 1972); Morris Rosenberg, *The Logic of Survey Analysis* (New York: Basic Books, 1968).

3. For a detailed discussion on training interviewers, see *Survey Research*, chapter 5 and *Interviewers Manual*. Also see *Polling*, op. cit., for a detailed discussion of this topic.

4. For a detailed elaboration on the use of mail questionnaires see "Mail Questionnaire Efficiency: Controlled Reduction of Nonresponse," *Public Opinion Quarterly* 31 (Summer 1967): 265-71; "The Utilization of Mail Questionnaires and the Problem of a Representative Return Rate," *Western Political Science Quarterly* 32 (Summer 1968): 44-53.

# 16

# Campaign Financing and the Aftermath of Watergate

Money has always been a factor in the American electoral process. The large-scale expenditure of funds is a development that began in the twentieth century and reached its zenith (and perhaps its culmination) with Watergate. It has been estimated that the Democratic National Committee spent approximately $25,000 to elect James Buchanan in 1856. Four years later, the Republicans spent about $100,000 to elect Abraham Lincoln, and a century later they spent over $50 million to elect Richard Nixon, an increase in cost of over 50 percent (see Figure 16-1). Even so, these amounts are only the tip of the iceberg; these figures are startling, but they underestimate the sums expended because so many have gone unreported. It is relatively easy to identify and report some obvious campaign expenditures, but what of the time spent by a congressman's secretary in an election campaign, the use by a candidate of a free billboard or jet aircraft for electioneering or volunteer helpers at the campaign headquarters? Aren't these also expenditures? If these sources were not available to a candidate, he either would forego them or pay for their cost. Perhaps the more basic and immediate question to consider at this juncture is: What impact does our political system have on the costs of running for public office?

215

Figure 16–1

Cost of Presidential General Election (in millions)*

| | 1932 | 1936 | 1940 | 1944 | 1948 | 1952 | 1956 | 1960 | 1964 | 1968 | 1972 |
|---|---|---|---|---|---|---|---|---|---|---|---|
| Republican | 2.9 | 8.9 | 3.5 | 2.8 | 2.1 | 6.6 | 7.8 | 10.1 | 16.0 | 25.4 | 69.0 |
| Democrats | 2.3 | 5.2 | 2.8 | 2.2 | 2.7 | 5.0 | 5.1 | 9.8 | 8.9 | 11.6 | 67.0 |
| TOTALS | 5.2 | 14.1 | 6.3 | 5.0 | 4.8 | 11.6 | 12.9 | 19.9 | 24.9 | 37.0 | 133.0 |

*In round numbers.

SOURCES: Adaptation from Herbert E. Alexander, *Political Financing* (Minneapolis: Burgess Publishing Co., 1972); *Financing the 1972 Election* (Boston: D. C. Heath & Co., 1976).

## The Importance of Costs

On the surface the American political system is straightforward, having scheduled elections, single-member districts, and a winner-take-all policy. There are seldom more than two parties vying for a public office, no complex vote-counting method of proportional representation, nor are elections called on short notice. This relatively simple pattern is, however, quite complex, including primaries of various sorts (runoff and presidential primaries), party conventions, and general elections for federal, state, and local offices. It has been estimated that there are over 500,000 elective public offices in the United States. While general elections for Congress and the presidency are set in November, each state selects its own primary, convention, and general election dates whenever it chooses; local governments may hold elections at varying times throughout a year. This fragmentation as to when elections are held reflects a higher pitch of competitive activity for all candidates at all levels, which has the effect of increasing the costs of campaigning. In other words the United States has no one "political season" with guaranteed attention from the voters, so candidates at all levels are placed in a position of continually competing for dollars and visibility.

The cost of politics increases as the electorate and the population expand. Most obviously, expenditures increase in direct proportion to the increase in registered voters. Even though there are campaign items that will not basically change the amounts of money spent (e.g., novelties, brochures, stickers), there are other types of campaign expenditures in which the cost of reaching the voters is fairly constant (that is, mass mailings—each new voter added to the rolls increases the cost of mailing literature).

One objective of political parties and candidates is to register new voters, and expenditure for these activities increases as the pool of potential voters increases. But population size can affect costs of a campaign even if the candidate is not interested in reaching any of the increased numbers. A case in point is the expenditure for mass media utilization. The advertising rates for mass media are based upon the size and not the composition of the audience; thus, the political campaign will pay according to the number of viewers or listeners, with no guarantee about the voting eligibility of these individuals.

Although the geographic size of a political constituency and the density of the population are also important factors, their impact upon expenditures is difficult to measure. On the most obvious level, a candidate's travel costs will vary greatly from small, densely populated constituencies to extended, sparsely settled ones. Such contrasts characterize many legislative and congressional districts in the United States (e.g., Alaska has one member of Congress for the entire state). Furthermore, travel expenses will also vary, even in constituencies of the same geographic size, according to the kind of campaign a candidate wages.

Another element in the escalation of campaign costs is the importance of the office to be filled. More money is spent to contest important offices; and the greater the number of important offices slated for election, the greater the total amount spent in the entire system.[1] Although the definition of "important office" is elusive, the formal powers associated with and the prestige of offices such as president, governor, U.S. senator, and congressman generally qualify these as important offices. The importance of an office may also be determined by whether or not it is regarded as a stepping stone to higher office, for the candidate may be willing to expend more money and may more easily secure contributions if the office he seeks may lead him (and his backers) to more powerful places in government. For example, the office of attorney general has substantial inherent power in most states and is often viewed as a stepping stone.

Another factor that affects campaign costs is the degree of party strength in a given area. There are widely varying patterns

217

of strength at the state and local levels, while naturally it might appear that both the Democratic and Republican parties are fairly evenly matched. As a result there exist today many one-party constituencies where the Republican or Democratic nomination is tantamount to election. In such cases the monies expended in the general election may appear relatively low when compared to a competitive two-party constituency, but the spending difference may be more than made up in the intraparty fighting that takes place in the primary election. For example, in the 1968 Texas Democratic gubernatorial primary, eight major candidates spent about $2.8 million; this represented an average of $1.82 per vote. In the general election the cost per vote dropped to less than half that amount, only 74¢ per vote. In the 1970 primary elections for U.S. senator in Florida, seven candidates spent about $1.7 million, compared to $553,000 spent in the general election.[2] Generally, there are more Democratic than Republican one-party constituencies in this country, and usually the Democrats have more primary battles even in competitive two-party states.

Chapter 1 presented a discussion of the fragmentation of party structure and how this affects the ways in which fund raising for campaigns becomes a decentralized and dispersed activity. Because of this fragmentation, chaotic organization, inefficient overlaps, and multiple solicitation by candidates ensue. As such, political parties find themselves hard-pressed to raise money as parties. It is the personal appeal of a candidate or officeholder or the voluntary campaign organization that is effective. An example of such solicitation is the $20 million collected on appeals by the Committee to Reelect the President in 1972. The movement of money in American politics tends to travel from the bottom and middle levels to the top—exactly as one would expect in a decentralized party. The implications are tremendous when an incumbent president such as Lyndon Johnson, through a vehicle known as the President's Club (made up of contributors of $1,000 or more), succeeded in reversing the direction of money flow by collecting funds that otherwise might have gone to local fund raising and then dispersing them back to state and local party campaigns. Any such device or practice that manages permanent financial centralization of party politics will have a tremendous impact on political parties.

218

Although campaign technology will vary from place to place, it has been this facet of campaigning that has escalated geometrically in the last two decades. The most significant recent advances in campaign technology have been in the use of television (Figure 16-2). Although available in almost all constituencies, it is not, on the other hand, practicable in many contests.

**Figure 16-2**
RADIO AND TELEVISION EXPENDITURE
PRESIDENTIAL GENERAL ELECTION
1956-1972 (in millions)

|             | 1956 | 1960 | 1964 | 1968 | 1972 |
|-------------|------|------|------|------|------|
| Democrats   | 1.8  | 1.2  | 4.7  | 6.1  | 6.2  |
| Republicans | 2.9  | 1.9  | 6.4  | 12.6 | 4.3  |
| TOTALS      | 4.7  | 3.1  | 11.1 | 18.7 | 10.5 |

SOURCES: Herbert E. Alexander, *Political Financing* (Minneapolis: Burgess Publishing Co., 1972), p. 10; *Congressional Quarterly* 31, no. 19 (May 12, 1973): 1134-37.

For example, in geographically compact constituencies of urban areas, television is often impracticable for those candidates running for congressional as well as state legislative offices. This is the case in the New Jersey area, where a large part of the population is served by New York City outlets.

Another change in campaign technology has been in the area of public opinion polls (see Chapter 15 for detailed discussions). Utilized both to determine whether a candidate should run and what kind of campaign he should wage, polls have become essential in the view of party leaders and candidates. A reliable statewide poll will cost at least $7,500, and polls or surveys are seldom one-time affairs. It is important for a campaign to take periodic surveys in order to keep a close watch on both the present thinking and the trend of opinion among the electorate.

In short, the new technology has increased the cost of campaigns because these new expenses have not displaced expenditures for older and more established campaign activities, but have added to them.

Over and above the general patterns discussed are the enormous differences in the cost of campaigns from place to place and year to year. What causes these differences? Although each campaign is unique, perhaps the most important factor, and the hardest to predict and to control, is the intensity of the race. The "winability" factor also affects costs. A well-known incumbent facing a candidate who is unpopular or unknown may feel secure in spending very little. On the other hand, his opponent may be unable to raise or be unwilling to spend very much money on what may seem a hopeless cause.

But when a race is thought to be relatively even, or if a challenger believes an incumbent is vulnerable, the costs of the election may skyrocket. The 1970 Ohio Senate race between Howard Metzenbaum and Robert Taft was a classic race wherein both the Democratic and Republican parties were equally strong and well-organized. At least $1.9 million was spent in that race, and in the end it was as close as had been originally predicted, with Taft winning by a margin of 70,420 votes out of 3,060,944 total votes cast.[3]

Other factors affecting campaign costs include the availability of money and the candidate's willingness to spend it. Some areas are too poor to generate much money for political campaigns, and some are not "important" enough to command national attention and nationally raised funds. Also, a wealthy candidate who is willing to spend his own money can drive up the costs, as can a candidate who can turn to other resources or who is willing to go into debt.

## Allocating Spending

Although the collection and disbursement of funds is at the heart of the campaign process, it is very difficult to find reliable, uniform data on the sources and uses of political money. Financial needs will vary from election to election, and the problem of drawing conclusions about campaign finances over a period of time becomes very complicated. With few exceptions, records of state campaign finances are sketchy, making it impossible to determine the patterns of income and expenditures over a continuum, except to say that they show an upward trend.

220

In examining how political funds are used, politicians generally respond to situational factors, which vary from constituency to constituency and from election to election. Furthermore, spending strategies and priorities will vary among candidates and party organizations. Party organizations tend to spend money on registration drives, canvassing, getting out the vote on election day, and coordination activities of various political committees and candidates. All this makes sense from the perspective of the party leaders, for it is their objective that their party remain in power and thus control the government.

Candidates, on the other hand, have a different perspective. Each wants to build an electoral coalition for himself in a particular election that will, in the end, spell victory. It is the intention of the candidate to extend his name recognition and to win votes on his platform beyond those votes gained by party identification or party activity. But he cannot commit his funds exclusively for such purposes, for he must spend money to inspire party workers, reinforce the committed party voters, and activate them to go to the polls. Figure 16-3 reflects the specialized functions performed by party committees and candidates.

More specifically, what does the money go for? The oldest and most frequently incurred expense is printing. In the early days of campaigning for the presidency, most printed matter appeared in newspaper columns. By 1840 more than just printed matter was used to bolster a campaign; pictures, banners, buttons, and novelty items appeared. According to Herbert Alexander, the Republican party in 1896 estimated to have sent out 120,000,000 pamphlets at a cost of $80,000 for shipping alone, and a total cost of $500,000. In all, there were 275 different pamphlets and many were translated into foreign languages.[4] To this day, this practice continues to be a very important item in any campaign.

In 1968 the Republicans spent $1.3 million on a centralized campaign materials center, which was responsible for designing, ordering, storing, and billing all the major items to be used in the campaign. A catalogue was prepared for field usage and special kits were assembled for servicing 116 rallies with custom-packaged materials. The following is a list of the needs and costs involved in a present-day presidential campaign:[5]

| Item | Cost |
|---|---|
| 20,500,000 buttons | $300,000 |
| 9,000,000 bumper stickers | 300,000 |
| 560,000 balloons | 70,000 |
| 400,000 posters and placards | 70,000 |
| 28,000 straw skimmers | 30,000 |
| 3,530,000 brochures, speeches, and papers | 500,000 |
| 12,000 paper dresses | 40,000 |
| jewelry | 50,000 |

Mass media—radio and television—are very important in most campaigns, especially presidential ones. In 1924 radio was used for the first time in a campaign. Since that year the dependence of candidates on mass media has continued to grow, and there is no end in sight. To a greater extent than ever before, the masters of the media—public relations men, pollsters, ad agency representatives, television production experts—form a new political elite.

Today no candidate can escape the exposure that the media provides. A great part of it comes cost-free because speeches and statements, however trivial, are likely to be reported. Other types of exposure can be controlled; certainly in their commercial uses of the media, the candidates do have full control. In fact, the costs of media today comprise about one-half of the total cost of a presidential campaign. In 1968 about half of Hubert Humphrey's postconvention budget went for media exposure—$4.4 million for time and space charges and more than $1 million for agency and production costs.[6] Figures from the Federal Communications Commission show that candidates and parties spent $59 million on radio and television broadcasting in 1969, as opposed to $35 million in 1964.[7]

In 1972 Richard Nixon spent $4.4 million, while the Democratic presidential candidates bought $9.6 million worth of air time.[8] This discrepancy in spending is reflective of the incumbency of the candidate and his built-in visibility, thereby requiring less media exposure. The media-centered campaign has raised many issues and created new dimensions for the entire range of campaigning. More specifically, it is evident from available data that it has certainly affected the costs of campaigns

Figure 16-3

Expenditures by Democratic Candidates and Party Committees: Connecticut, 1966–68

| | Senator[a] | Governor[b] | State Central Committee[a] | State Central Committee[b] | U.S. House of Representatives[b] | State Senate[b] | Town Committees[b] |
|---|---|---|---|---|---|---|---|
| Advertising | 63.5% | 77.7% | 27.8% | 48.9% | 47.4% | 34.1% | 21.5% |
| Headquarters and organization | 9.4 | 1.6 | 14.4 | 20.3 | 10.4 | 19.7 | 21.7 |
| Salaries and expenses | 13.2 | .9 | 17.4 | 18.7 | 9.7 | 6.2 | 27.0 |
| Materials | 11.1 | 11.8 | 14.5 | 5.4 | 26.0 | 33.7 | 17.8 |
| Transfers | 1.1 | 6.4 | 14.4 | 1.1 | .7 | 2.8 | 5.3 |
| Other | 1.7 | 1.6 | 11.4 | 5.7 | 5.8 | 3.4 | 6.7 |
| TOTALS | 100.0 | 100.0 | 99.9 | 100.1 | 100.0 | 99.9 | 100.0 |

[a] Data are for the 1968 election.
[b] Data are for the 1966 election.

SOURCE: David W. Adamany, *Campaign Finance in America* (North Sciuate, Mass.: Duxbury Press, 1972), p. 108.

and has created new problems in raising the money to meet the rising costs.

Travel is also an escalator of campaign costs. Geography and type of constituency will define the mode of transportation to be utilized, but in statewide or presidential campaigns, most candidates cannot escape the use of campaign planes—especially jets—for traveling. The days of special campaign trains are past: in 1956 a five-car campaign train cost $1,000 per day, plus full fare for each passenger. In 1968 Nixon spent $1.4 million and Humphrey $876,000 for air travel in quest of votes.[9] These chartered planes not only have flight crews but are replete with various types of office and telecommunications equipment; they are in effect airborne offices. For example, on John F. Kennedy's 1960 travel staff were a speech professor to teach the candidate voice control, a psychologist to evaluate the size, make-up, and reaction of the crowds, an official photographer, and a two-person stenographic team to transcribe every public word uttered by the candidate so that transcripts were available to reporters within minutes after a speech.[10]

The shadowy world of campaign finances has been briefly illuminated as a result of the Watergate revelations about "laundered" money, secret campaign donations, and various kinds of "slush" funds, but the world of political money still remains vague. Who donates? Why? Is political money a serious problem? If so, what has been done about it? What *can* be done about it?

A forbidding secrecy veils the budgets of candidates and parties, the causes of which can be attributed to several considerations: the hesitancy of contributors to be publicly identified, the concern that the candidates or parties (knowingly or unknowingly) might be violating the law regulating political finance, and a general fear by most concerned that even a modest political donation will seem profligate to a suspicious public.

Even if this barrier of secrecy could be pushed aside, the problem of identifying the sources of monies would remain unsolved. Not only are the American parties decentralized and fragmented, so are their finances. There are a plethora of overlapping, semiautonomous party and candidate organizations all having budgets, and they often transfer sums of money among themselves—perhaps, one might suspect, to purposely obscure the total finance picture. For example, in Jacob Javits' successful campaign in 1974 for reelection against Ramsey Clark (D) and Barbara Keating (C), Javits had a total of eleven different campaign committees working on his behalf as opposed to his two opponents' total of three.

Both Democrats and Republicans receive their largest share of monies from individual contributors. Personal financing and, for the Democrats, the contributions of organizaed labor, account for most of the remainder. It appears that the sources for each of the parties are quite different. According to David Adamany, the Democrats emphasize extrinsic exchanges because patronage and preferments are major sources. On the other hand, program and ideology are most important for the Republicans because they claim the support of those in the upper socioeconomic ranks—particularly those associated with finance, commerce, and industry—who seek conservative policies and who have both the desire and the wherewithal to make political contributions.[11] For both Democrats and Republicans, the personal wealth and credit of a candidate is an important asset, especially when other resources are in short supply.

Political campaigns historically have been underwritten by big contributors. Both the number of donors and size of contributions undergo striking changes from election to election. Incumbency, personal attractiveness, and ideology of the candidates are probably the main factors in this variation. In the 1950s the Republicans obtained a much larger percentage of their total funds from contributions in excess of $500 than did the Democrats. In 1960, however, contributions by the "well-heeled" were almost equally divided: 59 percent for the Republican cause and 58 percent for the Democrats. In a radical turnabout in 1964, the Republicans obtained only 28 percent of their funds from contributions in excess of $500, while the Democrats secured 69 percent in such amounts. In 1968 George Wallace garnered the largest number of contributors of any candidate, estimated at about 800,000. His contributions were primarily from citizens donating less than $100 each. On the other hand, the "fat cats" favored the Republicans over the Democrats by a 13-to-1 margin.[12] This was also the case in 1972, when George McGovern raised a total of $33 million, of which two-thirds came from donations of $100 or less.[13] The following table is an estimate of the largest number of contributors in six recent presidential election years.

Figure 16–4

| Year | $500 and Over Contributors | $10,000 and Over Contributors |
|------|----------------------------|-------------------------------|
| 1952 | 9,500  | 110   |
| 1956 | 8,100  | 111   |
| 1960 | 5,300  | 95    |
| 1964 | 10,000 | 130   |
| 1968 | 15,000 | 424   |
| 1972 | 51,230 | 1,254 |

SOURCES: Herbert E. Alexander, *Political Financing* (Minneapolis: Burgess Publishing Co., 1972); *Financing the 1972 Election* (Boston: D. C. Heath Co., 1976).

The role played by corporations and labor unions in campaign financing cannot be overemphasized. They are some of the largest institutions in our country, both in numbers of people and in economic resources, and, therefore, two prominent forces in the political arena. Federal law prohibits both unions and corporations from making contributions or expenditures in connection with candidates for federal elective offices. Two-thirds of the states have laws also forbidding such contributions, so donations are now frequently made by "individuals," even though they may come from corporations. In turn, these individuals are either given pay raises or bonuses to offset their contribution. Also, corporations indirectly donate money by settling for less than the full value of a bill owed them by a candidate; for example, in 1968, Eugene McCarthy's committees owed American Telephone & Telegraph $305,000 for telephone service, but wound up paying only $75,000. American Airlines, which was owed $285,459, received $141,903.[14]

In 1972 the reported pledge of International Telephone and Telegraph Company (ITT) to the Republican party for its convention was a most unusual bid guarantee. The controversy that later ensued was not over the propriety of the gift, but about an alleged connection between the pledge and the terms of the government's settlement of an antitrust suit against ITT.

Some corporations in 1972 did give money directly (however camouflaged) to the Nixon campaign. Numerous executives and their corporations have since been prosecuted and convicted.

It was not until 1936 that labor unions became significant contributors to political campaigns. In that year it was estimated that they contributed $770,000 to aid Franklin Roosevelt's re-election.[15] Like corporations, labor unions have also circumvented the law against direct contributions. They have formed auxiliary political organizations such as the AFL-CIO's Committee on Political Education (COPE), which collects voluntary contributions from union members for political purposes. It has been estimated that labor alone spent about $6.5 million in 1972 in support of candidates for federal office. Labor contributions in money and services are very important to a great many candidates for state, local, and congressional offices. Surveys indicate that among union members about one person in eight gives to a political campaign, as compared with about one in eleven for the rest of the electorate.[16] Although union leaders donate individually to campaigns, the number of contributors and amounts contributed are much less than for corporate executives.

In 1968, when George Wallace was directly appealing to the working people, labor went all out to thwart this attempt. In *The Making of the President 1968*, Theodore White relates the following:

> The dimension of the AFL-CIO effort . . . can be caught only in its final summary figures: The ultimate registration, by labor's efforts of 4.6 million voters; the printing and distribution of 55 million pamphlets and leaflets out of Washington and 60 million from local unions; telephone banks in 638 localities, using 8,055 telephones, manned by 24,611 union men and women and their families; some 72,225 house-to-house canvassers; and on Election Day, 94,457 volunteers serving as car-poolers, materials-distribution, babysitters, poll-watchers, telephones.[17]

There are other legal techniques by which candidates and parties raise their funds. Chapter 10 elaborates on these methods, which are limited only by their ingenuity and by the prevailing political norms.

The percentage of donors, habitual or sporadic, is likely to bear some relationship to the effectiveness of solicitation procedures, for even the faithful need to be reminded and stimulated. Personal contact appears to be the most rewarding method of solicitation, especially when pursuing larger gifts. Below are distributions of educational and income groupings for the nation in 1968.

Figure 16-5
Educational and Income Groupings of Donors

| Education | Percentage Who Contributed | Income | Percentage Who Contributed |
|---|---|---|---|
| Grade school[a] | 4.6 | $    0-  2,999 | 2.9 |
| | | 3,000-  5,999 | 4.1 |
| High school[b] | 4.7 | 6,000-  8,999 | 7.1 |
| | | 9,000-11,999 | 7.6 |
| Some college | 10.0 | 12,000-19,999 | 12.0 |
| College degree or more | 18.6 | 20,000 or more | 36.7 |

[a] Includes persons who completed any grade through eighth. Also includes persons with additional nonacademic training; for example, vocational education.
[b] Includes persons who completed any grade from ninth through twelfth. Also includes persons with additional, nonacademic training.
SOURCE: David W. Adamany, *Campaign Finance in America* (North Scituate, Mass.: Duxbury Press, 1972), p. 83.

There is a paucity of information available that relates to the true motivations of those who give. The causal relationship between giving money and the passage of legislation, for example, is extremely obscure and tenuous; too many factors are involved to gain a clear picture. A wide variety of factors affect those making donations to parties and candidates. Traditional party loyalty may lead some to become regular contributors, while ideological identification with a faction or a candidate may motivate others. Many contributors to the campaigns of Barry Goldwater and George Wallace fell into this latter category. Other reasons for contributing that are extraneous to party and candidate orientation are the belief in the two-party system, a sense of responsibility, a feeling of duty, simple patriotism, and a desire for good government.

Yet another reason for giving is to gain access or entré, to have a basis for talking with public or party officials at some future point in time. These contributors usually hope to gain influence over legislation which will affect them, or they might be potential bidders for public contracts or wish to obtain loans or licenses, to receive key appointments, and so on. This may be the reason that some donors "hedge their bets" and give to both parties.

Although it appears that much campaign giving stems from selfish motives, it could hardly be argued that altruism is always absent. The line between the two is often blurred, for almost any kind of giving involves some degree of satisfaction for the individual. As seen, motives are complex; a person may have more than one reason for donating.

The important factors are whether the recipient feels obliged to promote the interests of the donor, and what types of demands the latter may make on those he has supported. There is also the question of whether large segments of the population who do not or cannot afford to donate to a candidate are thereby disadvantaged. Candidates and political committees are often placed in the position of having to judge and evaluate the economic motivations of those willing to give.

## Campaign Finance Reforms

Three basic strategies have been attempted in trying to prevent abuses: *limitations* on giving, receiving, and spending of political money; *disclosure* of the sources and uses of campaign funds; and governmental *subsidies* of campaigns, including incentive arrangements.

229

The limiting of campaign spending is one of the oldest preventive measures enacted. Under the 1925 Corrupt Practices Act, a candidate for United States representative could not spend more than $2,500, a candidate for senator no more than $10,000. While higher amounts were permitted for larger states or districts, this was a completely unrealistic act that could easily be circumvented. Later amendments limited spending by any political committee to $3 million a year and contributions by individuals to each candidate or national affiliated party committee to $5,000 annually. Reporting was inadequate; reports were filed, if at all, after the election was over. Policing was almost nonexistent. For the most part these legislative acts did not cover primary elections or, for that matter, any activities between elections. President Johnson referred to the 1925 act as having "more loophole(s) than law."

It was in 1971 that campaign financing was drastically changed. The Revenue Act of 1971 for the first time provided tax incentives to contributors. The law states that political contributors may claim a tax credit against their federal income tax for 50 percent of their contributions, up to a maximum of $12.50 per single return, or $25 for a joint return, or they may claim a deduction on the full amount of the contribution, but not more than $50 on a single return or $100 on a joint return. This law also provides for a checkoff that allows taxpayers to designate $1 of their tax obligation toward subsidizing the presidental election campaign (the general election, the national party nominating convention, and up to one-half of the possible costs of the prenomination campaigns) beginning in 1976. It is estimated that as of 1976 this fund will total $90 million.[18]

The Federal Election Campaign Act of 1971, which went into effect in April 1972, was significant in that it abolished all ceilings on political contributions, except for candidates or their immediate families contributing to their own campaigns. Instead, the law instituted a comprehensive system of disclosure of all receipts, expenditures, and debts. All political committees that anticipate receiving or spending more than $1,000 in any year on behalf of federal candidates are required to register with the government. Periodic reports must be filed, including full data on every contribution of more than $100 and every expenditure of more than $100. The law requires continuing reports on all surpluses and debts until they are dissolved, and prohibits any contribution by one person in the name of another person.

Because this law required full disclosure of all contributions received, there was a rush prior to the April 7, 1972, deadline to contribute to the Nixon Finance Committee to Reelect the President. The Nixon fund raisers were able to raise nearly $20 million before this date. In fact, in a crash drive in the month before the Federal Election Campaign Act was to take effect, the Nixon fund raisers took in $11.4 million. Within two days of the deadline, they added $5 million to the Nixon coffers.

The second major change in this new law set limits on the amount that federal candidates could spend on campaign advertising (including radio, television, newspapers, magazines, outdoor advertising, and automated telephone systems) to 10¢ per voting-age person in each constituency. This law further limits advertising expenditures by providing that no more than 60 percent of the total allowed be spent on radio and television.

The disclosures that came about as a result of Watergate gave a sharp push to further regulations on political money. Late in 1974, after prolonged debate, Congress passed and President Ford signed the most sweeping campaign reform measure in America's history. The new act established more realistic limits on campaign contributions and spending. For example, a spending limit was set of $20 million for each presidential candidate in a general election and $70,000 for each congressional candidate. Spending limits were also set on presidential primaries ($10 million total per candidate for all primaries), senatorial ($100,000, or 8¢ per eligible voter, whichever is greater), and House ($70,000) primaries.

Contributions by candidates and their immediate families were limited to $50,000 for presidential races, $35,000 for the Senate, and $25,000 for the House. The new act also set limits on individual contributions of $1,000 per for each primary, runoff, and general election, and aggregate contributions of $25,000 for all federal candidates annually.

This new measure was a breakthrough in campaign spending law in that it provided for public financing of presidential campaigns. Under these provisions, a candidate who raises $5,000 in contributions of $250 or less in each of at least 20 states will qualify to receive $5 million in matching public funds for presidential primaries.[19] For the presidential general election, major candidates will automatically qualify for full funding, while minor candidates will be eligible to receive a proportion of full funding based on past or current votes received. If, however, a candidate opts for full public funding, no private contributions will be permitted. This law also repealed the 1971 provisions regarding media-spending limitations.

The new law further tightened disclosure, reporting, and accountability. An eight-member, bipartisan, full-time supervisory board, the Federal Election Commission, will oversee and enforce this landmark statute.[20] In essence, this commission has rule-making advisory and enforcement responsibilities and, therefore, has the potential of being the most politically sensitive agency in the entire government.

This Watergate-spawned campaign finance law is undergoing its first test under actual field conditions as politicians prepare for the 1976 presidential and congressional contests. Its impact is going to the heart of the American political system—money. Although it is premature to evaluate the full effect of this law (which is under serious constitutional challenge and which may be changed before the 1976 elections), the following observations can be made:

——Fund-raising patterns will be drastically changed. This law has put an end to the "fat cat" contributors by placing tight ceilings on contributions by individuals, organizations, and political committees. It appears that fund raising for House campaigns will not be affected. The limits will have a greater impact at the Senate and presidential levels. "It's a funny law," said John T. Calkins, a political aide to President Ford, "because it makes it necessary to raise less money than before but forces you to think more about how to raise it."[21]

——This law also affects the "well-heeled" candidate, who in the past has been able to finance his own campaign. Limits are placed on individual and family contributions.

——If this law had been in existence in the 1974 congressional elections, it would have affected one-fourth of the senatorial races regarding the limits imposed on spending. Most of the House races would have escaped the burden of having to adjust to lower spending limits. The arguments over the meaning of reduced spending boil down to the incumbency factors. How can the challenger offset these advantages? Can the benefits of incumbency be reduced by lower spending? It remains to be seen after this law is tested how these questions will be answered, but for now, at least, it appears there will be limits, without the extremes encountered in the past when incumbents vastly outspent their opponents.

——While the law initially discriminates against third parties, it may ultimately help perpetuate them. Minor-party candidates for president in· 1976 will not receive public financing at the start of their campaigns because, in order to get a proportional share of public money after the election, they must receive 5 percent of the vote and finish the campaign with debts. A candidate with more than 25 percent of the total vote would receive full public financing in the next election. Although third parties have been one-shot affairs under our system, it is conceivable that if they did receive 5 percent of the vote in one election, they would receive money in the following election long after they had reached their peak. As a result, it is possible that the law will institutionalize and perpetuate third parties.

——Prospective presidential candidates face this dilemma: In how many primaries can they afford to run? More than 30 states, including many of the largest, will have presidential primaries in 1976. In 1968 and 1972, primary campaigns alone cost candidates more than the overall prenomination campaign spending limit of $10 million set by law. For example, Richard Kline, Senator Henry Jackson's finance chairman, predicts that Jackson's campaign will spend no more than $7.5 million in the 1976 primaries. "We're setting aside $2 million for headquarters and travel costs," he said, "plus another $500,000 for the convention. That leaves $7.5 million for every one of these primaries. That's very little money."[22]

——In one sense the law makes former President Nixon's 1972 Committee to Reelect the President a model for future campaign organizations because of the premium it placed on accountants and managers, instead of politicians, for running the campaign. The law requires that budgets remain within spending limits, and therefore money cannot be spent casually, as in the past. To David Rosenbloom of Boston's Parkman Center, the new law will have a salutary effect on campaigns by forcing candidates to tidy up their operations and stop wasting money. "The law will moderate elections," and "people will more carefully budget their money and work through organizations that can mobilize people."[23] On the other hand, David W. Adamany argues that ". . . when you budget down to the last detail as the law requires, it precludes a candidate from dealing with events over which he has no control. Inflexible budgeting prevents politicians from being part of what is happening in society at any given moment."[24]

Overall, it would appear that this measure is a landmark act whose full impact will ultimately depend on the probity and wisdom with which the Federal Election Commission administers it.

State legislatures, also feeling the reverberations of Watergate, have responded with a flurry of measures to reform their campaign finance laws. During 1973 and 1974, as many as 40 state legislatures enacted 67 measures dealing with the limitation of campaign contributions and spending and the monitoring of ethical standards for politicians.[25]

When the dust had finally settled from Watergate, significant changes had occurred at both the federal and state levels on the financing of political campaigns. On the surface it would appear that our society has moved even closer to resolving the conflict between political equality and economic inequality. The final results are, of course, still out, but they should begin to emerge very shortly.

## NOTES

1. David W. Adamany, *Campaign Finance in America* (North Scituate, Mass.: Duxbury Press, 1972), pp. 56-57.

2. Herbert E. Alexander, *Political Financing* (Minneapolis: Burgess Publishing Co., 1972), pp. 2-3.

3. Ibid.

4. Ibid.

5. Ibid., p. 9.

6. Herbert Alexander and Harold Meyers, "A Financial Landslide for the G.O.P." *Fortune* (March 1970).

7. Ibid.

8. *Congressional Quarterly* 31, no. 19 (May 12, 1973): 1134.

9. Alexander, *Political Financing*, p. 11.

10. Ibid.

11. Adamany, *Campaign Finance in America*, p. 171.

12. *Congressional Quarterly* 38, no. 40 (October 2, 1970): 2417-20.

13. *Congressional Quarterly* 30, no. 42 2643-55; and no. 43 2720-27.

14. *Fortune*, op. cit., pp. 106-7.

15. Alexander, *Political Financing*, p. 27.

16. Hugh A. Bone, *American Politics and the Party System* (New York: McGraw-Hill, 1971), pp. 401-2.

17. Theodore White, *The Making of the President 1968* (New York: Atheneum, 1969), p. 365.

18. *Congressional Quarterly* 33, no. 16 (April 19, 1975): 787.

19. Alabama's governor George Wallace was the first presidential candidate to qualify for preconvention campaign expenses. *Congressional Quarterly* 33, no. 16 (April 19, 1975): 787-88.

20. Two members will be appointed by the House speaker, two by the president of the Senate, and two by the president, all of whom are to be confirmed by Congress. The House clerk and the secretary of the Senate are ex officio members.

21. *Congressional Quarterly* 33, no. 24 (June 14, 1975): 1241.

22. Ibid., p. 1247.

23. Ibid.

24. Ibid.

25. For a detailed discussion of these various changes, see *Congressional Quarterly* 32, no. 35 (August 31, 1974): 2360-65.

# 17

# CONCLUSION:

# The Future
# of Campaigning

The spirit and technology of American politics continues to undergo substantive changes with every passing year. The nation's traumatic experience of seeing the political process flagrantly corrupted at the highest levels in the Watergate affair has increased the public's wariness of becoming involved with politics and politicians. At the same time, citizens may have become appreciative of the need to protect more jealously their prerogatives as shareholders in the political system. Only time will tell how well the lessons of recent years have been learned.

An important indicator of newly developing attitudes toward politics will be found in the extent to which citizen participation in politics increases or decreases in the near future. If the current low rate of voting continues and if greater numbers of people fail to become actively involved in campaigns, the future of American politics is likely to be rather dismal. A small political elite might well preempt those political functions that in a democracy require broad-based participation. If this elite is benevolent, there might be little *visible* change in the workings of the political system. But there will always exist the possibility that this ruling group might decide to ignore those aspects of democracy that are vital even though no one seems willing to support them actively. This would profoundly transform the nature of our political system and would likely do so in a way that would provide no recourse for those who disapproved.

The alternative to such systemic deterioration is to be found only in a rejuvenation of the national political spirit that can foster a renewed commitment to making "the system" work. This entails a willingness not only to participate, but also to develop the skills essential for *effective* participation. This undertaking is no simple matter—political techniques are reaching new levels of complexity that create difficulties even for professional political workers. By no means can political action be viewed as a mere lark for part-time participants; such an approach ensures ineffectiveness. The political parties, candidates, civic organizations, and educational institutions must recognize and respond to the demands of politics. Training in the rudiments of politics should be made readily available to any citizens interested in becoming involved.

This training must be developed in the context of the ever-changing technology of politics. Aspects of campaigning such as media usage, data analysis, and polling remain developing arts. "Electronic candidacies" and their attendant dangers are very definitely matters for present concern. The communications media can "create" candidates through their capability to provide a high degree of exposure in a short period of time. As noted in Chapter 8, there exists a frightening potential for abuse of this capability by an unscrupulous candidate. There is no absolute method of guaranteeing responsible behavior by a candidate, but some safeguards can be utilized in such matters as setting standards of conduct for advertisements and other broadcast appearances. Since live broadcasts cannot be screened in advance, the only logical protection against abuse is to be found in allowing adequate response time by an opposing candidate. A further measure might include disallowance of live paid broadcasts by a single candidate in the twenty-four-hour period immediately preceding an election. This would help guard against the possibility that a candidate might make outrageous charges with too little time for rebuttal by his opponent.

The increasingly sophisticated methods of demographic data analysis that are now available provide politicians with consistently accurate portraits of the electorate. Characteristics of individuals that are likely to influence voting behavior can be detected and evaluated in ways that will aid a candidate in

238

planning his appeals to various classifications of voters. An analysis of socioeconomic indicators, coupled with well-planned opinion polling, can be used in the construction of a political simulation, determining how given voters will respond when certain stimuli (i.e., campaign issues) are introduced. How such techniques will be implemented may vary. This methodology can be utilized to help candidates and elected officials better determine the attitudes, needs, and wants of their constituents, thus allowing for improved representation. On the other hand, such an approach could lead to improper manipulation of voters by playing on their fears and expectations for the sole purpose of affecting their voting behavior. The only effective safeguard against dangers of this sort is a fully informed citizenry, reasonably knowledgeable in matters concerning the political activities that might be in progress.

Even the most basic aspects of campaigning are constantly being refined. With the increased importance of computers in canvassing (as discussed in Chapter 5), in-person door-to-door electioneering has become a science in itself. A campaign with an adequate budget can computerize lists of voters and barrage them with mailings, telephone calls, and cavass visits in accord with projections of how best to turn out favorable votes. This approach is virtually an entirely new political dimension in terms both of planning requirements and efficacy. Hit-and-run canvassing, or informal campaign planning of any sort, belong to the past.

In addition to the ongoing development of specific campaign techniques, American politics continues to undergo major change in the overall structure of the electoral system. Traditional political entities have become weakened. Once-powerful party "machines" are now rarely able to mobilize blocs of voters in automatic support of the party label. Current loyalties tend to be to candidate or cause, not to party as voters today have no qualms about asserting their independence.

Campaigning for public office has become an almost continuous process, with planning for campaigns spanning virtually the entire period between elections. It is not unusual for candidates to be announced and organizations to be fully operative well over a year prior to an election. This, in turn, requires that politics take the form of a business, with a steady flow of activity and a constant need for money. Politics as big business has spawned a new breed of professional campaign experts—advertising and public relations specialists, management consultants, media planners, and others who have not, in the past, been considered part of the world of politics. These exponents of a new political technology possess no magic formulas for winning elections, but rather have developed new ways to approach the traditional task of finding the voters and eliciting their support.

Thus, the future of American politics, although constantly growing and utilizing new techniques, will be inextricably bound to the "nuts and bolts" traditions that are the foundation of American electoral activity. Just as it is the great mass of voters who are the objects of politicians' appeals, it will be these same voters who will determine, by their responses, the course of the politics of the future. The technology that stimulates involvement will become dominant, and the voters who choose to participate will control the most significant share of political power.

# SELECTED BIBLIOGRAPHY

## Political Campaigning

Adamany, David W. *Campaign Finance in America*. North Scituate, Mass.: Duxbury Press, 1972.

Agranoff, Robert. *The New Style in Election Campaigns*. Boston: Holbrook Press, 1972.

Alexander, Herbert E. *Political Financing*. Minneapolis: Burgess Publishing Co., 1972.

Boyarsky, Bill, and Boyarsky, Nancy. *Backroom Politics*. Los Angeles: J. P. Tarcher, 1974.

Broder, David S. *The Party's Over*. New York: Harper Colophon, 1972.

Brown, Sam. W., Jr. *Storefront Organizing*. New York: Pyramid Books, 1972.

Bruno, Jerry, and Greenfield, Jeff. *The Advance Man*. New York: William Morrow, 1971.

Chester, Lewis; Hodgson, Godfrey; and Page, Bruce. *An American Melodrama*. New York: Viking, 1969.

Crouse, Timothy. *The Boys on the Bus*. New York: Random House, 1973.

Dutton, Frederick G. *Changing Sources of Power*. New York: McGraw-Hill, 1971.

Gallup, George. *The Sophisticated Poll Watcher's Guide*. Princeton, N.J.: Princeton Opinion Press, 1972.

Herzberg, Donald G., and Peltason, J. W. *A Student Guide to Campaign Politics*. New York: McGraw-Hill, 1970.

Hess, Stephen. *The Presidential Campaign*. Washington, D. C.: Brookings Institution, 1974.

Kahn, Si. *How People Get Power*. New York: McGraw-Hill, 1970.

Kingdom, John W. *Candidates for Office: Beliefs and Strategies*. New York: Random House, 1968.

Lane, Robert E., and Sears, David O. *Public Opinion*. Englewood Cliffs, N.J.: Prentice-Hall, 1964.

Levin, Murray B. *Kennedy Campaigning*. Boston: Beacon Press, 1966.

May, Ernest R., and Fraser, Janet. *Campaign '72: The Managers Speak*. Cambridge, Mass.: Harvard University Press, 1973.

McGinniss, Joe. *The Selling of the President 1968*. New York: Trident Press, 1969.

Minow, Newton, et al. *Presidential Television*. New York: Basic Books, 1973.

Murphy, William T., Jr., and Schneier, Edward. *Vote Power*. Garden City, N.Y.: Anchor Books, 1974.

Napolitan, Joseph. *The Election Game and How to Win It*. Garden City, N.Y.: Doubleday, 1972.

Pool, Ithiel de Sola; Abelson, Robert P.; and Popkin, Samuel L. *Candidates, Issues, and Strategies*. Cambridge, Mass.: M.I.T. Press, 1965.

Riordan, William L. *Plunkitt of Tammany Hall*. New York: E. P. Dutton, 1963.

Rosenbloom, David L. *The Election Men*. New York: Quadrangle Books, 1973.

Stewart, John G. *One Last Chance*. New York: Frederick A. Praeger, 1974.

Stout, Richard T. *People*. New York: Harper & Row, 1970.

Van Riper, Paul. *Handbook of Practical Politics*. New York: Harper & Row, 1967.

Whalen, Richard J. *Catch the Falling Flag*. Boston: Houghton-Mifflin, 1972.

White, Theodore H. *The Making of the President 1960*. New York: Atheneum, 1961.

Witker, Kristi. *How to Lose Everything in Politics (Except Massachusetts)*. New York: Mason and Lipscomb, 1974.

## Politics Parties

Burnham, Walter D. *Critical Elections and the Mainsprings of American Politics*. New York: W. W. Norton & Co., 1970.

Duverger, Maurice. *Political Parties*. New York: John Wiley & Sons, 1967.

Eldersveld, Samuel. *Political Parties: A Behavioral Analysis*. New York: Rand McNally, 1964.

Epstein, Leon D. *Political Parties in Western Democracies*. New York: Frederick A. Praeger, 1967.

Katz, Daniel, and Eldersveld, Samuel. "The Impact of Local Party Activity upon the Electorate." *Public Opinion Quarterly* (1961): 1-24.

Key, V. O. *Politics, Parties and Pressure Groups*. New York: Thomas Y. Crowell Co., 1964.

——*Public Opinion and American Democracy*. New York: Thomas Y. Crowell Co., 1966.

LaPolombara, Joseph, and Weiner, Myron. *Political Parties and Political Development*. Princeton: Princeton University Press, 1966.

Leiserson, Avery. *Parties and Politics*. New York: Alfred A. Knopf, 1958.

Lipset, Seymour, and Rokkan, Stein, eds. *Party Systems and Voter Alignments*. New York: The Free Press, 1967.

MacDonald, Neil. *The Study of Political Parties*. New York: Random House, 1961.

Matthews, Donald, and Protho, James. *Negros and the New Southern Politics*. New York: New York University Press, 1957.

Michels, Robert. *Political Parties*. New York: The Free Press, 1962.

Neumann, S., ed. *Modern Political Parties*. Chicago: University of Chicago Press, 1956.

Ostrogorski, M. Y. *Democracy and the Organization of Political Parties*. London: Macmillan Co., 1902.

Ranney, Austin, and Kendall, Willmoore. *Democracy and the American Party System*. New York: Harcourt, Brace and Co., 1956.

Schattschneider, E. E. *Party Government*. New York: Holt, Rinehart & Co., 1942.

——*The Semi-Sovereign People*. New York: Holt, Rinehart & Co., 1960.

Sorauf, Frank J. *Party Politics in America*. Boston: Little, Brown & Co., 1972.

Sundquist, James L. *Dynamics of the Party System*. Washington, D.C.: Brookings Institution, 1973.

Turner, Julius. "Primary Elections as the Alternative to Party Competition in 'Safe Districts.'" *Journal of Politics* (1953): 197-210.

Wildavsky, Aaron. "A Methodological Critique of Duverger's *Political Parties*." *Journal of Politics* (May 1959): 303-18.

## Voting Behavior and the Electorate

Adrian, Charles. "Some General Characteristics of Nonpartisan Elections." *American Political Science Review* (1952): 766-76.

Alford, Robert. "Voting Turnout in American Cities." *American Political Science Review* (1968): 796-813.

Berelson, Bernard, et al. *Voting*. Chicago: University of Chicago Press, 1954.

Burdick, Eugene, and Brodbeck, Arthur, eds. *American Voting Behavior*. Glencoe, Ill.: The Free Press, 1959.

Burnham, Walter D. "The Changing Shape of the American Political Universe." *American Political Science Review* (1965): 7-28.

Campbell, Angus, et al. *The American Voter*. New York: John Wiley & Co., 1960.

——*The Voter Decides*. Evanston, Ill.: Row, Peterson Co., 1954.

——*Elections and the Political Order*. New York: John Wiley & Co., 1966.

Cowart, Andrew T. "Electoral Choices in the American States." *American Political Science Review* (1973): 835-52.

Dobson, Douglas, and St. Angelo, Douglas. "Party Identification and the Floating Vote." *American Political Science Review* (1975): 481-90.

Flanigan, William H., and Zingale, Nancy. *Political Behavior of the American Electorate*. Boston: Allyn and Bacon, 1975.

Goldbert, Arthur. "Social Determinism and the Rationality as a Basis of Party Identification." *American Political Science Review* (1969): 5-25.

Gosnell, Harold. *Machine Politics: Chicago Model*. Chicago: University of Chicago Press, 1937.

——*Grass Roots Politics*. Washington, D.C.: American Council of Public Affairs, 1942.

Hennessy, Bernard. *Public Opinion*. Belmont, Ca.: Wadsworth Press, 1970.

Kelley, Stanley. *Political Campaigning*. Washington, D.C.: Brookings Institution, 1960.

Kelley, Stanley, and Mirer, Thad. W. "The Simple Act of Voting." *American Political Science Review* (1974): 512-91.

Key, V. O. *Southern Politics in State and Nation*. New York: Thomas Y. Crowell Co., 1949.

——*The Responsible Electorate*. Cambridge, Mass.: Harvard University Press, 1966.

Lane, Robert. *Political Life*. New York: The Free Press, 1959.

Lazarsfeld, Paul, et al. *The People's Choice*. New York: Columbia University Press, 1948.

Lee, Eugene. *The Politics of Non-Partisanship*. Berkeley: University of California Press, 1960.

Lipset, Seymour. "The Psychology of Voting." *Handbook of Social Psychology*. Cambridge, Mass.: Addison-Wesley, 1954.

——*Political Man*. New York: Doubleday and Co., 1960.

Lubell, Samuel. *The Future of American Politics*. New York: Harper & Row, 1952.

Merriam, Charles, and Gosnell, Harold. *Non-Voting*. Chicago: University of Chicago Press, 1924.

Polsby, Nelson, and Wildavsky, Aaron. *Presidential Elections*. New York: Charles Scribner's Sons, 1968.

Porter, Kirk. *A History of Suffrage in the United States*. Chicago: University of Chicago Press, 1918.